The Archive of Empire

THE LEWIS WALPOLE SERIES IN
EIGHTEENTH-CENTURY CULTURE AND HISTORY

The Lewis Walpole Series, published by Yale University Press with the aid of the Annie Burr Lewis Fund, is dedicated to the culture and history of the long eighteenth century (from the Glorious Revolution to the accession of Queen Victoria). It welcomes work in a variety of fields, including literature and history, the visual arts, political philosophy, music, legal history, and the history of science. In addition to original scholarly work, the series publishes new editions and translations of writing from the period, as well as reprints of major books that are currently unavailable. Though the majority of books in the series will probably concentrate on Great Britain and the Continent, the range of our geographical interests is as wide as Horace Walpole's.

The Archive of Empire

Knowledge, Conquest, and the Making of the Early Modern British World

Asheesh Kapur Siddique

Yale

UNIVERSITY PRESS

New Haven and London

Published with assistance from the Annie Burr Lewis Fund.

Published with assistance from the foundation established in memory of
Amasa Stone Mather of the Class of 1907, Yale College.

Published with assistance from the Office of the Vice Chancellor for Research and
Engagement, University of Massachusetts Amherst, and the College of Humanities and
Fine Arts, University of Massachusetts Amherst.

Yale University Press books may be purchased in quantity for educational, business,
or promotional use. For information, please e-mail sales.press@yale.edu (U.S. office)
or sales@yaleup.co.uk (U.K. office).

Set in Bulmer type by Westchester Publishing Services.
Printed in the United States of America.

Library of Congress Control Number: 2023947509
ISBN 978-0-300-26771-6 (hardcover : alk. paper)

A catalogue record for this book is available from the British Library.

This paper meets the requirements of ANSI/NISO Z39.48-1992
(Permanence of Paper).

10 9 8 7 6 5 4 3 2 1

For Veena, Mohsin, Mohona, and Xuân

Contents

Acknowledgments

THIS BOOK OWES ITS CREATION TO many great and dedicated educators. I would never have gotten this far had my teachers at the Green Acres School and at the Sidwell Friends School not maintained their confidence in me even when I gave them little reason to do so. At Princeton University, Christopher Bush, Angela Creager, Robert Darnton, Tony Grafton, Marie Griffith, P. Adams Sitney, Cornel West, Sean Wilentz, and especially Dan Rodgers opened up new worlds, helped me understand what questions matter, and laid the seeds from which this project grew. I am also grateful to Linda Colley and Bill Jordan for introducing me to English and British history. At Oxford University, Lawrence Goldman helped me become a better scholar.

It was a privilege and an honor to research and write the first version of this project as a doctoral dissertation at Columbia University under the direction of Christopher L. Brown. Chris's advice, support, and friendship over these many years have guided me through the trials of the profession. His questions and suggestions have long inspired and enlivened this project. I could not have asked for a better advisor. The insights of Evan Haefeli, Matthew L. Jones, Pamela Smith, and Carl Wennerlind are similarly felt on every page, and I am profoundly grateful for their engagement and inspiration. During my time at Columbia, Susan Pedersen made me a better historian, and I am extremely grateful for her kindness, time, and support. I also thank Eric Foner, Samuel Moyn, Deborah Valenze, Joanna Stalnaker, and Emma Winter for their instruction and encouragement.

The gift of time and support of two postdoctoral fellowships allowed me to expand the ambitions of this project. With these opportunities came extraordinary mentorship, resources, and time, first as a member of the Society of Fellows in the Humanities at the University of Southern California, and second as a fellow at the Center for Humanities and Information at Penn State University. At USC, I was profoundly fortunate to have been supported by Peter Mancall, Nathan Perl-Rosenthal, the late Tom Habinek, and especially Jacob Soll. Thank you, Jake, for everything. An indirect benefit of my time at USC was the chance to participate in the

Huntington Library's wonderfully supportive research community: my thanks to Lindsay O'Neill, Amy Braden, Daniela Bleichmar, Juan Gomez, Steve Hindle, Vanessa Wilkie, Sara Austin, and Roy Ritchie. At Penn State, my gratitude goes to Eric Hayot, Pamela VanHaitsma, and John Russell. Beyond these two institutions, I have been incredibly fortunate for the ongoing mentorship of Paul Halliday and Phil Stern since the late days of graduate school. At a manuscript workshop in 2022, generously funded by a Mutual Mentoring Grant from the Office of Faculty Development at the University of Massachusetts Amherst, Paul, Phil, Hannah Weiss Muller, and Josh Piker gave me incredibly inspiring and thoughtful feedback on a draft version of the manuscript. The book is so much better thanks to their engagement.

My thanks also go to my many wonderful colleagues at the University of Massachusetts Amherst's Department of History, who have been enthusiastic supporters from day one. Particular thanks go to Joye Bowman, Anne Broadbridge, Richard Chu, Jennifer Fronc, David Glassberg, Daniel Gordon, Jennifer Heuer, John Higginson, Marla Miller, Jason Moralee, Brian Ogilvie, Sam Redman, Heidi Scott, Garrett Washington, and Kevin Young for their collegiality, mentorship, and encouragement. I am particularly grateful to Kiran Asher, Kate Freedman, Anne Kerth, and the late Kathryn Schwartz for their friendship. Kate, Anne, and Kathryn (who is much missed) read many versions of these chapters, and their advice and camaraderie have improved this book and sustained me.

At a time when support for research in the humanities is dwindling at a pace both tragic and alarming, I am particularly grateful to the institutions that funded my many years of archival and library investigation. Without their support, this book simply would not exist. Particular thanks go to the Social Science Research Council and Mellon Foundation for an International Dissertation Research Fellowship and Columbia University for a Graduate School of Arts and Sciences–Mellon Foundation International Travel Fellowship, which supported two years of archival research; the Alliance Program for a Doctoral Mobility Grant, the Omohundro Institute's Lapidus Fellowship in Transatlantic Print Culture, and the American Philosophical Society's Nancy Halverson Schless Resident Research Fellowship, all of which helped jumpstart writing; and the Huntington Library for a Research Travel Grant to the United Kingdom that enabled further time in the archives.

The awarding of an Andrew W. Mellon Fellowship for Assistant Professors from the Institute for Advanced Study enabled me to spend a transformative, unforgettable year as a member of the IAS's School of Historical Studies between 2021 and 2022, where I substantively rewrote and reimagined the manuscript under absolutely ideal circumstances. It is a profound privilege to have spent time in an environment so deeply and inspiringly committed to the humanities as a research enterprise. I am incredibly grateful to the institute's permanent faculty and staff for their investment in my scholarship: to Francesca Trivellato for her encouragement, mentorship, and suggestions; to Nicola Di Cosmo and Myles Jackson for their friendship, kindness, and humor; to Suzanne Conklin Akbari for important dialogues about historical knowledge; and to Danette Rivera, Alexis May, Marcia Tucker, Caitlin Rizzo, Karen Downing, and Joshua Horowitz for making my experience simply magnificent. I was so fortunate to overlap at the IAS with scholars who enriched this project through their concrete suggestions, confidence-boosting conversations, and warm friendship; particular thanks go to Ken Alder, Andrew Amstutz, Ana Lucia Araujo, Jonathan Bach, Samuel Baker, Andrea Bohlman, Delia Casadei, Celia Chazelle, Rosanna Dent, Christopher Faraone, Douglas Flowe, Jérémie Foa, Patricia Gaborik, Lucia Galli, Asaf Goldschmidt, Karen Graubart, Byron Hamann, Matt Hersch, Rush Holt, Ayesha Irani, Maya Jasanoff, Nate Jones, Emily Kadens, Diana Kim, Yukiko Koga, Whitney Laemmli, Peter Lake, Emily Merchant, Maureen Miller, Takashi Miura, Rob Nelson, Eleftheria Pappa, David Potter, Jillian Porter, Ram Rawat, Ann Reynolds, Matthew Shafer, Sayuri Shimizu, Sandy Solomon, Anna Wilson, and Joseph Witztum. My thanks as well to Heinrich von Staden, Glenn Bowersock, and Helmut Hofer.

I have had the good fortune to present aspects of this project to many audiences over the years. Their comments and engagement have immeasurably improved my thinking. Particular thanks go to the hosts and audiences at Columbia University's Heyman Center for the Humanities and University Seminars program, Harvard University's Center for History and Economics, the Colonial Society of Massachusetts, the Huntington Library, the Max Planck Institute for European Legal History, Queen's University (Canada)'s History Department, the University of Georgia, the University of Pennsylvania's Workshop in the History of Material Texts, the University of Toronto's Centre for Industrial Relations and Human

Resources, the History of Political Thought workshop at Stanford University's Humanities Center, and the Yale Early American Historians workshop for their kind invitations and stimulating engagement. It was largely through these and similar opportunities over the years that I benefited from feedback, questions, and advice from many scholars, including Tim Alborn, Bob Allison, Bob Bellinger, Herman Bennett, Shira Brisman, Daniel Carey, Joyce Chaplin, Jeffrey Collins, Manuel Covo, Elizabeth Cross, Will Deringer, Nicholas Dew, Maria-Pia Donato, Jonathan Eacott, Hannah Farber, Caroline Fowler, Mitch Frass, Joanne Freeman, Durba Ghosh, Claire Gilbert, Devyani Gupta, Jessica Hanser, Woody Holton, Jane Hooper, Matthew Hull, Ben Kafka, Zoë Laidlaw, Brian Larkin, Zachary Lesser, Erik Linstrum, Ted McCormick, Peter Mitchell, Fabien Montcher, Sandra den Otter, Guy Ortolano, Nathan Perl-Rosenthal, Mark Petersen, Steve Pincus, John Pollack, Kapil Raj, Bhavani Raman, Jessica Ratcliff, Daniel Richter, Craig Robertson, Emma Rothschild, Padraic Scanlan, Jerome Singerman, Sujit Sivasundaram, Sanjay Subrahmanyam, Fidel Tavárez, Meg Williams, and Rebecca Woods. Within this wide community of scholars, I am especially grateful and indebted to Noah Millstone and Nick Popper. They have not only profoundly inspired so much of my own thinking but generously read and commented on much of this book and encouraged me from our first conversations.

A book about archives owes everything to archivists. My thanks to the staff of the institutions where I conducted the research for this book: the National Archives in London, the National Records of Scotland, the British Library (Western Manuscripts, Asian and African Studies, and Rare Books), the National Maritime Museum, the Foyle Special Collections Library (King's College, London), the Bodleian Library (Special Collections), Senate House (University of London), the John Rylands Library, the Huntington Library, the William Clements Library, the National Library of Scotland, the Centre for Research Collections (University of Edinburgh), the Historical Papers division of Wits University, the Newberry Library, the Historical Society of Pennsylvania, the Morgan Library, the Beinecke Rare Book and Manuscript Library, the Postal Museum (London), the Royal Society, the United Kingdom Hydrographic Office, the American Philosophical Society, and the Wellcome Institute. Particular thanks go to the staffs of the Manuscript Reading Room and Asian and African Studies Reading Room at the British Library, the Map Room at the National Archives in London, and the National Records of Scotland, who put up with my presence for years on end and offered assistance and kindness that went beyond the call of duty.

It has been a pleasure to work with Yale University Press. Adina Popescu Berk's confidence and enthusiasm for this project over several years kept me going. Ash Lago and Eva Skewes have been most helpful in keeping me organized and on track. Mary Pasti steered the ship to harbor with kindness and a keen eye for detail. The anonymous peer reviewers of this project at both the proposal and manuscript stages read my work with generosity, offering profoundly insightful suggestions that sharpened my arguments. I am particularly grateful to Dr. Margaret A. Hogan for her outstanding copyediting and to Meridith Murray for preparing the index. I am grateful to UMass Amherst's Vice Chancellor for Research and Engagement, UMass Amherst's College of Humanities and Fine Arts, and the Aaron Warner Fund at the University Seminars, Columbia University, for subventions to facilitate the publication of this book, parts of which were presented to the Columbia University Seminar on British History.

The questions at the heart of this book—about how people make meaning through texts—grew out of conversations that I've been having since the first days of college with Maya Maskarinec. I am so grateful for our friendship. Over the years I worked on this book, I was sustained and indulged by the wisdom, kindness, and good humor of Nishant Batsha, Rhae Lynn Barnes, Sam Biagetti, Andre Deckrow, Suzie Ferguson, Abby Fradkin, Heather Froehlich, Matt Ghazarian, Debra Glasberg, Toby Harper, Alma Igra, Katie Johnston, Colin Jones, Suzanne Kahn, Abram Kaplan, Noah Kazis, Ana Keilson, John Kuhn, Jessica Lee, Weiwei Luo, David Marcus, Raleigh Martin, Melissa Morris, Sean O'Neill, Nathan Perl-Rosenthal, Keith Pluymers, Allison Powers Useche, Justin Reynolds, Pollyanna Rhee, Alex Roberts, Noah Rosenblum, Tim Shenk, Josh Shepperd, Danny Steinmetz-Jenkins, Alex Taylor, Simon Taylor, Dominic Vendell, Peter Walker, Jeffrey Wayno, Jude Webre, Jennifer Wells, and Natasha Wheatley. The itinerancy involved in researching and writing this book resulted in friendship with Mara Caden, Catherine Chou, Rishad Choudhury, Nick Crawford, Josh Ehrlich, Mircea Raianu, Alec Zuercher Reichardt, Aileen Robinson, and Tehila Sasson. What you hold in your hands (or read on your screen) results from our years of conversations about empire, information, and power, all begun when we met in the archives.

Finally, I am profoundly grateful for the support of my family on three continents whose own lives and journeys have been knit together by the consequences of the complex history partly investigated in this book, and especially to my parents, Veena Kapur and Mohsin Siddique, and my sister, Mohona, for their support and love over a lifetime. My deepest debt is to Xuân Pham, who is a constant reminder that life's greatest enjoyments lie beyond the archive.

Note on the Documents

EARLY MODERN SPELLING WAS highly variable; all documents are quoted as written or as they appear in published editions.

Furthermore, early modern manuscripts were not consistently paginated or foliated. Rather than impose pagination, I have endeavored to represent sources exactly as they appear in the relevant archives.

The Archive of Empire

Introduction

THE PROLIFERATION OF DATA AND its collection, ordering, and use by modern states and companies are among the most striking features of global society today. Empowered by satellites, computers, Transmission Control Protocol/Internet Protocol (TCP/IP), mobile communications, global navigation systems, and artificial intelligence, governments and corporations face the challenge of compiling, analyzing, and brokering information about human behavior that is being produced, circulated, and stored at an unprecedented and continuously accelerating scale and speed. Both public and private actors marshal this information to shape and execute projects of resource extraction, rule, and profitmaking in relation to what are increasingly multiethnic, multilingual, and multiconfessional constituencies whom they seek to bind together through the artifice of commitments to shared political or consumerist norms. The modern technological infrastructure of data management is dazzling, disquieting, and seemingly unprecedented because of both the scale of collecting this infrastructure enables and its facility for storage, search, and retrieval. But the problem of using information to govern in relation to human difference has far deeper roots. The reason lies in the persistence of *empires* across the globe for roughly the last 4.5 millennia: polities that attempt to incorporate, through conquest, trade, and settlement, multiple peoples with heterogenous cultural backgrounds under the authority of a sovereign, and face the attendant challenge of collecting, ordering, and deploying information about culturally different peoples to produce political order.

Perhaps no single political formation since the fall of Rome faced the problem of governing in relation to cultural difference more acutely than the British Empire. In the period spanning the sixteenth to the early twentieth centuries, Great Britain—an island polity roughly the size of the modern U.S. state of Oregon—laid claim to what became an empire that at its height spanned a quarter of the globe and encompassed millions of people of linguistic, ethnic, and religious backgrounds with nothing in common with either their rulers or each other except the shared circumstances of imperial rule. How did the British Empire gather, organize, and deploy information in relation to governing difference? Scholarship on empire and information, spurred especially by a series of lectures given by Harold A. Innis at the University of Oxford and published in 1950 as *Empire and Communications,* has focused almost exclusively on the modern period, when technologies like steam, telegraph, mass print, radio, and television defined the limits and possibilities of imperial communication.[1]

But we know far less about how forms of media shaped imperial rule in an earlier period when none of those technologies existed. Given that one of Innis's major themes was the transformational impact of parchment and paper on government, this lacuna is paradoxical, for it was precisely those technologies that decisively shaped the information order of early modern Europe and its empires.

This book provides an answer through an examination of how the early modern British Empire aspired to make power coherent through writing. It argues that between the early seventeenth century and the early nineteenth century, governing institutions attempted to rule what came to be an empire spanning two oceanic spheres by transposing a technique of making knowledge central to early modern statecraft into the project of constructing overseas institutional formations: correlating incoming information about the conduct of subjects and aliens in physically distant spaces with a set of normative conceptions of good governance derived from accounts of how humans have behaved in the past. I trace how officials sought to produce political order through the deployment of sovereign reason expressed in writing and show how the empire's demographic transformation complicated that work. Expansion raised the question in the minds of administrators as to whether written records contained the knowledge requisite to govern the non-English-speaking populations who inhabited the lands over which the British asserted sovereignty. This book explores the conflicting ways administrators answered that question and the shared mode of archival reasoning in which contestation occurred.

The Archive of Empire begins by tracing how practices of creating, circulating, and preserving sovereign writing characteristic of early modern statecraft came to be applied from the seventeenth century onward to

English administration in North America, the Caribbean, and South Asia. Archives of documents generated by officials in the conduct of administration functioned as sites for generating knowledge, facilitating the maintenance and justification of rule. Both royal and corporate administrators relied on archives, created through the dispatch of documents to and from colonial agents, as sources of authority and information from which they could develop policies addressing present-day concerns of government based on the examples of past precedents. They learned this technique of administration by archive from the information order that came to characterize the statecraft of late Elizabethan England. That period saw the development of two phenomena whose extension into imperial politics in the seventeenth and eighteenth centuries this book examines. The first phenomenon was the development of an "information state" in which councilors attempted to produce and control knowledge about political affairs by analyzing the contents of contemporary correspondence in relation to authoritative bodies of textual evidence in their possession.[2] Circulating written documents between the metropole and officials abroad, administrators sought to both direct the conduct of officers and collect geographic, demographic, diplomatic, and economic information. London administrators analyzed the contents of these documents to ensure that the manifestation of imperial sovereignty on the ground remained consonant with metropolitan expectations. Officials then filed the records within developing organizational systems as they sought to form a body of precedential knowledge under their control that could guide the work of decision-making in the present and future. They read this information in a manner that sought to confirm their preexisting conceptions of how empire was supposed to work, not because they were open to the possibility of changing their ideas. The second phenomenon reflected the failure of officials' aspirations to control the possession and dissemination of this knowledge: the rise of a political public sphere through which the secrets of state and corporation were regularly appropriated in political discourse by their critics and opponents via the constant leakage of records beyond the official channels to which their creators intended them to be confined.[3]

The experiences of many of the actors who were victimized by imperial rule—including enslaved Africans and their descendants, and Native Americans—had no significant presence within this system. Several

generations of decolonizing scholarship on the "archive" have painstak-
ingly demonstrated that the voices of the colonized can be heard only with
difficulty or inaccurately from imperial administrative records and have
pioneered methods of reading such texts with the goal of recovering subaltern experience, while also emphasizing that the violent processes of
empire-building make these experiences in many ways unknowable.[4] Although mine is a different project, I take seriously the argument that it is
impossible to "turn to readings 'against the grain' without a prior sense of
[colonial archives'] texture and granularity."[5] To that end, this book explains how conditions of alterity emerged in the first place and traces their
material consequences in structures of imperial knowledge. Crucially,
non-Europeans in the British Atlantic were thought about very differently
than non-Europeans in British Asia. From the perspective of an imperial governing and commercial elite who understood Native Americans
as outside the compass of the political subject and were committed to the
ideological fiction that enslaved Africans were property, not people, neither fit within the archival regime of governance. Their exploitation never
prompted reference to records in order to be justified. In the vastly different context of imperial South Asia, however, officials sought to apply the
archival epistemology to govern "Indians." There, they endeavored to rule
not simply on the basis of records from English sovereigns but also from a
variety of grants and delegations of power from Mughal government that
resulted in the corporation's literal inhabitation of Mughal offices under
the ultimate authority of the Mughal emperor. Imperial administrators
in India came to see the exercise of Mughal offices as incumbent on the
acquisition and deployment of a different set of archives than those available in the metropole.

Following the emergence by the 1690s of an administrative infrastructure governing an extended polity that contemporaries increasingly understood as an "empire," official archival systems came to be profoundly
enmeshed in political contestation and struggles over how that empire
should be ruled.[6] Like their Elizabethan and Stuart predecessors, the officials who created imperial archives aspired to control the circulation and
use of information by designing these systems to be closed, self-referential,
and secret. But like their predecessors, they failed. Just as the materials ostensibly under the privileged control of the English state in the late fifteenth
and sixteenth centuries came to be regularly appropriated by its agents, op-

ponents, and actors interested in making claims on government rooted in the authoritative act of referencing records, so too did the documents of imperial government flow beyond the control of official institutions. Competing interest groups sought to mobilize both the rhetoric of documents and the actual material contents of archives in order to construe policy proposals related to imperial governance as "authoritative." In these contentious debates, records were used for a variety of purposes. One political practice saw records invoked *post facto* as justification for decisions and actions. Another practice involved studying records for their propositional content, which then might inform a reader's future behavior. Other actors might not read records at all but instead simply refer to them in political debate, print them as "proof" of a policy position, or display them as a material manifestation of authority. Underlying these and other modes of using records was a widely shared understanding that a statement of fact about matters of government could not stand apart from its referentiality to a physical document that either actually existed or that people might plausibly be led to believe existed. The proliferation of these practices, moreover, reflected that these protocols and techniques of document use collectively constituted a powerful style of political reasoning: a way of making a claim in which the presentation of the claim's evidentiary basis was considered as integral to its persuasive effect as its discursive enunciation.[7]

War and conquest drove administrators to deploy the political practices of archival governance to conceptualize ways of ruling an empire that contemplated the membership of non-British subjects. Administrators sought to posit the existence of non-English and non-Latin language archives created out of the materials of conquered peoples. They analogized these archives as equivalent to the metropolitan collections in their capacity to produce authoritative political knowledge. In the Atlantic world, the practice of analogy bolstered metropolitan power. At the same time, in the course of the crisis of imperial authority in British North America during the 1760s and 1770s, the idea that archival documents might legitimate a state's policies came to be critiqued by rebels and a different idea of the relationship between writing and sovereignty advanced in its place within the political discourse of the American Revolution. With respect to South Asia, officials on the ground sought to posit the existence of a non–English language archive that they believed was better suited than metropolitan records to govern "Indians."

By the early nineteenth century, the terms of political discourse had come to change in a manner that began to push the archive out of the field of contestation. New forms of knowledge ascended in the estimation of administrators as better suited to solving problems of government, and the consequence was the transformation of archives from tools of rule into sites of "history." Central to this transformation was the rise of a set of entwined ideas around the nature of government and information: first, a concept of officials as accountable not only to sovereigns but also to a "public," and second, the idea that this public needed access to information in order to render officials accountable. As the sixth and final chapter of the book shows, the archive would play a different role in this shifting constellation of power—one that signaled the recession, both temporally and ideologically, of an early modern concept of sovereignty and its particular braiding of power and information. This development was seen in the diminishing administrative power of archivists, a broadening of access to archives, and an ideology of political knowledge that disconnected "policy" from the materiality of information.

The Language of Early Modern Statecraft

"Bureaucracy"—defined as a system of executing rule predicated on a "separation between politics and administration"—is the organizing category through which the world excavated in this book has been conceptualized.[8] But applied to any political formation before the mid-eighteenth century, the term "bureaucracy" misleads. Unlike the "state," "bureaucracy" formed no part of the conceptual vocabulary of early modern government, and the people involved in running states, churches, and corporations never referred to themselves using its cognate, "bureaucrats."[9] Instead, the word was first invoked by critics of the early modern European state, initially in France during the 1760s, to refer at once to the meddling of government in "things" with which it "should not concern itself," as well as to servants of government who were "not appointed to benefit the public interest."[10] In the aftermath of the French Revolution, the word became an epithet that Napoleon's opponents hurled against "the multiplicity of employments" under his rule, which they believed embodied an "invisible and mischievous power" that usurped "the natural and civil rights" of "the people."[11] Indeed, only in the Napoleonic period did the word "bureaucracy" come to be widely used in the English language. Inherent in the concept was the idea of state servants thwarting something that only ascended to normative status in political discourse in the late eighteenth century—"natural and civil rights"—while at the same time evading the form of public accountability the bearers of those rights demanded. As such, the birth of bureaucracy was conjoined to the emergence of the ideology that its formulators sought to make into a reality—popular sovereignty. But until the crises of legitimacy that befell European monarchies during the Age of Revolutions, and despite the rise of "rights talk" in the seventeenth century, the exercise of political power in Europe and its empires was widely understood to inhere not in the consent of the "people" to their rulers but instead in the possession of "privileges" conferred by sovereigns and monopolized by an elite. Applied to the early modern period, therefore, "bureaucracy" imports an anachronistic vision of early modern states and companies as primarily concerned with responsiveness to democratic demands, when they were not. Before the "old regime" became *ancien,* it was simply *the* regime; to understand how early modern government worked requires attending to its practices, not simply their critics.[12]

Rather than bureaucrats, those who ran early modern governments understood themselves to be officials: holders of "office," a word derived from the Latin *officium* and which by the sixteenth century had become a fundamental term of European discourse on government.[13] By occupying an office within the body of a sovereign organization (whether monarchy, church, guild, or corporation), an official took responsibility for the performance of a set of associated duties understood to be essential to keeping a part of the overall system functioning. "Office" was thus primarily understood as a position one held and only secondarily as a physical location one occupied. The identity of these officials lay in their manifestation of the specific forms of conduct and reasoning defined by the head of the body as requisite to the performance of these duties. The heads of these sovereign bodies detailed and delineated the precise definitions of these forms of conduct, reasoning, and duties, which occupants of office were expected to execute. The stimulation for early modern thinking about the nature of office and government came not from reading Max Weber but rather from Cicero, whose *De Officiis,* written in 44 BCE, was well regarded in early modern Western Europe as "the Best of Books" for "the Study and Exercise of Virtue," a "Manual of Precepts" that instructed readers in "the Government of our Selves, in all the Offices, Actions, and Conditions of Human Life," including that lived in the service of sovereigns, as one of the work's English translators noted in 1680.[14] From Cicero, as one eighteenth-century writer put it, "Divines have borrowed their Systems, Legislators their Constitutions, Statesmen their Maxims, and Magistrates their Practice."[15] Cicero provided a vocabulary for thinking about official conduct and a guide for acting in office, such that by turning to his work "in whatever State of Life a Man is in, whether Publick or Private, of Governour or Governed," an early modern administrator expected he would "find Rules how he ought to demean himself in any of those Capacities."[16]

In contexts characterized by relative spatial proximity between rulers and ruled, the communication of these "Rules" could occur through the physical and spoken performance of relationships of deference and authority through courtly rituals before the observant eyes of the powerful. But as states extended the geographic range of their claims to dominion over land and water, distance prompted rulers to supplement the verbal and gestural communication of their command with inanimate objects that they invested with the ability to bear their power into spaces where their physical bodies could not so easily be present. From perhaps the second century BCE until about the fourteenth century CE, the dominant substrate on which such communication took place was parchment, made from animal hide. Paper—initially invented in China and made out of plants, introduced into the Arab world in the eighth century via long-distance trade, and transformed under the Abbasids into a substance produced out of linen rags—joined parchment as the medium of European textual cultures from its introduction by Muslims into the Iberian peninsula in the eleventh century. Comparatively easier to produce than parchment (as well as harder to fabricate because it is more susceptible to tearing), paper by the beginning of the sixteenth century overtook the animal-based substrate as the quotidian technology through which European commercial exchange, ecclesiastical governance, secular administration, and scholarly cogitation came to be conducted. Parchment continued to be used as a prestige material on which information deemed especially important—such as grants of royal or church privilege—was recorded and preserved.[17]

Commercial and territorial expansion placed these officials and their substrates in contact with cultures of governance that operated on procedural and material protocols which were profoundly different, not only from those of Europeans but also from one another. In South Asia, for example, parchment was incomprehensible as a substrate for many regimes since its production involved the slaughter of animals considered divine by demographically numerous and politically powerful communities such as Hindus, Buddhists, and Jains. Rather, South Asian polities used a variety of materials—including the copper plates employed early in the Common Era by ruling dynasties such as the Mauryas, palm leaves within Hindu court culture, and birch bark and cloth in the Buddhist monastic communities of Kashmir—to inscribe, circulate, and store knowledge. These forms of documentation persisted and coexisted alongside the paper-based modes of recordkeeping that entered South Asia from the thirteenth century via the conduit of Islam. The First Peoples of the Americas presented an equally distinctive approach from the parchment-paper world of Europe and the substrates of South Asian governments. While the myth that Native Americans transmitted knowledge orally, not through writing, may persist as a schoolroom commonplace, it is empirically untenable in light of decades of research exploring the communication practices, including signs, wampum (shell beads strung together), and pictographs in which people circulated and preserved information about trade, war, and justice. Applied to many of the societies in the Americas, the characterization is also clearly erroneous, as it cannot account for phenomena such as the pictographic inscriptions on animal skins, rocks, and beads of societies of the Great Plains, or the bark "codices" of pre-Columbian Mesoamerican civilizations.[18]

As Europeans brought their parchment-paper culture of government to Atlantic and Indian oceanic geographies through war, conquest, migration, and trade, they mobilized these substrates as instruments of communication among a variety of powerful interests, including their officers, whom they invested with the authority to execute command at a distance; the "native" peoples into whose homelands they violently encroached, and with whom they fought, exchanged, enslaved, and at times cohabitated; and their subjects, over whom they sought to assert power at vast spatial remove. It has become common to characterize the process of expansion undertaken by the English Crown and companies in both the Asian and Atlantic hemispheres as one of "negotiation," whereby central authorities delegated privilege and power to far-flung subjects in order to maintain their obedience at a distance.[19] But the terms of negotiation in each arena were distinct. In the Atlantic world, the imperial constitution was forged via both the extension of royal prerogative through the appointment of Crown officials and delegation to representative bodies such as assemblies, as well as the extension of the protections of the common law to white imperial subjects. Other European colonizing projects, most notably the Spanish and Portuguese, developed defined legal categories that comprehended "natives" as "subjects" of the reigning sovereign. But in the context of English expansion, the concept of "subjecthood"—in theory, as simple as fidelity to the monarch—was comparatively less clearly delineated in law and administration, and in its settler-colonial iteration in the Atlantic world entirely excluded "native" peoples.[20] "Negotiated" governance between center and periphery—as well as the immense contestation such negotiation generated both within the metropole and between metropolitan and colonial spaces—occurred in the British Atlantic in a shared linguistic and conceptual framework. In South Asia, by contrast, a corporation chartered as the Governor and Company of Merchants of London Trading into the East-Indies and known familiarly as the East India Company conquered territory and monopolized trade on the basis of a complex set of delegated charters and authorities granted both by English and "Asiatic" sovereigns. While Europeans denigrated the latter as despots oppressing "natives" simultaneously caricatured as unfit for liberty, the grammar of negotiation encompassed concepts borrowed from Indians and their languages in combination with European political idioms.

    While the terms of sovereignty were often the subject of grand reflection in early modern political thought and have received extensive scholarly attention, the practices of rule through which they were manifested have been comparatively understudied.[21] When attended to, these practices have also been conceptually misunderstood. Insofar as "paperwork" evokes the mechanisms by which bureaucracy operates—the material technologies through which citizens and states make demands on each other as they manifest representational modes of sovereignty—the word is not a useful descriptor for the kind of documents early modern governing bodies created in the execution of rule.[22] Early modern subjects, of course, made claims on sovereigns using written forms such as petitions, letters, and affidavits. But until the late eighteenth century, they framed these claims in the terms of specifically early modern expectations of what states and state-like bodies might provide, such as "justice" and "protection," not in the vocabulary of "efficiency," "agency," and "freedom," which came to define the particular conception of politics that the rise of popular sovereignty ultimately rendered normative.[23] Moreover, such documents were dwarfed in volume and importance by the records that early modern governing bodies generated to regulate themselves as they tried to project accounts of sovereign reason from the centers of power on to officials tasked with implementing these commands at a distance. It is this kind of documentation—officials communicating with other officials, the governing body speaking to itself—that early modern states and institutions primarily circulated and preserved, that they invoked as justification for their authority and conduct, and that their critics sought to turn against them. Indeed, as this book shows, in conceptualizing how to govern over conquered subjects, imperial officials were most interested in controlling, organizing, and redeploying the documentation of the internalist functioning of the rulers whom they displaced.

In addition to "office" and "subject," four other terms—"record," "archives," "experience," and "politics"—were central to the vocabulary of early modern administration. From about the 1300s, the term "record" was used in English to refer contemporaneously to three phenomena: first, the practice and the product of writing down evidence, especially (though not exclusively) in a legal matter; second, a document produced by a governing or commercial body; and third, as fact preserved, especially in the form of writing and often with reference to events in the past.[24] In the medieval period, secular and ecclesiastical rulers alike began to conceive of administration as involving the collection, interpretation, manipulation, and dissemination of records. While record creation had a long history in the regions that became Europe, its volume accelerated from the eleventh century, with written texts in many forms, from decrees, inscriptions, and scholarly compendia to literary texts, charters, and legal proceedings, proliferating across different governing regimes. By the early seventeenth century, the sites where these records were stored had come to be referred to as "archives," loci for the collection and preservation of records in diverse documentary forms such that, by virtue of controlling such institutions, the possessor exercised, or claimed to exercise, some form of political dominion.[25] Accompanying these technological and infrastructural developments was a nascent theory of sovereignty that numbered among its characteristics the control and use of information—both its networks of production and circulation, and its storage in archives. Beginning in the city-states of the Italian peninsula in the fifteenth century and spreading westward in the sixteenth century to France, Spain, and eventually England, both secular and ecclesiastical administrators across Europe developed a vision of successful government as incumbent on the collection and control of information. They conceived of the interpretation, dissemination, and manipulation of such information in support of their policy ambitions as a quality of effective rule. The early modern information state governed by aspiring to control the flow of written records within administrative systems, and to use these records as the basis on which to make policy decisions considered sound by virtue of their referentiality to records.[26]

"Experience" was also a keyword of this vocabulary of administration. By the sixteenth century, English officials were invoking experience as a useful form of knowledge for the conduct of government—specifically, knowledge of the causes of human behavior. Unlike the knowledge of why God did things, which the fallibility of reason rendered humans incapable of discerning, it came to be widely believed that explanations for why *humans* did things ought to be decipherable to other humans. This humanistic knowledge of civil affairs could be produced by correlating incoming information about how people behaved in the present time with accounts of how they had behaved in the past. Information about how people behaved in the present could be garnered by training trusted servants in how to observe and describe phenomena, sending these servants to travel in territory with instructions to write down what they saw and learned, and then requiring that these disciplined travelers return the substrates on which they had written their descriptions back to the center of power. The incoming material could then be analyzed by metropolitan officials in comparison with the authoritative records of administrative precedent in the archives, thus producing wisdom from which government decision-making could proceed. The material could then be stored in these archives according to protocols of organization and classification in order to enable future officials to make use of it.[27]

Another fundamental part of this vocabulary was the term "politics." As recent scholarship has emphasized, "politics" is not a transhistorical category but rather a contextually specific and temporally bound way of seeing the world and conceptualizing the exercise of power within it. In early modern Europe, "politics" had multiple, complex, and contested meanings, defined both with and against the ancient Aristotelian category of the *polis* and the more proximate Renaissance concept of *prudenza*. Fundamentally, it was invoked as a way of thinking about the causes of human events as conforming to a system of rules and patterns that were knowable but might be hidden (and deliberately so) by actors, thus requiring techniques of investigation that would render visible otherwise obscured intentions and facilitate the governance of behavior. There were many different ways to be political in this context, but a prominent one, whose deployment with respect to the conduct of extra-European affairs this book investigates, was by writing down and preserving observations of human activities to enable the development of knowledge about political matters. Such knowledge could then be deployed by actors to advance their preferred visions of government and "policy" (sometimes spelled "policie" by contemporaries), a term that referred both to a course of action proposed and pursued by a governing body and also the idea of acting in a prudent or shrewd manner to achieve the desired end of such an action.[28] The production, manipulation, and circulation of writing was a crucial form of "political" activity. The meaning of these terms, which collectively constituted this vocabulary of early modern administration—"office," "subject," "record," "archives," "experience," "policy," and "politics"—were, moreover, dynamic and capacious enough that actors with conflicting interests applied them to divergent, contentious ends.

The lived experiences of people under imperial government, whether as subjects, aliens, or officials, did not of course actually correspond to the fantasies of coherence that administrators scribbled on parchment and paper. Implicit in the discourse of official documents was an insistence on the capacities of language and writing to exactly depict social realities they were in fact constructing. To delineate the meanings of administrative repertoires, however, is not to imply that fantasy ever matched reality. Rather, it is to insist that political history cannot be understood without accounting for attendant specific and contextual meanings of "politics," and that making sense of the authenticating methods that people have used to construct political truths is vital to a project of writing the history of the "political."[29] Indeed, it is precisely the disjuncture between prescription and what happened on the ground that makes the massive technological, financial, and logistical investment of actors to nonetheless try and produce fictions of order even stranger and therefore worthy of investigation.

The Arrangement of Office

A small group of British officials constituted as a board overseeing underlings tasked with specific duties and ranked according to seniority: this was the basic arrangement of all offices involved in the regulation of plantation and trade, including the Secretary of State, the Treasury, the Admiralty, and government in colonies and settlements. This organization reflected the constitution of the royal council itself, a body whose origins traced back to the *witan*, the Anglo-Saxon institution made up of powerful landowners who advised kings and queens. The salient constitution of this body as a Privy Council began to occur in the 1530s and 1540s, when it was composed of advisors selected by the reigning monarch as trusted councilors who met semi-regularly and whose work was facilitated by a clerical staff.[30] Prior to the Restoration, the regulation of trade and colonization fell to a series of temporary committees established under the Privy Council. In 1660, Charles II established a Committee of the Council for Foreign Plantations which later that year divided responsibility between two sub-councils: a Council of Trade, with sixty-two commissioners, and a Council of Foreign Plantations, with forty-nine commissioners. Until 1696, the Privy Council periodically reconstituted this committee in different sizes; that year, the council established a Board of Trade, composed of eight salaried commissioners, with the seniormost, known as the first lord of trade and usually selected from the House of Lords, presiding, and the other seven commissioners selected from members of the House of Commons. The board also had a number of unsalaried *ex officio* commissioners who did not regularly attend its meetings. In establishing the board in 1696, the Privy Council designated the appointment of an eleven-person clerical staff to assist the body, including a secretary, to be nominated by the Privy Council (an office held singularly except from 1753–1758 when two secretaries occupied the position); a deputy secretary or chief clerk;

four clerks whose salaries were determined by seniority, and who were often assigned specific responsibilities; two office or chamber keepers; two messengers; and a female cleaner known as the "necessary woman." Over the 1700s, the size of the establishment fluctuated slightly, with the number of clerks numbering between four and six between 1696 and 1708, expanding to seven in 1708, and then nine in 1764. During the eighteenth century, three other offices were added within the board's establishment: a counsel to advise on matters of law not considered important enough to merit consultation with the Crown's primary legal advisors, the attorney general and the solicitor general (1718); a porter to carry messages (1724); and a "solicitor and clerk of reports" (1730), who carried out searches of the records of the board, especially in response to growing demands of reports on trade from Parliament.[31]

The conciliar arrangement shaped the organization of other offices that came to exercise duties associated with the governance of overseas activity. From the Restoration, the office of Secretary of State was divided between two secretaries, and occasionally a third, including from 1709 a secretary charged with Scottish affairs (discontinued in 1746), and from 1768 a secretary tasked with managing affairs relating to the Atlantic world colonies. With respect to diplomatic relations, the secretaries assumed primary responsibility for different geographic areas, which from 1689 came to be referred to as the Northern and Southern Departments. Under the secretaries served other officers, including the aptly titled undersecretaries, as well as clerks, messengers, and necessary women, who performed cleaning activities. Over the 1700s, new offices were added to the establishment, including translators, interpreters, housekeepers, and law clerks, as well as writers of the *London Gazette,* the official journal of government. In 1782, the Northern and Southern Departments were reconstituted as the Home and Foreign Offices. While the total size of the Secretary of State's establishment fluctuated over the early modern period, the staff never numbered more than about sixty-five salaried officials prior to 1782. The Treasury, which experienced greater growth than other offices during the eighteenth century, generally had under its arrangement a board of commissioners whose number fluctuated as high as ten but was usually around five or six during the eighteenth century (at times, there was a singular lord of the treasury, who presided); one secretary until the establishment of a second one in 1711; the chancellor of the exchequer; and a staff of clerks, housekeepers, messengers, solicitors, and other officials.[32]

Before the mid-seventeenth century, English ventures in the Atlantic world took on a variety of governing forms. Whether the operating principles of information management described in this book for the late seventeenth and eighteenth centuries really applied to English enterprise in those earlier periods remains unclear. What is clear is that in the aftermath of the revocation of the Virginia Company's charter by the Privy Council in 1624, colonies began to assume administrative forms increasingly dictated by the monarchy, which imposed its principles of information management on them. Over the seventeenth century, English colonies in the Atlantic world increasingly took one of three constitutions: proprietary (meaning founded by private investors or interests), chartered (in which case a specific group was granted a charter from the Crown to establish the colony), or royal (meaning that the colony was under the direct supervision of the Crown). The structure of Crown colonies generally replicated the division of English government between an executive body with an advisory council and a legislature divided between upper and lower houses. Modeling the role of the Privy Council as an advisory body to the monarch, governors were advised in the administration of the colony by a council, usually composed of local influential and wealthy subjects nominated by the governor and approved of by the Board of Trade. The colonial council was invested with the power to review and debate legislation, and in this respect acted as a check on the governor's executive power. The council also operated as the upper house of the colonial legislature. However, the governor retained ultimate responsibility for overseeing administration. The Privy Council invested him with the power to appoint subordinates—customs officials, judicial officers, and clerks, for example—and it was with and through the governor that London administrators corresponded and conveyed information to the rest of colonial society. Below the gubernatorial and conciliar levels in each colony lay a pastiche of administrative institutions and positions, such as town councils, sheriffs, justices of the peace, and coroners, whose numbers and remit were highly varied depending on locale but often modeled off of English counterparts. Selected by governors or elected by local property-holding elites rather than appointed by metropolitan institutions (with whom they had limited interaction), these local administrators (like all colonial officials) were nonetheless subject to the ultimate sovereignty of the Crown and its delegated authorities for imperial administration.[33]

The organization of the East India Company presents a distinct but equally elaborate scene. The patent granted in 1600 by Elizabeth I to the merchants trading to the East Indies incorporated them as a legal personality, defined the division of the body into offices, and prescribed modes of institutional self-governance. The patent called for an annual election, in which the "generality"—meaning the entire membership—chose leaders, including the personnel to serve on twenty-four committees. These committees and their specific functions were also designated in the patent. The Crown patent granted the company the power to make rules for governing itself so long as these were not contradictory to the laws of England; the power to "impose" "Penalties" on members of the body who violated such rules; and the ability to appoint "apprentices," "freemen," and "factors" to make voyages and conduct the business of the company at a distance. The patent also detailed the customs duties that the company was to pay the Crown in exchange for the exercise of trading privileges.[34] The company's 1621 *Lawes or Standing Orders* described a complex set of officers and duties whom the generality was to elect annually—a governor at the head of the company, a treasurer to manage its finances, a range of committees tasked with administering specific tasks, and a secretary who was not a member of either the generality or the committees and who was responsible for managing the entirety of the company's written records.[35] The company established "factories," or settlements from where its servants traded, from the Persian Gulf to the Bay of Bengal and into China, Sumatra, and the Philippines. It appointed specific servants to govern trade and political relationships at these factories according to explicit written instructions.[36]

In both the Atlantic and Indian Ocean worlds, communication between metropolitan officials and their counterparts on the ground depended on circulating documents through often precarious infrastructures. Many have seen in the company's *Lawes* the forging of a system of information circulation in which, according to Matthew S. Hull, "vouching was done by artifacts, not people," and in which actions came to be seen as undertaken in the name of the corporation "only through a connection with a piece of paper."[37] In Bhavani Raman's words, the East India Company's "dominance was forged by the sword, built on the spine of the accountant's ledger, and held together by written correspondence" across vast space, requiring an enormous network of messengers, sailors, ships, packet boats, logs, and registers to coordinate and control activities at factories from Aleppo on the Red Sea, Bombay and Surat on the Arabian Sea, and Madras and Calcutta on the Bay of Bengal to Bantam on the island of Java.[38]

Such descriptions of a government stretched across space and bound by an infrastructure of communication comprising both artifacts and people could also be applied to the British Atlantic world, where a similarly complex web of merchants, officials, and messengers moved the material substrates on which information was recorded among ports, administrators' quarters, and assembly chambers. In neither context was this communication seamless. In the Atlantic, there was no consistent packet boat service between America and England until 1755, when Benjamin Franklin, then a postal official, spearheaded the implementation of a regular mail ship among Falmouth, on the coast of Cornwall; New York; and Charleston, South Carolina. Prior to that date, all documents were sent through ordinary merchant vessels, resulting in highly variable transmission times. The dispatch of written information between the London headquarters of the East India Company and its trading outposts and settlements across the globe depended on the company's East Indiamen, the fleet of ships that sailed its trading routes carrying servants, cargo, and mail. In both contexts, routines of circulation were subject to the contingencies of distance, wind, weather, war, piracy, and other factors that made delay, loss, and waiting fundamental to the experience of communication. Before the invention of steam in the nineteenth century, ships took between five to nine weeks to sail between the North American colonies and Britain, ten to fourteen weeks to sail between the West Indies and Britain, and between three to six months to sail between India to Britain (not accounting for the additional time required to move people and correspondence between the ports where vessels docked and the interiors where they might be needed).[39] Communication between London and Asia was further circumscribed by a sailing season that saw voyages to Asia occur between December and April in order to take advantage of winds, and return sailings occur between September and November. Consequently, the exchange of information between India and Britain experienced a significant time lag—sometimes as long as eighteen months—that did not begin to shorten until technical and navigational innovations from the late 1770s onward.[40] In the Atlantic world, seasonality of a different kind created obstacles to communication, with the climatic conditions induced by the "Little Ice Age" in North America during the eighteenth century leading to a consistent pattern of reductions in the flow of shipping and thus written information when the weather turned cold.[41]

The Material of Office

Early modern offices relied on supplies in order to function. Primary among these were parchment, paper, ink, quills, binding, and books. Although the earliest evidence for paper documents within English archives (in the form of merchant letters) dates to the late 1290s, parchment, usually referred to as *membrana* and made out of the skins of mammals, especially sheep and cattle, was the primary substrate of government in the medieval period. Demand for parchment was fueled by the medium's centrality to the practices of monastic recordkeeping and the administration of royal justice. Medieval and early modern people understood parchment as having gradations of quality, and they tied the use of a particular grade to their estimation of the importance of the specific information being recorded. Content considered to be of particular value was written on vellum (made of calf skin). Information deemed comparatively quotidian was written on sheets made from cheaper materials such as sheepskin. Parchment could be cut into different sizes, including sheets small enough to be rolled for storage in a manner that imitated the preservation of papyrus in the ancient world. From the first century CE, parchment sheets began to be combined together and secured with tacketing (made out of strips cut from larger parchment sheets or from cloth) into what came to be called quires. These quires were themselves eventually combined into objects that by the late first century CE were being referred to as codices. The codex was easier to use than the roll because it could be written on, on both sides, read with one hand, and contain multiple texts, and because its pages could be enumerated to facilitate organization. Codices were bound with twine and sometimes placed between hard covers made from leather-covered wooden boards or folded parchment. From the 1500s, these hard-cover codices came to be referred to as manuscripts, a derivation from two

post-classical Latin words: the adjective *manuscriptus,* meaning handwritten, and the noun *manuscriptum,* meaning written document.[42]

Prior to the late fifteenth century, evidence suggests that there was
virtually no paper manufacturing in the British Isles, with paper imported
from continental Europe—mainly from northern France and the Piemonte
region of the Italian peninsula—by merchants who then sold it to English
printers. The paper was generally of the so-called Chancery size (about
32 × 45 cm), with three other sizes—median (about 35 × 52 cm), royal
(about 43 × 62 cm), and imperial (about 49 × 79 cm)—appearing within
Western European markets by the mid-1500s.[43] This paper was made out
of fiber, mainly extracted from linen cloth, rags, hemp, and flax, which
artisans combined with water to soften and congeal into an oatmeal-like
combination that they fed through screens to form sheets. Papermakers
allowed the sheets to dry and then covered them with a finishing agent
(such as starch) to render them firm for writing with ink. Parchment was
initially written on with a calamus, part of a reed dipped in ink. From
the fourth century, the calamus came to be replaced by the quill, made
from a bird feather, which remained the dominant writing instrument in
Europe and its empires until the invention of the fountain pen in the nineteenth century. Paper mills began to be established in England itself in
the 1490s, though with limited commercial success until the late seventeenth century. In the interim, most English printers and offices relied on
French paper, sold to them by merchants who competed against periodic
government bans on French imports during periods of war, and by French
Huguenot papermakers who in 1686 from King James II received a charter
of incorporation as the Company of White Paper Makers.[44]

Metropolitan offices supplied themselves with paper, parchment,
other necessities, and binding services by making contracts for their provision with merchants known as stationers, who were connected to the paper market and possessed the skills of binding. Different government and
corporate bodies made contracts with stationers "for furnishing" a given
office "with Books, Stationery, Wares, binding of Books, and all other
things belonging and appertaining to the several Trades of the Bookseller,
Bookbinder, and Stationer," as the Treasury described the process in a
1770 report.[45] This practice began to shift in 1786, when the Treasury
established a government Stationery Office, which gradually took over
the patents that individual offices had made with commercial firms and

coordinated the establishment of stationery contracts at wholesale prices with private businesses for printing, paper, and binding across offices.[46] Both officials and subjects in the Atlantic colonies relied heavily on local printers who imported stationery supplies from Europe to produce newspapers, pamphlets, and occasional government documents. The terms of the Navigation Act of 1663 and its reinforcement in subsequent legislation required subjects to buy paper and other supplies from English outlets and only through English merchants; most of the imported paper was Dutch, French, and Italian in origin, and it was also available illicitly from those merchants who managed to circumvent customs inspectors. At the same time, a colonial paper industry slowly began to emerge between the 1730s, when there were eight paper mills in North American colonies, and 1740s, when that number jumped to thirteen; however, the rise of a substantial North American paper industry was a post-independence phenomenon.[47] Printing presses came to the West Indies in the eighteenth century, prior to which officials and subjects relied on sending writing to be printed to North America or the metropole; paper and other supplies were also imported from North America and Europe.[48]

No paper industry comparable to what developed in the Atlantic world ever emerged in imperial South Asia; East India Company officials at times used local "Patna paper," made from rags and plant fibers, but were generally reliant during the seventeenth and eighteenth centuries on paper and stationery supplies sent from Europe. The Portuguese had brought printing presses into Goa in the mid-sixteenth century, and missionaries from the Society for Promoting Christian Knowledge did the same for company factories during the 1710s. It was only in 1761, however, that the company established a printing press under its direct control after seizing one from the French during the Battle of Pondicherry.[49]

How Archives Make Knowledge

Archives form the foundation on which historians construct accounts of the past. Indeed, archives are so foundational to the process of making historical knowledge that their protocols of arrangement, contents, and even physical structure—in other words, their *givenness*—can seem to exist out of time itself. This book challenges that sense of the givenness and timelessness of the archive, one that the practice of historical scholarship, despite its insistence on contingency, can at times unwittingly produce. Instead, I ask how that foundation formed in the first place. This book pursues this project by recovering the underexamined techniques and repertoires through which imperial systems of archiving took form. It shows how archives shaped the conduct of both administration and political contestation, and traces change in cultural attitudes toward archives and practices of using them. I examine these practices in relation to the epistemologies of early modern administration itself, not in terms of the anachronistic categories of "bureaucracy" and "bureaucrat" that have animated previous studies. My work complements recent scholarship on knowledge and early modern state formation that emphasizes the importance of claims to expertise, "useful knowledge," and technical authority by those who aspired to public service; to order within institutions of the state, corporations, and the household; and to patronage by governing bodies and commercial endeavors.[50] But I focus on the comparatively underexamined question of how concepts of expertise and authority developed *within* official systems themselves. Institutions created their own internal concepts of expertise, which complemented and at times relied on projectors and others who claimed epistemic authority from beyond these official systems. Attention to this internalist system is a vital complement to the emphasis in recent scholarship on hybridity, nonofficial actors, and liminal spaces in the formation of imperial epistemologies that often took shape as part of projects of resistance to official modes of knowledge and power.[51] Without examining the operation of these official knowledge structures, it is unclear what precise epistemologies those who challenged imperialism were defining themselves against. This book proceeds on the conviction that these official forms of knowledge, though often invoked, are not in fact fully understood, and that their meanings and functions were far more internally contested than scholarship has appreciated.

Understanding how empires—and imperial archives—worked requires attending to the totality of their geographic breadth. The idea of writing the history of empire in such a capacious manner takes inspiration from the twentieth-century scholarship associated with the so-called imperial school of British history, especially the towering work of Vincent T. Harlow. Harlow and others sought to connect the Atlantic and Asian spheres of Anglophone expansion with the aim of explaining if and why there was a transition between a first British Empire, allegedly focused on the Atlantic world and motivated by trade and white settlement, and a second British Empire whose robust form emerged in the late eighteenth century through territorial conquest in South Asia and rule over non-Europeans. Much of that project merits critique: for example, the trade/conquest distinction fundamental to the first/second empire framework is an anachronism that misses the profound entwinement of commerce and conquest in the early modern period, both in the minds and practices of actors at the time.[52] But Harlow's inclination to "think the empire whole" was on point. Indeed, historians attentive to the metropolitan contexts in which English enterprise developed in the sixteenth and early seventeenth centuries have perceptively and powerfully revealed the important political, economic, and ideological parallels—and at times ties—among ventures of settlement, trade, and conquest in the Atlantic and Asian worlds.[53] *The Archive of Empire* extends this pan-imperial analytical vision to later periods, while placing far greater emphasis on the vocabularies and practices that animated this early modern world.

It is true, of course, that a vast chasm of space and difference separated the Atlantic and South Asian theaters of the early modern British Empire, and this circumstance partly explains why they are rarely studied with reference to each other. In 1607, the Virginia Company claimed a settlement at Jamestown on the banks of the river they named after their patron, King James I; that same year, eight thousand miles away, the East India Company established its first factory at the prosperous Mughal port of Surat on the mouth of the Tapi River in western India. These settlements imbricated English people into profoundly different cultural, economic, and social worlds—and the narrative of their consequent development has tended to be told separately. There are good reasons for this. The early modern Atlantic and early modern South Asia were not the same kind of places—geographically, demographically, or culturally. In the Americas, the British eventually built an empire of settlement that in the scale of its population came to number in the millions; by contrast, company servants were always massively outnumbered by South Asians.

But distance can also be deceptive. Viewed from the metropole, the endeavors were profoundly proximate. Much of the initial activity of both the Virginia and East India Companies occurred in the same place: in the city of London, at the Philpot Lane house of Sir Thomas Smythe, governor of the East India Company for most of its first two decades who also sat on the Virginia Company's board and served as its first treasurer. Smythe's membership in these ventures was exemplary of the profound overlap between the personnel involved in different seventeenth-century overseas activities.[54] The expansion of Crown administration over Atlantic world trade and settlement in the 1620s moved the metropolitan locus of its governance only two miles east along the Thames River to the palace of Whitehall. After the East India Company transferred its headquarters in 1661 to Craven House on Leadenhall Street, the distance was reduced to merely a mile. Understanding the subsequent development of empire requires attending to how the metropolitan proximity of its rulers and their shared political cultures radiated into vastly different parts of the early modern world.[55] However, the proto-nationalist approach to writing imperial history—what three scholars have recently critiqued as the tendency to study the spaces of early modern empires "only in reference to the nation-states that emerged out of them"—has made it difficult to see how this radiation occurred.[56] There are, of course, many ways of writing the history of early modern imperialism that avoid the trap of the nation-state framework, such as by comparing specific local contexts in which metropolitan schemes came to be deployed, complicated, and undone.[57] These approaches could certainly be applied to the history of imperial archives: one can imagine, for example, a comparative history of British, French, and Dutch modes of imperial recordkeeping, or between Mughal and East India Company archival practices, or between Haudenosaunee and English methods of transmitting information.

This book, however, is not a comparative history. Although the project of a comparative account of the development of imperial systems in the Atlantic world and around the Indian Ocean is certainly conceivable, it is unlikely to be particularly illuminating or compelling: direct comparison between two units in which so many variables were different rarely is.[58] Instead, *The Archive of Empire* offers what might be termed a radial history: it examines how a political epistemology that widely came to characterize administrative thinking in early modern England was deployed in parallel into two distinct worlds, vastly different both from one another and from the metropole, to work out problems of rule at a distance. The book demonstrates how early modern British imperial administrative thinking and behavior—no matter where or in relation to whom it was deployed—were shaped, empowered, and constrained by a political practice in which authority was understood to involve the collection, circulation, and deployment of written information.

An intra-imperial story could, of course, be told through any number of lenses. The migration and movement of peoples, both willingly and through coercion, across the vast, ever-changing, and porous expanse of the imperial world offers one avenue—indeed, it has been the approach taken by much recent work on "global" empire.[59] Yet, for all the power such a perspective holds to evoke the social, contingent, and indeed violent interactions through which empire was made, a focus on mobility and the biographies of those who moved can at times make it difficult to see the powerful structural and institutional dynamics through which empire changed, especially in regard to their emanation from imperial centers. An equally persuasive answer might be political economy. Like all other projects of state formation in the early modern world, the British in both America and Asia faced the problem of acquiring sufficient resources to project power over space and govern the terms of their circulation and distribution. The effort to find solutions to this problem—via war, trade, diplomacy, and conquest—fueled structural change.[60] Indeed, by taking political economy as a lens of connection, recent scholarship has perceptively demonstrated the profound linkages among the developing market worlds of European empires' Indian and Atlantic spheres.[61] But even "political economy" was structured in relation to a set of specifically early modern conceptions of the political itself.[62] The profoundly important and extensive work that has been done to revive the temporally specific meaning of the "economy" as it pertained in the early modern world has yet to be matched by a similarly robust effort to historicize "politics."[63]

Finally, by historicizing the archive, rather than accepting its givenness, this book challenges accounts of imperial state formation that have emphasized the variables of war, demography, and financial crisis as the primary levers of structural change—insofar as the structures on which they are argued to bear include those of official knowledge. These accounts, while powerful in many respects, assume the solidity of the archive, fixing it as a foundation on and out of which the history of sovereignty can be written. Yet, *The Archive of Empire* demonstrates that there is another way of writing that history: one that turns sovereignty's institutional manifestations inside out to reveal the messy processes of making through which power aspires to cohere.

Animating Imperial Bodies

D U R I N G A N I M P A S S I O N E D S P E E C H delivered in Parliament in 1775 attacking efforts to preserve the thirteen North American colonies within the British Empire, Edmund Burke critiqued the idea that official administrative documents could bear sovereign authority. "Letters of office," "instructions," and "suspending clauses" were "dead instruments" and "passive tools"; hence, he argued, "these things do not make . . . government." "The spirit of the English Constitution," not written records, kept the imperial body politic alive. Absent that spirit, the empire was dead, and the colonies ought to be left to their own devices.[1]

About a decade later, however, Burke enthusiastically sought to use documents of office to hold an imperial government accountable. Leading the parliamentary prosecution of the East India Company's governor-general Warren Hastings and his associates for crimes committed in the company's territory in Bengal, Burke consistently demanded that the corporation's Court of Directors furnish him with copies of "the Company's records" to facilitate his case, even going so far as to successfully pressure the company to induce Hastings to "deliver up their whole Correspondence or authentic Copies thereof" "not already contained in the Company's records"—records that Burke then cited as "authorities" proving that Hastings had acted "against the express orders of the Court of Directors."[2]

There was nothing contradictory about Burke's behavior. Instead, he demonstrated a shrewd understanding of the inseparability of documents, archives, and the concept of constitutional sovereignty in the early modern British state and empire—and the power of manipulating both the ideology and practice of documentary governance to advance specific interests. It was a style of politics that Burke's service to the administrative state had rendered intimately familiar to him. As the London agent for the New York colonial legislature in the 1770s, Burke had appeared before executive bodies like the Board of Trade to lobby on behalf of the assembly's interests, compiling and presenting written evidence in support of his client.[3] In both his administrative and legislative offices, he enacted political practices of controlling and manipulating written information to advance policy priorities, practices that lay at the bedrock of how the politics of imperial government worked in the early modern British Empire. To animate political bodies and exert power across both territorial and oceanic space, rulers developed regimes of disseminating, collecting, and storing documents so they could mobilize the wisdom of the past to develop policies to maintain present rule and plan for its future maintenance. Documents—their creation, circulation, strategic citation, and archiving—were essential to the exercise of sovereignty and the practice of making arguments about how it should be exercised. Indeed, as Burke's example demonstrates, even the *denial* that an opponent's records held validity was part of the style of political reasoning that underlay the practices of writing, disseminating, and preserving which collectively constituted early modern archival governance. Precisely because of the centrality of written records to the practice of rule, their control was a battlefield of contestation between those rivaling for power.

Building an Archive of the Atlantic World

In England, the link between power and knowledge as manifested in records materialized into practices of statecraft during the Reformation. In the medieval period, ecclesiastical institutions performed many of the most document-intensive functions of administration, such as collecting taxes and notarizing births. Hence, much written information circulated outside the compass of secular power, housed not in institutions directly controlled by monarchs but instead in churches, monasteries, and other sites under corporate authorities. Aspects of these standard administrative practices of delegation to corporate bodies and other private interests—including the power to control information—remained central to the workings of the English state for centuries to come.[4] But in 1536, two years after forming the Church of England, King Henry VIII extended his "Tudor revolution in government" into the sphere of political knowledge when he sent Crown officials to seize the administrative records that had accumulated in the hands of the medieval church. As Henry reallocated authority over administrative matters from sacred institutions to newly established secular offices, written information on the status of matters administrative in the realm flowed into the hands of the monarchy. Henry's successors Elizabeth I and James I formalized this information infrastructure with the chartering of new institutions, such as the State Paper Office in 1578, through which the Crown aimed to assert control over official records.[5]

Accompanying this organizational revolution was a conceptual one in the very nature of politics. If politics had been defined in medieval Europe in terms of Aristotelian categories of personal virtue, by the end of the fifteenth century the conceptual terrain had begun to shift. "Politics" now came to be thought of not only in terms of the ancient conception but also as "politique," governance based on the neo-Platonist idea that truth lay behind the misleading surface of visible reality, which required rulers to deploy cunning to gain the wisdom about humans' secret motivations in order to govern effectively.[6] Increasingly, politics was understood by officials as composed of a system of knowable rules and patterns. They believed that political wisdom could be generated by collecting information about how people behaved in the present and comparing it with evidence of how they had behaved in the past. Information about present-day human behavior could be gained by sending trusted servants to travel, spy, and observe both human and natural phenomena, record their findings in writing, and report them to their higher-ups. Authoritative information about past human behavior could be found in the written records generated by earlier observers over the ages. By correlating this incoming information about the present with archival documentation about the past, administrators believed they could produce reliable guidance on matters of statecraft. Moreover, if they controlled the circulation of these records, administrators assumed that they could ensure they retained a monopoly over this essential component of power. Administrators would be able to cite, replicate, and circulate these records in forms such as manuscript tracts, memoranda, and letters as evidence to support the adoption of specific policies. Such activities involved the construal of records as providing confirmation of the feasibility of existing ambitions as well as the reading of documents for information that could spur the development and justification of new policies. Officials vied to accumulate copies of records in their own private collections and then deploy them against their political opponents. They viewed the possession and control of documents as constitutive of the expertise that allowed them to make definitive claims about contentious policy matters.[7]

England's expansion over the seventeenth century complicated this braiding of power and information. Ventures of trade and settlement were executed under the protection of the Crown. But monarchs also sought to offset the expense and risk of trade and settlement in far-flung maritime and territorial spaces by authorizing bodies of merchants and settlers to undertake these ventures on their behalf while devolving significant powers of administration to merchants and settlers themselves in exchange for a portion of any profits. During the early seventeenth century, monarchs granted corporations and proprietors written charters empowering them to settle, trade, make laws, and collect taxes from inhabitants in specific geographic areas. The process of granting these charters—known as "letters patent"—placed the English state in a set of complicated jurisdictional relationships with such private interests, ones that were, in turn, complicated even further by the affective, commercial, legal, and diplomatic ties these corporate communities forged with non-English peoples in European, Mediterranean, Atlantic, African, and Asian spaces.[8] Information ranked among these complications: by exercising direct powers of administration, corporations and proprietors, not the state, controlled what was known about the commercial opportunities presented by overseas expansion. Companies themselves were acutely aware of this advantage, and they sought to regulate access to their archives as well as to manipulate the use of these collections to achieve desired ends.[9] Monarchs were aware of their comparative disadvantage, and when over the course of the seventeenth century they asserted royal authority over corporate activities, control of information formed part of their strategy.[10] Just as the monarchy had taken hold of the records of the incorporated body of the medieval church in creating a state church during the English Reformation, it asserted authority over Atlantic world settlement and trade by seizing corporate records. In 1623, the monarch's body of advisors, the Privy Council, ordered that the Virginia Company "immediatly" deliver to them "all Charters, Books[,] . . . Letters, . . . and all other writings . . . belonging to . . . the Plantations of Virginia and the Summer Islands." The council proclaimed that it would hereafter possess and manage "all charters, writings, and seals of the Company," which it directed to be "left in the custody" of its clerk so these records could be "used" by royal officials "at their pleasure."[11]

These documents formed the basis of an archive whose system of organization coalesced during the 1670s under subsequent bodies formed by the Privy Council, specifically the Council for Foreign Plantations (1670–1672) and its successor, the Council for Trade and Foreign Plantations (1672–1674). The Council for Foreign Plantations kept three kinds of records—a "Journal" recording its proceedings, a book of general letters into which it copied correspondence, and a series of "entry-books" that classified papers under different titles. The Council for Trade and Foreign Plantations continued these practices and added two new letter-books of "In-Letters" from the colonies and "Out-Letters" to them, with indexes of entries made at the back of each letter-book.[12] Between 1675 and 1696, the Privy Council formed a series of Committees of Trade and Plantations.[13] At each new establishment, the council instructed the preceding committee to deliver its records to the succeeding body. Thus, in the commission establishing the first of these committees in 1675, the Privy Council demanded that any member of the previous bodies "who have or shall have any Books, Papers, or Writings touching any matter or thing acted or done" in relation to the governance of the colonies "deliver or cause the same to be delivered" to the new administrators.[14] On March 13, 1675, the committee formally ordered "that all Bookes and Papers which were lately on possession of the Councill of Plantations be enquired after and taken into the Councill office, and that a true List of all such Papers be made, Also that Enquiry be made for Globes, Mappes, Sea Charts, and Journalls."[15] At the committee's next meeting, on March 18, John Locke, acting as "late Secretary of the Councill of Plantations," provided a "list of all such Papers as he received" but reported that he had never received any "Globes and Mapps," prompting further demands for these to be transferred.[16] Over the course of its existence, the committee accumulated records in a similar manner, ordering clerks to previous councils of trade to surrender documents, instructing imperial officials to deliver any papers in their private possession, and expanding the inherited archive through the issuance of orders, generation of minutes, and receipt of documents from officials.[17] This burgeoning body of records was placed under the management of the committee's clerks, whom it reimbursed on July 11, 1676, for the cost of "stationery Ware" and "Paper Bookes" for writing and keeping records.[18]

The committee designed this archive to be used in terms of the same aspirations held by the administrators who had built the state archive in

the Elizabethan era: consulting the records to determine ways of governing in the present that aligned with previous practices. For example, at its
May 24, 1675, meeting, the committee ordered the making of "a generall
Collection" of "Commissions and Instructions given to foreign Governments," a "List of the Governors' Names," and "all Charters relating to
Grants in America." The committee specified that it wanted these documents arranged in this manner so that "it may appear" to the Privy Council "at what time, and by what means" the various colonies "came under
the Sovereignty of His Majesty, and in what Manner They now hold and
depend upon him." Following the practice of late Elizabethan archival administration, officials used techniques of comparing incoming information
with records already under their possession to make decisions on policy
matters. Similarly, when it considered the complaint of a captain regarding "repatriation" for the seizure of his ship in Jamaica by the Spanish,
the committee ordered "that the Councill Bookes be searched for all the
late Compaints of hardshipps don by his Majesty's Subjects by those of
Spain."[19] The secretaries associated with this committee—Robert Southwell, who briefly served in mid-1675, and then his successor, William
Blathwayt—instituted a system for organizing the documents. Following
the May 24 directive to prepare collections of charters, commissions, and
instructions, Southwell informed his superiors that "it was impossible for
him to make searches up and down in the offices and put together the
Patents and Charters of all the Plantations . . . without some help." The
committee moved to make "some allowances" to hire more clerks.[20] After
an accident incapacitated Southwell in early 1676, the task of organizing
the records fell to Blathwayt.

Blathwayt's method of arranging the committee's papers by geographic region was modeled after the system instituted in the State Paper Office by Sir Joseph Williamson for the organization of diplomatic
correspondence. Blathwayt was familiar with Williamson's system, having served as a clerk to Sir William Temple during the latter's ambas-
sadorship at The Hague, during which time he corresponded with and
procured manuscripts for Williamson, who served as keeper of the State
Paper Office from 1661 until his death in 1701.[21] Blathwayt thus implemented an archiving regime for the central administration of the English
Atlantic colonies based on a system of information management that
originated in the context of managing foreign relations. Under Blathwayt,

the entry book system expanded to encompass distinct books for each colony in which were recorded all incoming and outgoing correspondence and related papers concerned with the specific place.[22] In the initial entry book for a given colony, the board's clerks usually began by copying first the colony's charter and then the earliest records related to the colony. They included both the records generated by officials in the colony and the proceedings of metropolitan institutions, especially the Privy Council, touching on the affairs of that colony. These books also contained indexes of each volume's contents.[23] Subsequent entry books followed this design of copying records into a single book and then indexing them.[24]

The Privy Council augmented this archive as its administrative activities over the remainder of the seventeenth century generated a growing body of records. These activities included appointing officials to execute the council's directives with respect to settlement and trade in the Atlantic world. Investing these officials with specific responsibilities and tasks for executing policy, the council demanded that they regularly provide written proof of their obedience to metropolitan directives, which in turn generated records that were used to monitor performance and inform policymaking. In its "Instructions" to its various committees, the council expounded a view of imperial governance centered on the collection of information about trade and its use to formulate policies for improving administration. It ordered the committees to "consider, and propound how to remedy inconveniencys of the English Trade" by making "due enquiry into" the question of "how the forraigne Plantations may be made most usefull to the Trade & Navigation of these Kingdomes."[25] Executing these directives, the committees applied the document-based methods of administration that had coalesced in the practices of English statecraft since the Elizabethan era to the governance of the nascent Atlantic empire. Using these documents, metropolitan administrators collected and recorded the experiences of merchants, governors, and settlers; exchanged information among themselves so as to inform decision-making; and inculcated officials into norms of governing practice through written prescriptions. Executive officials also developed systems of organizing and preserving these records so they could be used to inform future policymaking. In these ways, the early modern English state's information order projected outward across oceanic space.[26]

After the Glorious Revolution, William III's Privy Council sought to ground these practices of inquiry on a firmer institutional foundation. The Williamite Council endeavored to replace the committees of trade with a permanent Board of Trade that would carry on written inquiry and records-based policymaking with respect to the empire. But the political climate after 1688 was very different from the 1620s environment in which the first committee was formed. In the intervening decades, the Crown's claim to sovereignty in imperial affairs had faced multiple challenges, including from settlers and privateers who defied the chartered trading monopolies the Crown had granted to corporations such as the Royal African Company; from colonists who rebelled against the attempted reorganization of provincial government in the North American northeast into a Crown-controlled Dominion of New England; and, of particular importance, from Parliament, which challenged royal prerogative over imperial trade by passing the Navigation Acts of 1651, 1660, and 1663 and sought to create its own Board of Trade, partly on the claim that the legislature was better suited than the Crown to manage the informational challenges associated with imperial governance. In establishing the Crown-controlled board in 1696, the Privy Council worked to reassert its authority by institutionalizing powers to both inquire into and make policy about imperial affairs in the hands of a body of royally appointed administrators. Parliamentary opponents of the board feared that it would mute the powers of administration over the empire that the legislature had won in the aftermath of the revolution. Ultimately, the board was established as an advisory body to the Privy Council, one that could collect information on commercial affairs, draft instructions to governors on how laws should be executed, and make policy recommendations but without the power to legislate, which remained with the council itself and Parliament.[27]

The 1696 establishment of the Board of Trade placed these advisory and investigatory activities on what proved to be a more durable institutional foundation. The board's creation formed part of William III's efforts to assert monarchical control over the administration of trade and Atlantic settlement in the aftermath of the dissolution of the Dominion of New England and the crisis of state finance resulting from wars with France. As part of this program, the Crown sought to take possession of records related to Atlantic imperial governance. The Privy Council's commission to the board thus empowered it to take into its care "all Records, Grants and Papers remaining in the Plantation Office or thereunto belonging."[28] When the board first met in Whitehall on June 25, 1696, the commissioners began by appointing William Popple to the office of secretary and tasking him with the management of the body's written correspondence and archive.[29] The board spent early meetings coordinating the renovation of rooms in Whitehall for its use and contracting with a stationer "to furnish this Board with all sorts of Stationery Ware proper for their Service."[30] The board issued an order to Thomas Povey, the clerk of its predecessor body, "for the Books & Papers of the late Plantation Office" to be transferred into the board's possession—papers that were delivered between July and August 1696.[31] Popple, who now had responsibility over the management of these papers, created an inventory describing the transferred records. He assigned the papers twenty-one subject headings, mostly corresponding to the relevant colony or corporate body to which they pertained. Papers within each subject heading were grouped into bundles, each given a letter designation. For example, "Papers Relating to New England" were grouped into eight bundles labeled with the letters A through H. Each document was assigned a number according to its place within each bundle, which in the inventory of the transferred records was arbitrary; it was not based on the size or date of the paper, and papers were not arranged in chronological order either within or across bundles.[32] After a fire in Whitehall in December 1699, the board ordered the secretary to transcribe records into copybooks as a means of "securing the Books and Papers in this office" from damage, and obtained "a Competent Number of Sacks . . . for carrying away the said Books upon any such accident."[33]

At each of the board's meetings, members considered the contents of the documents received from the colonies and other offices of state and decided on courses of action to advise in response. The clerical staff then archived the documents in a manner designed to facilitate the possibility of future consultation. Until the 1770s, the chief clerk of the board recorded in the meeting minutes the titles of documents received from the colonies. The documents from each royal colony (in which the governor was directly appointed by the Crown) were filed within their own series, while documents from proprietary colonies (where the Crown granted private interests known as proprietors the powers of administration) were classified under a heading of "Proprietaries." If they became royal colonies, they too were filed in a distinct series. There were also more general series, such as "Plantations General," in which documents deemed to pertain to multiple colonies were filed; "Miscellanies"; and "Trade," a category that began in 1717 and absorbed three previous series: "Trade Foreign," "Trade Domestic," and "Trade and Fishery." After the board had considered a document, the clerk assigned it a letter corresponding to the bundle to which it was to be assigned, numbered it in relation to the rest of the documents in the bundle, and filed it correspondingly. The clerk recorded the title of the document, initially in an entry book (assigned a letter) and later in a numbered register. From 1703, the board's clerks began to generate separate "calendars" listing documents in small paper books corresponding to each bundle.[34] Around this time, it seems, clerks also began creating indexes listing papers according to several modes of categorization. Some of these indexes simply listed papers within a bundle in order of appearance in the file, by date of creation, or under subject keywords (such as "Admiralty," "Africa," or "Plantations").[35] Other indexes were more elaborate: in addition to listing papers under keywords, they included cross-references to the entry of the paper's receipt as recorded in the board's "Journal," the entry book in which the paper had been recorded, and the place of the paper in the bundle.[36]

The Board of Trade's use of records demonstrates how this system of information management shaped practices of administration. As the primary site for the receipt of incoming correspondence from officials in the colonies, the board also served as the metropolitan hub of written information about current conditions in the Atlantic world empire. Measuring the efficacy of ongoing administrative practices—as described by governors and other officials in this incoming correspondence—against the precedents of its archival holdings, the board applied the form of expertise tied to control over written information (crystallized under Elizabethan administration) to the conduct of overseas rule. It distilled these precedents into written "Instructions" given to Crown officials on their appointment to an office. Mirroring the instructions issued by early modern states and institutions to ambassadors, diplomats, and travelers that trained them to observe and report on political and natural phenomena according to disciplined conventions, the board's instructions codified both executive decrees and royal interpretations of parliamentary legislation into a single document, reviewed and approved by the Privy

Council. The instructions prescribed rules for the conduct of officials and the production of administrative information. Officials were instructed to constantly correspond with the board and keep it appraised of "all occurrences necessary for their Information, relating either to the . . . Laws of Trade and Navigation, or to his Majesty's Revenue of Customs and other Dutys under their Management."[37] Mirroring the practices of earlier royal councilors, the board's members examined the incoming correspondence for evidence of governors' compliance and for information concerning the conduct of trade in the colonies.

Using this information, the board made policy recommendations to the Privy Council; forwarded relevant documents to other executive offices with imperial jurisdiction, such as the Admiralty and Treasury; and archived incoming documents in series corresponding to the colony to which they pertained, mirroring the organization of diplomatic correspondence with foreign states in the State Paper Office.[38] Just as the organization of diplomatic records in the State Paper Office was intended to facilitate the administrative decision-making of the Secretary of State, the board's archival management was designed to facilitate the use of these records in the contentious politics of imperial policy. As royal and parliamentary officials exercised competing claims to legislate for the colonies, they demanded that the board provide them with documents that they could use to legitimize their preferred policies and undermine those of their opponents. Mirroring the practices of earlier officials with respect to domestic and diplomatic affairs, many of these imperial officials sought to compile personal collections of government records, which they could then invoke as authorities in partisan battles. In these ways, practices of political knowledge that saw administrators weaponize records against the political ambitions and programs of their opponents came to shape the conduct of imperial governance (a topic examined in greater detail in chapter 3).

Emulating earlier officials who circulated manuscripts and records as authoritative proof of the wisdom of particular policies, the board itself entered into these disputes by citing, excerpting, and interpreting records as proof that Crown policy in imperial affairs was grounded in the authority of written precedent. The board had the advantage in this regard of unrestricted access to administrative records, which it enjoyed alongside the rest of the Privy Council, whereas other interested parties, such as members of Parliament, had to obtain conciliar permission to consult the records of trade and plantation and could only request specific documents. The board's leveraging of records in policy disputes was particularly evident in its campaign in the early eighteenth century to "resume" control over the charters issued by the Stuart monarchs to proprietors and colonists. Stuart rulers had granted privileges in the form of written charters to English people to settle, own, and cultivate colonies and exercise considerable jurisdiction over the management of their internal affairs. But in the aftermath of 1688, Williamite and Hanoverian monarchs pushed to invalidate these charters and replace proprietors with Crown-appointed governors. The post-1688 constitutional settlement, however, inhibited the monarchy from acting without legislative consent, requiring that the Board of Trade submit legislation to Parliament to gain approval for revoking the charters. Thus, in 1701 and then again in 1721, the board introduced parliamentary bills that proposed to strip proprietary and corporate colonies of their charters and place their governments under royal jurisdiction, a policy known as resumption. Although neither effort succeeded, the board's lobbying exemplified how it applied the archival epistemology to the politics of imperial policy.[39] In both 1701 and 1721, the board mobilized the records under its purview to substantiate its policy ambitions, construing them as authoritative proof of resumption's constitutionality. On each occasion, the board's advocacy took the form of manuscript reports arguing for legislative approval for resumption, prepared on behalf of the Privy Council and circulated to Parliament.

The board began the 1701 report by stating that it had compared "severall Papers" recently sent to the Privy Council from the proprietary colonies of East and West New Jersey with records "of the like nature that were already in our hands." The process of reading the incoming documentation from the Jerseys against the archival authorities demonstrated the dubious constitutionality of proprietorships. Despite the grants issued by Charles II to the colonies' proprietors, the board's members reported that "we do not find that any sufficient form of Government has ever been settled in those Provinces." Instead, the proprietors had proceeded with a mere "pretence of right to Govern," which produced "many inconveniencies and disorders" in administration. The proprietors' behavior ran counter to the commercial interests of the empire: in appointing governors for their colonies, the proprietors had acted "without his Majesties Approbation" and defied the legal order of commerce, especially the Navigation Acts

instituted for "preventing Frauds and regulating abuses in the Plantation Trade." Both "the preservation of those Territories to the Crown of
England" and "the private Interest" of their inhabitants required that the
"pretences" and "pretended Right" of the proprietors be replaced by a
royal governor.[40] Reasoning in a manner that would have been intelligible
to earlier generations of English officials who practiced administration by
comparing incoming information with archival records, the board aimed
to support the Crown's claim to control the imperial economy by invoking the discrepancy between current conditions in the proprietorships as
recorded in contemporary documents and the juridical order of empire as
promulgated with reference to archival precedents.

Construing the meaning of these documents to support its current
policy ambitions, the Board of Trade rearticulated this vision of imperial sovereignty against the threat of corporate and proprietary power in
1721. In this report, the board evaluated how well "the Laws and Constitutions" of the colonies (as approved by the Privy Council and then
copied into the board's archive) were being executed in the colonies. The
board did this by comparing the archival documents against the contents
of answers to a questionnaire it had circulated earlier that year to governors and colonial agents soliciting information on current administrative
conditions. It concluded that even as colonial laws were "Copy'd from
those of Great Britain," their execution in the colonies "f[e]ll short of"
metropolitan expectations "in many particulars." Laws from colonies that
retained charter privileges were described as deviating the most from metropolitan expectations, and the board argued that correcting the problem
required the government to enforce "due Obedience" to royal "Commands" "in the Proprietary and Charter Governments." For example, with
respect to Massachusetts, the board emphasized that "altho' the Governmt
of this Province be nominally in the Crown," the "unequal Ballance of"
the colony's "Constitution" "lodged too great a power in the Assembly,"
causing in turn "great disorder" and "too great an Independance" from
the "Mother Kingdom." Such "Mischiefs" could only be "redressed" if
the Crown "resume[d]" the proprietary charters. Paramount among these
"Mischiefs" were the "Misfeazancies" that the existence of "Proprietary
Governments" introduced into the regulation of commerce. "Daily Experience" demonstrated that "illegal Trade is not to be prevented in a
Proprietary Government." The solution lay in the Crown's takeover of the

charters, for the proprietorships "might undoubtedly be more Effectually restrained if they were all of them under Your Majesty's immediate Government, and were by proper Laws compelled to follow the Commands Sent them by Your Majesty."[41] Comparing the incoming information on current conditions of governance with the documentation of promulgated constitutional norms contained in the archive, the board mobilized written authorities to advocate both for the particular policy outcome of resumption and for control over trade to be lodged squarely in its hands.

In the 1721 report, the board also explicitly aligned its view of how trade should be governed with its vision of the imperial information order. In addition to continuing its attack on proprietorships, it used the report to respond to a worrisome threat: other administrators' encroachment on its control of documents. Its power in this regard had been challenged in 1702 when the secretary of state, the Earl of Nottingham, instructed governors to correspond directly with him, rather than the board, a circumstance that some of Nottingham's successors in the office sought to continue.[42] In its battle to win parliamentary approval for resumption, the board advocated placing all colonies under the administration of royally appointed governors and returning control over the flow of information to its own hands. Noting that the proprietary colonies' constitutional status empowered them to participate in "a Trade destructive to that of Great Britain," the board argued that restoring its complete control over correspondence was essential to solving the problem. Because governors, assemblies, and subjects could address correspondence to any office that exercised some kind of jurisdiction over imperial affairs—including the Treasury, the Secretary of State, the Privy Council, and the Admiralty— the board wrote, the "present Method of dispatching Business relating to the Plantations" was "lyable to much delay and Confusion." It advocated replacing this multichannel system of communication with one that "Charged" it with "the dispatch of all matters relating to the Plantations" and "wholly confined" the "Business" of recordkeeping to its purview.[43] The board's lobbying in relation to both the 1701 and 1721 bills exemplified the deployment of techniques of administrative knowledge-making through archival precedents within the sphere of legislative contention. An early modern concept of sovereignty that invested "Papers" with both political and epistemological authority was thus applied to governing empire in a manner that confirmed institutional ambitions. The board's repeated deployment of this technique throughout the early eighteenth century exemplified the recurring power of archival arguments in the politics of administration.

Building the Corporate Archive

The constitutional and administrative contexts in which the East India Company operated in the seventeenth century were fundamentally different from those in which the English state ultimately found itself in the Atlantic world. As a joint-stock company formed under a charter granted by Elizabeth I on December 31, 1600, it was empowered by the Crown to specifically form its own "Laws, Constitutions, Orders and Ordinances" insofar as they were "not contrary or repugnant to the Laws, Statutes, or Customs" of England.[44] But unlike other types of early modern companies, such as guilds, the joint-stock form of the East India Company meant that it was governed not by traders but by shareholders, with those who had invested the most capital in the corporation commanding the highest administrative posts, supervising sub-councils and committees to which they delegated the performance of specific tasks. Moreover, in contrast to the constitutional circumstances emerging in parallel in the Atlantic world, the company's membership was bound together not by obligation to the Crown and its privy councilors but instead by obligation to capital investment and a shared commitment to defending and using the privileges specified in its charter: monopoly over trade and settlement granted to the company by the Crown in return for portions of revenue and political support from the corporation's rich and powerful investors. The company's corporate constitution was, moreover, shaped by other kinds of agreements that did not prevail in royal administration in the Atlantic world, especially grants and privileges made to it by Asian powers, which in turn placed it in juridical and administrative relationships based on non-European forms of law.[45] In 1698, for example, the company purchased from the Mughal governor Prince Azim-ush-Shan the rights to collect land revenues from the villages that collectively made up the settlement of Calcutta, known as *zamindaris,* which in turn meant that one of its councilors at Calcutta held the Mughal title of *zamindar*—the English assuming a non-English office.[46] By contrast, seventeenth-century English colonists in the Atlantic world sought to replicate the model of subordinate kingship initially practiced in the Spanish Empire whereby Native rulers were understood to be under the sovereignty of a European monarch, whose authority they would then execute in their dealings with other Native communities. In this endeavor, the English proved spectacularly unsuccessful, most famously demonstrated by their inability to control the Indian leader Powhatan despite his 1608 "coronation" by the Virginia Company captain Christopher Newport as at once king over the Powhatans and a subject to the English sovereign.[47]

These different structures of imperial government in the Atlantic and Asian worlds, respectively, evolved from shared epistemological roots in a post-Reformation-era political culture in which effective governance was conceived to encompass the control of written information and the manipulation of administrative documents to advance policy priorities. If the Privy Council made sure to specify rules of recordkeeping to its servants in the context of "Instructions" as a method of command and control, so too did corporations, both imperial and domestic. Corporate bodies were determined to ensure that their servants "keepe the Bookes of the Company, and fairely, and orderly to enter in them the particulars heere-under expressed, and in such manner as hee shall be directed by the Governour, Deputy, or Auditors," as the Somers-Island Company dictated in 1622. As with Crown administration, the clerks and secretaries of these bodies managed the flow of documents, swearing oaths that they would "faithfully keep all the Books and Records" of their corporate employers; manage the "Custody" of the bodies' seals, "Letters Patents, Deeds," and other documents; and keep them "locked up" so that only the corporation's leadership had access.[48]

The East India Company was no exception in this regard. The corporation specified detailed rules, oaths, and procedures through which its administrative apparatus was to operate and how its records were to be kept in ways that preserved their secrecy while facilitating their use by leadership.[49] These rules were described in the company's *Lawes or Standing Orders,* published in 1621, and then reiterated in subsequent instructions and manuals given to servants, which cemented documentation as the binding fiber of the corporate body. As in Crown offices like the Board of Trade, labors of records management were delegated to the company's secretary, who with clerks under his direction kept minutes of the meetings of the body's leaders (defined as the governor or chair, deputy, treasurer, and twenty-four committees) and the generality (meaning the rest of the members), as well as various subcommittees. In the *Lawes or Standing Orders,* the company defined protocols for the management of written information: "Upon receipt of publique Letters from the *Indyes,*" the governor of the company was to "assemble a Court of Committees, and in their presence" open, register, and then read "in open Court" such letters. Also to be read openly in court were "all the Letters directed to particular men from the Companies Factors or Commanders in the *Indyes,*" a circumstance through which the company sought to prevent its own factors from defying its trading monopoly through private commercial activity. Recordkeeping responsibilities were divided between multiple offices. The Treasurer's Office, for example, both kept the company's accounts and was charged with holding "Custody" of the Crown's "Letters Patents to the Company" and the company's seal, treaties, and contracts, which it was to keep "in some convenient place of the Companies house." The company's secretary was to take all the notes of the meetings, write its letters, "performe the Messages," register all of the letters, and "keepe a Booke" "by Alphabet" of all the members of the corporation. Any court directives that pertained to one of the company's committees was to be copied out of the secretary's notes by a separate officer, the remembrancer, and then sent to the committee. The remembrancer was also to attend the meetings of the various committees in order to "take true Notes" of the proceedings. Indeed, almost every company official had recordkeeping prescribed as part of their duties, even the "Clarke of the Slaughter-house," who was to "keepe a true Accompt of the Receipts of all the Beefes & Hogs" purchased and killed to provision sailors on the company's voyages. Unlike the Crown offices, however, the corporate structure of the East India Company meant that there were important internal divisions within the body through which the leadership sought to control the generality's own access to information as part of its strategy of establishing authority and preventing the circulation of secrets.[50]

Like the metropolitan officers of the corporation, the company's servants at its factories in Asia were rule-bound with respect to recordkeeping. According to the *Lawes or Standing Orders,* two factories were to exercise oversight over the company's establishments in the east Indian Ocean (at Bantam on the island of Java) and west Indian Ocean (at Surat on the western coast of India) respectively. These two principal factories were to "keepe Bookes of all the Letters which they write" to the subordinate factories, copy them "fairely" into "other Bookes," and send them "yearely . . . unto England" for the inspection of the metropolitan leadership, along with "a Journall" in which officials at Bantam and Surat were to "briefly set downe day to day" "all the notable occurrences." Factory officials were also to appoint servants "to keepe faire Bookes of Accompts," store them "in an open place . . . so every Factor in each Factorie" could "see and know the true passages of the Companies Affairs," and send copies of them regularly to England. They were to send all private letters to the Court of Directors, so the corporate leadership could inspect them in case they included proprietary commercial information.[51]

The company's commands that its factors and metropolitan servants keep "perfect" and "Exact" "books" according to prescribed "Rules & Directions" were sticky, reiterated throughout the seventeenth and eighteenth centuries with a fundamental degree of consistency using the same genre of document employed by the Privy Council to communicate rules and expectations to Atlantic world administrators: "Orders and Instructions."[52] In these documents, which the company's Court of Directors issued to governors, servants, and sailors and which were eventually called "General Letters," the court stressed good recordkeeping and the regular return of records as essential to both hold officials accountable and discipline their observations into forms of writing that could be mobilized as policy knowledge. In authorizing voyages, the company instructed sailors to keep "Continuall and true Journalls" of everything that happened on the voyage, and then return them to the court "for [the] better direccon of posteritie."[53] Such "faire Books of Accounts," the court wrote, were to be recorded "with as much plainness as possibly you can" and always "to be delivered" to London after the voyage "for the use of the Company."[54] Captains were ordered to "keep a Journall or Book of . . . Navigation, throughout the whole voyage, and duely to observe and record all materiall accidents and occurrances therein, which books at your returne for England, wee expect to have presented unto us."[55] Similarly, the company required that in factories "there be kept a Journall of each daies proceeding, wherein lists of all goods sent in and out of the factory; all sales and prices; and the names of all who sold or bought were to be kept." "Transcripts" of these documents were to be made and "sent us" while the "Originalls" were to remain "in the several factories."[56]

In such instructions, the court stressed that the creation of inventories, the keeping of accounts, the cultivation of knowledge about places, and the provisioning of documentary proof of good conduct were all essential to the health of the corporate body. These orders were, moreover, to be lasting and indefinite until changed by the Court of Directors: as the body explained in 1702 to Bombay and Surat, "when we tell you that what Generall Orders we have formerly given, We look upon to be of lasting use, not only when first directed, but in all future times while the same or such like occasions continue, and we doubt not but you so understand them."[57] The company also commanded the different factories to exchange information among themselves, writing for example in 1654 to Fort St. George (in the modern Indian city of Chennai) that it was essential "that a continued and good correspondency should be held between" it and "our two Presidencies of Surratt & Bantam."[58] The company used the "General Letter" to respond to specific communications and issues raised by its servants on the ground, instructing how these should be resolved.[59] The court expected a "punctual and speedy complyance with all Orders and Instructions" that it sent to servants.[60] The security of records was of the utmost importance: if a company ship was at risk of being overtaken by an enemy, captains were instructed "to sink all your Packetts received from us or for us to prevent the Enemys knowing their Contents and to that end you must keep a Shott or Piece of Lead fastend to each of them."[61] Better to let documents drown than risk commercial knowledge falling into the hands of a rival.

As with the governing instructions issued to Atlantic world officials, the East India Company's commands to servants for diligent recordkeeping and the regular transmission of records back to the metropolitan leadership were sticky, reiterated consistently from the late seventeenth through the eighteenth century in various guises but with little change in content. The supra cargo—the officer on a ship who represented the owner of the cargo and had the responsibility for its security and sale—was consistently instructed to "fail not to enter your Consultations in a Book which you are to Sign and keep regular Books of Accounts, not omitting to put down before you Sleep the transactions of the day past with relation to Buying, Selling, delivering out and receiving in Expenses Disbursements, Presents, &ca."[62] Presidents and councilors of the company's forts were ordered to keep "Dyarys's and Consultation Books," "margined and indexed," and to send them to London "that we may be the more readily turn to every considerable head therein contain'd."[63] The court generated precise rules and directions for the form of letters sent back by such councils. For example, in 1701, the court wrote to one governor and council that

> Before we come to take notice of the Materiall parts of that Letter We shall give you some direction for the future methodizing of your Letters which you will do well likewise to observe in your advices . . . (That is to say) to range the whole under these General heads viz.t

> First touching Shipping gone out or returned and goods sent from hence.
>   Secondly Concerning Investments of Goods proper for Europe and wherein deficient or blame worthy if so
>   Thirdly of matters relating to our Trade in Generall and therein any Transactions relating to the Country Government and our Accounts in particular.
>   Fourthly Concerning our Revenues and fortifications
>   Fifthly Touching factors & Writers Officers and Souldiers and their Accounts.
>   Sixthly Concerning such Matters as relate to the New Company our Competitors—After which you may add such other Occurrences as you shall judge not properly reducible to these Generall heads aforesaid.

The court then went on to arrange its own observations and responses according to the above heads, providing an example of the form of the written protocols it expected its servants to replicate.[64] Both officials at factories and ship captains were expected to regularly return documents to the company at the earliest convenience. Ship captains were instructed that "on your first arrival in any port of England or elsewhere from whence you have an opportunity of writing to us you do with your first Letters send us not only an account of your arrival and of your Voyage with Copy of your Bill of Lading [a document listing the contents of a shipment of goods] . . . but also an account in writing of all private trade parcells and goods whether Tokens or otherwise that are on board your Ship."[65] Governors and councils were instructed to send the court "yearly Books of Accounts by Shipping, and frequent Accounts of your Expences, presents, Remains, Goods bought and other matters fitt for our notice."[66] Failure to do so brought on the court's rebuke of "ill management" and strict reminders that the company's servants "must constantly comply with" metropolitan command.[67] "We will never again bear with the want of our Books of Accounts yearly. . . . We will never again rest Easy if We have not the Consultations sent Us" regularly, the company emphasized, continually making clear the demand for records to councils and governors such "that none hereafter may pretend Ignorance or excuses for failures in these Articles." "If they do fail," the court warned, "we will rid our hands of them be they who they will and will no longer content our Selves with bare chiding."[68]

The company routinely reiterated expectations around recordkeeping to officials, treating the protocols for the management and preparation of papers in the *Lawes or Standing Orders* as a "Generall Rule for all time to come."[69] Councils and governors were ordered by the court to constantly audit and examine the accounts of traders and factors in order to "take care that they don't privately make away with or conceal" profits that rightfully belonged to the company.[70] The company threatened merchants who failed to keep "regular Consultations" and "Regular Books of Accounts" with the "Penalty of forfeiting your Comission" as a company-authorized ship.[71] The instructions given by the court for the correct composition of records were profoundly granular. As it specified to Fort St. George in 1711, while

> the Margining your Consultations and putting the same in the nature of an Index in the beginning of the book is well done and will be helpfull to you as well as here, it would be much more usefull if the Secretary did rank the said Marginall notes in an alphabeticall order and under the Severall Letters which the principall words of the order relate to for Instance if any orders were made relating to the Frederick Then in ye Alphabet under F you would soon find it out so if any orders were made for what the Secretary was to do put a short line under S expressing the Substance of that order and in what folio to find it and the like for all other Persons or things or else to make a Generall title for each of the Severall Standing head Officers as President, Accountants, Warehousekeeper, Pay Master, Collector of the Land Customs, Collector of the Sea Customs &c.a

and for each factory of settlement you Correspond with or send orders to And under each of these Generall titles enter the Substance in one line in the Alphabet of what such orders contain and at the end of it the folio they are entered in by this means you would with a little trouble and much more dispatch presently turn to any thing you want and this Index might be kept up weekly as the Consultations are enter'd and the same you might do for the account of Broadcloth Lead and other Goods whether Europe or India which you have occasion to make orders about in Consultacon the Alphabet to a Ledger will easily show you the method.[72]

Even when the court praised councils that had taken "constant care" in the keeping of their accounts, the court also was granular in specifying that "there are some Entrys which must be better taken care of," something the directors blamed on "the Secretarys carelessness."[73]

As the company reiterated the rules and expectations for the conduct of correspondence, it also refined its system of archiving documents—which in the *Lawes or Standing Orders* saw responsibility distributed across several offices—in light of the practical experiences of administration. As the company's official apparatus grew in size and complexity over the course of the eighteenth century, these protocols also evolved. Changes in its administrative structure led to new challenges for managing documentation. These included its takeover between 1702 and 1708 of an English company trading to the East Indies, chartered in 1698 by William III, which saw the incorporation of the rival's "Bookes and Paper" into the company archive.[74] Some of these challenges in turn produced changes in the structure of records management. For example, in March 1706, the court delegated responsibility for assessing and, if necessary, drafting responses to letters from India to a Committee of Correspondence.[75] The company's own use of its archive in turn generated refinements and alterations in records management. In 1716, the Court of Directors sought to address claims for redress by Mary Gayer, wife of Sir John Gayer, the governor of Surat in western India from 1694 who had been imprisoned by the Mughal emperor Aurangzeb in the course of war with the company between 1700 and 1710. Looking for records to help determine compensation for Mary Gayer, a group of arbitrators appointed by the company discovered that the archive held in the office of the accountant was in disarray: one of the journals from Surat had been "cut off" from its cover and "stolen away," and "great quantityes" of the company's "Packets, and other Papers" were found "thrown on heaps" in one of its warehouses. In response, the Court of Directors appointed a committee to "make a strict enquiry about the Book so cut off from the Cover and stole away," and to make recommendations for both "a proper place wherein to lay the Company's packets & other papers" and a person to care for them so that they could "be ready at hand when wanted."[76] After reading the report, the court authorized the appointment of a "proper Person" "at a reasonable Salary, to have the Custody of all such of the Company's Books and Papers as are not in immediate use, so as to [ar]range and dispose them" such that "easie recourse" could be made "to them upon all occasions."[77] Four years later, however, the court declared that the company's "Papers, Packets and Old Books" still stood "in the utmost confusion," and ordered its secretary to arrange them in a "proper Repository." Over the next several decades, the offices of the accountant and the secretary traded responsibility for managing the records.[78]

Like the Board of Trade, the company used the records as precedents to shape decision-making and as confirmatory supports for particular policy interests. Perhaps the most quotidian use of records involved auditing those received from the factories to ensure the integrity and profitability of the company's commerce. This task was assigned to a hierarchy of officers, beginning with court-appointed auditors, who were to inspect accounts recorded by the various offices, and the company's own bookkeepers organized as "accountants generall," who were to "carefully review" the work of the auditors. A separate group of auditors—"auditors in the Court of Committees"—were specifically tasked with investigating any discrepancies found and delivering a report to the Court of Directors. At the top of the hierarchy were the "auditors generall," two in number, who were to undertake a quarterly audit of all the accounts generated by company servants. Through this division of official labor, the company sought to create an institutional culture centered on a particular idea of accountability in which (as the *Lawes or Standing Orders* described the system) "little or no trust" was "imposed in any particular mans accounts" on their own but instead rendered trustworthy only through a "checke" via reference to the "accounts of other men"—information validated by its correspondence to other information, rendered tangible, recoverable, and transferable through written records.[79]

The practice of accounting within the company thus became one of the sites where the archival epistemology of governance was made manifest. Accounting was fundamental to every level of its operations, and as a document-intensive administrative practice, it involved the corporation's servants in recurring labors of record creation according to strictly defined protocols. Indeed, in its *Lawes or Standing Orders,* the corporation devoted an entire section to specifying how the work of accounting was to be performed such that its entire membership would be clear on "the order and method" that the accountants general "shall observe and performe in the Mannaging and digesting [of] the Accompts of the Company."[80] Not only did the company's accountants endeavor to secure the profitability of its commerce; they also performed the work of supplying the Court of Directors with written precedents for making and executing decisions on a range of issues, including determining the appropriate level of compensation for families of sailors who drowned on company ships, settling debts, and, perhaps most importantly, managing the corporation's transfer books, in which sales of the company's shares were recorded.[81] Just as the company's accountants were regularly instructed by the court to "examine" the corporation's "Bookes of Accounts, Consultations, and other Books received from time to time, from all parts of India," so too were the company's own practices of accounting themselves subject to constant internal scrutiny, examination, and reform by the body itself, with different committees within the organization's hierarchy regularly inspecting one another's accounts in order to assess accuracy and recommend practices through which other servants could ensure their accounts were "methodical[ly] kept."[82] As the volume of the accountant office's records expanded, the court dedicated more and more space within the corporation's warehouses for "the more convenient lodging & keeping" of the archive.[83] Using the records prompted refinement of the methods of their organization: for example, when the Court of Directors learned in 1711 that a committee appointed to assess the "Generall State" of the company's trade could not complete its work "because the Books in the Accountant's Office are not yet brought up," the court ordered that "a proper method" "for the speedy, and regular bringing up" of accounting books be devised.[84] Through this system of inspection, audit, and assessment, the company endeavored to "regulate and rectify" its books so as to keep them "balanced" and in good order.[85]

If accounting was a core imperative toward which the company consistently directed its archival strategies, the legal and rhetorical defense of its commercial privileges was another. The utility of its archive as evidence in trials in a variety of courts was well known among merchants, who often appealed to the Court of Directors for "recourse" to the company's "diarys, the Letters to & from India & all papers which any ways relate[d]" to their situation, hoping that presenting such papers in litigation would "strengthen" their "cause."[86] The volume of such requests seems to have eventually strained the capacities of the corporation, prompting the directors to promulgate a rule in 1725 that they "would not for the future upon any occasion whatsoever suffer any Books or Papers to be produced in Try-alls wherein the Company are not concerned," unless granted an exemption, and to in some instances require that disputants pay the company's secretaries directly for the costs of copying and finding records.[87]

Instead, the Court of Directors generally sought to direct its clerical resources to assisting applicants in whose situations the corporation perceived itself to have a direct interest. As with other early modern administrative bodies, the company strategically circulated and cited records as authorities to advance these interests. Sometimes, this meant commissioning particular reports to be printed and circulated, though it is often unclear whether such printings actually occurred or whether the resulting texts simply do not survive.[88] In texts that did clearly appear under its sponsorship, the company often accompanied its arguments with appendixes consisting of transcriptions and reproductions of letters and other official documents which (they believed) substantiated these views. An early example was the company's response to the 1623 attack by the Dutch East India Company on its trading factory on the island of Ambon in modern Indonesia, the so-called Amboyna massacre, which shaped imperial ideology for centuries to come. In 1624, the company prepared, printed, and circulated its own account of the events in the form of a pamphlet, most likely written by the company sea captain John Skinner, offering *A True Relation of the Cruell and Barbarous Tortures and Execution, Done upon the English at Amboyna in the East Indies, by the Hollanders There Residing*, authenticated by reference to the "wrytings" of the company servants said to have witnessed the proceedings firsthand.[89] The company reprinted the 1624 text several times during the series of Anglo-Dutch Wars that broke out in 1652 and raged on and off for the next two decades in new editions in which it promised "A farther Account of the Deceit, Cruelty, and Tyranny of the Dutch" "Faithfully Collected from Antient and Modern Records."[90] The Company continued to inveigh against the Dutch in subsequent publications, authorizing its own views through appendixes of transcribed documents that it claimed substantiated its positions.[91]

What the Court of Directors described as "the great Encrease . . . of the Correspondence" generated by the company's receipt of the *diwani*, or grant of the office of revenue collector, for Bengal, Bihar, and Orissa prompted the appointment in 1769 of a dedicated officer, the examiner of Indian correspondence, to manage the records for the purposes of preservation and potential consultation in decision-making, and to prepare drafts of correspondence from the court and its committees to servants across Asia. In response to the court's requests for information, the examiner was "to inspect, examine, and make the necessary References to and Observations on the Important Branches of the Indian Correspondence."[92] The court augmented the staff of the Examiner's Office over the next several years, appointing a "Compiler and Writer of the Company's Foreign Correspondence with their Settlements in the East Indies" in 1770, and in 1771 a "Register and Keeper of India Records" instructed to "arrange, number and register" the "confused and disorderly" records.[93] The court enhanced the organization of the records in the late 1780s, instituting practices of creating abstracts of records to make the operation of the Examiner's Office more "regular."[94]

Lord North's Regulating Act of 1773 introduced significant changes into the company's administrative structure. The act extended Crown control and oversight of the corporation's activities in response to the administrative calamities it had experienced in Bengal, while preserving the company's trading privileges. At this point, a governor-general, advised by four councilors, all based at the company's establishment at Fort William, was to take charge of "the Ordering, Management, and Government of all the Territorial Acquisitions and Revenues" of the company. Officials at other forts were in turn directed to "constantly and diligently" "transmit" "Advice and Intelligence of all Transactions and Matters whatsoever that shall come to their Knowledge, relating to the Government, Revenues, or Interest" of the company to the governor-general. The act specified the appointment of Warren Hastings as first governor-general, with John

Clavering appointed as his lieutenant and three other officials—George
Monson, Richard Barwell, and Philip Francis—named to his council for
terms of five years, to begin after the public proclamation of the arrival of
the governor-general and the councilors to Fort William.[95]

The act empowered the governor-general with the authority "to
make and issue such Rules, Ordinances, and Regulations" pertaining to
the company's territories, to be registered and enforced in concert with a
"Supreme Court of Judicature" that would exercise "full Power and Authority" over all civil, criminal, admiralty, and ecclesiastical disputes but
which could not try any charges brought against the governor-general or
councilors themselves. This Supreme Court, also housed at Fort William,
was to serve as the custodian of "all the Records, Muniments, and Proceedings" of the company's courts. All laws and orders made by these
bodies were to be transmitted back to the Court of Directors, which reserved the power to nullify such laws and which would ensure that a copy
was "affixed in some conspicuous and publick Place in the India House,
there to remain and be resorted to as Occasion shall require." Additional
copies were to be sent to the Privy Council, which also reserved the right
to nullify laws. Indeed, such laws made by the governor-general and council would not be "valid, or of any Force or Effect," until "duly registered
and published" in the Supreme Court's registry. Testimony before the
courts was to "be reduced into one or more Writing or Writings on Parchment" by the court's officers, with a copy signed and sealed by them and
sent to the Court of King's Bench, whose clerks were in turn to make an
oath of the receipt of the decision and that it had "not been opened, or
altered, since he so received it." The clerk was then to read the document
aloud so it could be considered by the Court of King's Bench. In turn, the
Court of Directors was compelled to give "a true and exact Copy of all
Parts of the said Letters or Advices as any way relate to the Management
of the Revenues" of the company to the Treasury, and a similar copy of
such letters as in "any way relate to the Civil or Military Affairs and Government of the said Company" to the Secretary of State.[96]

The 1773 act constituted a significant moment in the information
order of the early modern British Empire. Two systems of administration,
one in the Atlantic world and one in the Asian world, both centered on
mobilizing archival authorities to enforce metropolitan command and substantiate policy ambitions, now came to be commonly within the purview

of the Secretary of State and its associated clerical officials. At the same time, the demographic contours of the empire were shifting: where once the majority of subjects were English speakers, now English speakers would coexist with "others." Could the metropolitan archive continue to serve as a source of precedential knowledge? Or would administrators seek a different version of the past, rooted in the experiences of non-English speaking subjects?

Subjects of the Archive

WHERE WERE INDIGENOUS AND enslaved people within these imperial archives? Did they appear within the vast troves of paper and parchment generated by imperial institutions, and if so how? From the vantage point of nineteenth- and twentieth-century British imperialism, one might expect ample documentation about non-Europeans to have proliferated in the archives' early modern predecessor. The circumstance of "ruling over hundreds of millions of conquered subjects, most of whom were Black or brown, and neither enslaved nor free," Caroline Elkins has recently observed, presented the modern British Empire with a fundamental problem: "How could Britain justify and maintain its domination of conquered peoples at a time when liberal ideals were rendering its own nation-state increasingly democratic?"[1] Asking the same question of the early modern British Empire, however, raises complications—and not only because liberal ideals, nation-states, and democratic expectations were yet to be born. While early modern imperialists exploited nonwhite populations prolifically and ruthlessly, they did not consider many of those whom they brutalized "conquered subjects." This circumstance explains the seeming paradox that two of these populations, Native Americans and African-descended peoples—whose exploited labor and contestation by and with British imperial government and settler populations is of vast importance to imperial history—appear in highly circumscribed ways within official records.

In contemporary cultural discourse, the term "archive" has become synonymous with the idea of any record of past thought and action, including but not confined to writing—a capacious definition that has enabled a powerful, vital expansion of who is considered a part of historical narratives and the forms of knowledge production through which their lives can be understood. This concept of the archive perceptively recognizes that despite the formal exclusion of enslaved peoples, Indigenous peoples, and nonmale people from the category of the "human" and the

54

corresponding "body politic" by governing regimes, they were nonetheless constitutive presences in the making of political, social, and economic life. Yet, it is at the same time vital to recognize that early modern administration operated on a contextually precise definition of the archive as "records of governance" that, in turn, created the conditions under which such groups came to be subordinated within regimes of knowledge production in the first place, and their experiences and material traces excluded from the evidentiary paradigm of historiography.

Precisely because governing institutions in the Atlantic world interacted with Native American and African and African-descended peoples through violence without the administrative formality of conquest, thus placing them outside the status of "subject," all were largely invisible in the archive even as they were inseparable from the history of empire. While Native and African-descended peoples were not exploited in the same ways, they were both absent within the justificatory apparatus of early modern archival reasoning. Put another way, the justifications made by early modern empires for territory dispossession and enslavement often involved referring to and citing from a body of texts, but administrative records were not especially important within this corpus. This was because the political use of this corpus (which included the Bible, the works of classical historians, the writings of Christian theologians like Saint Augustine and Thomas Aquinas, digests of Roman law, and antiquarian histories) to justify war, dispossession, and enslavement long preceded overseas expansion.[2] Imperial institutions in the Americas thus countenanced the exploitation of these groups while collecting information about them that facilitated that exploitation even as the institutions presumed their own legitimacy. By contrast, over the course of the eighteenth century, East India Company officials increasingly conceived of the corporation as ruler over nonwhite Indian *subjects*. They applied the archival epistemology of rule to the administration of this vision by conceiving of the governing project as emanating from "Indian" records. The practice of producing and collecting written knowledge about Indians in India thus came to be a focal point of the information regime of the East India Company, while collecting information on Indians in the Americas and African-descended peoples in the Atlantic world remained relatively marginal to the priorities of both corporate and Crown government in those geographic theaters.

To "Learne the Language of Yor Countrie"

In 1773, the imperial official and writer Thomas Pownall wrote a pamphlet analyzing the place of Asia within the imperial constitution. In his view, the British Empire had been transformed in 1765 when Robert Clive, the East India Company's governor in Bengal, forced the captured Mughal emperor Shah Alam II to sign the Treaty of Allahabad. By this document, the Mughal emperor granted the company the status of *diwan* over the provinces of Bengal, Bihar, and Orissa, which empowered the corporation to collect land revenue in these territories. In practice, Pownall emphasized, the company had used this grant, called the *diwani*, to exercise much broader powers—so broad, in fact, that the corporation was now ontologically indistinct from a territorial ruler.[3] "The exercise of the sovereignty of populous and extensive dominions in the East Indies, have come into the hands of the East India company," he argued, "and in consequence of power arising from this exercise of sovereignty, and of influence from this possession of the revenues, the same company have as merchants" "acted as sovereigns." In less than a decade since the treaty, Pownall continued, corporate administration had proved disastrous. The company's rule was characterized by a "want of wisdom and power" among its metropolitan leadership at home and "ungovernable disobedience" abroad by servants whose "plundering, pillaging, and rapine" had wreaked havoc in India.[4]

Pownall blamed the company's maladministration on its exercise of a set of powers that he believed were entirely unremarkable when viewed in relation to the history of the British Empire. The royal charter defining the company's constitutional status bore an "unvarying similarity," "clause by clause, word by word," to those that "have been given to all other colonists and emigrants" in the empire, Pownall wrote. These charters made clear that throughout the empire, colonists held "rights of possession" but not sovereignty over territory, since the latter was "alway[s] reserved" for the Crown. But something strange had occurred in the territories formerly controlled by the Mughal Empire and now by the company. There, according to Pownall, the "sovereignty of the native government of the country within the bounds of the East India Company" had been "abolished and annihilated" by conquest. But the corporation was now "executing the government of the country, under its own [i.e., Indian] laws" "by the ministration" of Indian offices and officers. The company was "STATE-HOLDER," yet, the administration of the territory was "still left in its old form of state" and "still exercised upon its old rules of government, and by its old officers of state and police." A pair of constitutional crises therefore prevailed, he contended. First, Indians were now under the sovereignty of an English ruler who governed them not in accordance with the English constitution but instead through the "native" laws that had prevailed before conquest. Second, while the Crown had granted the East India Company powers to trade, acquire, and possess territory on its behalf, the corporation was no longer an appendage of the British government; instead, Pownall warned, *"the merchant is become the sovereign,"* "independent of the supreme sovereignty of the state."[5]

Pownall's account of where non-English peoples were situated in relation to the body of this company-state was in stark contrast to the constitutional configuration of Native Americans in British America. The corporate sovereign's relationship to the peoples living in the *diwan* was not one of diplomacy with a geographically proximate but jurisdictionally separate population. Rather, the company was the sovereign *over* Indians, making them part of a European imperial formation. According to Pownall, the constitutional status of these Indians in India was entirely unprecedented. "The nature and spirit of our constitution" meant that "all acquisitions of territory made by the subjects of Great Britain . . . vest in the crown." Thus, in Pownall's opinion, the only legitimate sovereign in India could be the monarch and the only authority the imperial constitution, which was made up of administrative decrees, common law, and parliamentary legislation. But the company governed as *diwani* using Indian, not English, laws and administrators.[6]

What Pownall diagnosed as a novel constitutional dilemma might instead be contextualized as a particular variation on the structural problem at the heart of empires themselves: governing in relation to difference. In the context of the Atlantic littoral and American continent, the British Empire solved this by placing difference outside the compass of constitutional self-definition. In South Asia, by contrast, collecting and organizing knowledge of Indians in India was fundamental to the East India Company's project of rule.[7] In short, in the context of government and administration, there was no singular Other against which early modern "Britishness" was defined.[8] With respect to the "East Indies," the Crown had long envisioned that company servants would not cultivate intermediaries to deal with native powers but instead learn the customs and languages of Indians and then deploy them themselves in commerce and rule. In her letter authorizing the first voyage of the company, addressed to the "Kings of Sumatra and other places in the East Indies," Queen Elizabeth stated that the merchants sailing to the East Indies would "learne the language of yor countrie, and applie their behavior, as it may best sorte, to converse wth your Maies subjects, to the end that amitie and friendshipp beinge entertayned and begun, the same may the better be continewed, when our people shal be instructed, how to direct them selves accordinge to the fashion of yor countrie."[9] Accommodating local custom was central to the Crown's vision of how the company would actualize sovereignty in Asian territorial and maritime space—and accommodation required collecting, organizing, and interpreting information about such customs.

The company encoded these expectations for collecting information about the peoples of the "East Indies" into the instructions that it issued to sailors and factors. Company officials were instructed that "upon the delivery of her Majesties Letters to the princes of those places where our ships shall arrive" "to Commerce and traffick with the people of those Countries or place," the factors were to gather "better information" for delivery to future sailors as to "how to carry them selves in those places . . . as tyme and experience of those places shall direct you" to acquire.[10] The Court of Directors considered gathering and recording local knowledge in writing as central to the conduct of trade and settlement. Thus it instructed factors to return both their "accounte Journall" and any "other . . . obseruacons touching the affaires of those Countries" to London, in the hopes that the on-the-ground "intelligence" would render the corporation "better directed in our further proceedinge to settle in those partes."[11] Appointing councils to supervise trade and settlement in specific places, the court emphasized that servants should learn local languages and customs so that native inhabitants would not stiff the corporation in commercial exchange. In 1702, for example, the court suggested that in the low season, "some of our Servants that are not of Council" should "be employed in small Stocks in the Severall Augunges or places where Cloth and other goods are made and bought," where they would "not only gain experience in the Knowledge and true value of goods" but also "perfect themselves in the Language and Customes of the Country and Knowledge of the Government and so quallify themselves to serve use when they shall come into higher Stations at the head ffactory, but this likewise will be a Check upon the Black Merchants."[12]

The East India Company's interest in cultivating "Knowledge" of the "Government" as well as "Language and Customes of the Country" reflected a broader interdependence in early modern Europe between scholars and administrators for information about non-European worlds. Institutions such as long-distance trading companies were vital to the construction and operation of the infrastructures of patronage, communication, and exchange through which the circulation of texts and ideas occurred.[13] Participants in these networks of knowledge exchange relied on governing, religious, and commercial institutions—from the Levant Company to the Jesuits to royal diplomats—to facilitate and finance the collection and transmission of these materials.[14] The East India Company's belief that its servants could "quallify themselves" as useful members of its corporate body politic by mastering "the Language and Customes of the Country and Knowledge of the Government" of South Asia thus reflected a broader cultural milieu in which the pursuit of commercial and territorial sovereignty and the production of scholarship became mutually dependent activities. Commercial success was understood to require that servants immerse themselves in Asian styles of conduct, cultivating and practicing cultural fluency so that their behavior comported with and even mirrored local norms. These tactics have been examined with particular reference to the company's diplomatic interactions with Mughal rulers, and they expressed themselves in other contexts as well.[15] For example, in a 1704 letter to its council in Persia, the company advised, "We think it would be very much for our advantage that some of our own people in all places should better understand the Native Language there and the more the better[,] Especially in Persia and therefore have Entertained Six youths for writers at ffive pounds a year . . . to reside" at the overland trading post of Susa and the port of Gombroon on the Strait of Hormuz. "We chose them so young," the court continued, "as hoping they will the sooner learn the language, The Tongues of youths being more plyable and easier fitted to the accenting of words then generally is in those of more advanced years and we thereby recommend it to their Superiours to take care they be kept close to the learning of the Language, and if they could arrive at the writing of it, it would be yet better we should not grudge any reasonable charge for their Education therein and if they should be neg-ligent advise us that we may remedy it."[16] In 1713, the council at the com-pany's trading establishment of Fort St. George in Madras (now Chennai) reported that the Persian master there had died, that servants had been forced to study on their own (with at least one servant reported to have made "an unusuall progress in the Persian language"), and that the Court of Directors should give "encouragement to those who are Masters of the Eastern language."[17] The court replied by encouraging the precocious servant's Persian study, expressing its "hope" that "he will continue that Study till he is Master of Writing it as well as the speaking."[18] In a similar vein, the court in 1701 instructed its council in China to "putt one or two of the youths that are most apt & ready upon learning the Chinese language, which wee think may be of service to our affaires."[19]

The company was most interested in having servants learn Persian because it understood this to be the language of the Mughal court, whose sovereignty it continuously interacted with in India.[20] But getting them to learn was not easy. In January 1709, the Fort William council reported that it had employed "a Master to teach the Youths Persians," but "few would Stick to it."[21] The court responded a year later by lamenting that "our young Men are so unwilling to learn to Speak and Write the Persian Language" that "wee shall suspect they have neither inclination nor ability to serve us when they will not take pains to learn that which they will be so usefull to themselves as well as us." The corporation also encouraged servants to learn the so-called country languages spoken by Indians under Mughal rule, and to that end instructed Fort William to promote one par-ticularly adept official as "an Example to others to show how well wee are pleased with our Young Servants learning the Countrey Languages."[22] In response, the Fort William council sought to reassure the court that it had constantly "encourag'd" "the Company's Servants" "to learn the Indostan & Persian tongues" by having "a Tutor in the house to teach Persians," and by sending servants to learn Hindustani.[23] The court sent further encouragement, stressing to councils about the "benefit likely to redound" to servants "in their Trade & Converse and general usefulness" from learning Hindustani or Persian.[24] By the early eighteenth century, the company was firmly convinced that "our own People who are acquainted with the Natives and lie all the year amongst them . . . would do better" at trade "than those who are almost if not altogether Strangers in the Countrey."[25] It saw cultural competency, rooted in language study, as essential to its success.

The East India Company invested in bridging the linguistic divide in other ways. For example, it wielded missionaries to translate imperial rule into Indian vernaculars, mobilizing Protestantism as an instrument for building political order, prosperity, and civil harmony within its trading settlements in Asia, and for spreading Christianity beyond them.[26] In the early modern period, the company did not conceive of the mass education of Indians in the English language but instead sought to accommodate its evangelical impulses to local linguistic cultures. From the early seventeenth century, the company employed chaplains to sail on its voyages and ensure the moral upkeep of servants. Once they reached India, the ministers were tasked with trying to convert any non-Protestant European merchants whom they encountered. The company's ambitions broadened following the formation in England of the Society for Promoting Christian Knowledge in 1698 and the Society for the Propagation of the Gospel in 1701. Robert Boyle, best known in his capacity as a natural philosopher and member of the Royal Society but who was also head of the Company for the Propagation of the Gospel in New England from 1662 and a director of the East India Company from 1669, played a crucial role in these efforts. Boyle supported the production of the Eliot Bible in North America, the first Bible printed in North America in any language and printed in Massachusett, the language of the Algonquian people living in Massachusetts. From the 1640s he sponsored translations of works on Christianity into "Oriental" languages like Arabic and Malay and used the company as a distribution network for sending them to factories to facilitate conversion. In the early 1680s, Boyle tried unsuccessfully to have the company sponsor language-training programs for missionaries in Arabic, Persian, and Malay at Oxford. Boyle's efforts established the terms of the company's relationship with missionaries during the eighteenth century. It was to support the transportation of missionaries to India who would learn local vernaculars and Christianize without Anglicizing. Simultaneously, servants at the company's Asian factories began to send texts in languages such as Parsi, Avestan, and Persian back to London to be copied, translated, and circulated among both learned and mercantile communities in Europe in order to further both scholarly pursuits and improved administrative knowledge of Company India.[27]

The company continued to sponsor this traffic in book circulation and the production and diffusion of translations of Protestant propaganda into Indian languages.[28] In doing so, its leadership demonstrated a belief that the practice of gathering information about Asian cultures was relevant to its conception of the work of a company-state.

In a similar vein, the company instructed its senior officials in India to encourage and use local servants who wished to learn or had learned local languages.[29] Although the Court of Directors continuously stressed this to factors during the first five and a half decades of the eighteenth century, Robert Clive's military success made cultivating linguistically competent servants both more imperative and more complicated. From at least the 1640s, Indians had served in the company's military during wars with French, Portuguese, and Asian powers, but the number of Indians employed in the corporation's army massively increased from 1757.[30] For the councils appointed to govern each of its three presidencies, or trading forts in India during the 1750s and early 1760s—Fort William in Calcutta, Bombay, and Fort St. George in Madras (now Chennai)—conquest raised intertwined questions of sovereignty and administration in relation to customary practices but very little clarity. Was the company to receive territory by grant from defeated rulers like the Nawab of Bengal, or, as the Bengal council deliberated in 1757, would the company need "to take Possession by force of the Lands to be granted" to it?[31] Would Indians living in the territory that the company now claimed to rule be integrated into a corporate administrative and military infrastructure with nowhere near the cultural expertise to effectively communicate with locals, or would they be governed differently? How was the company to actually collect the land revenues of Bengal?

These circumstances introduced considerable quandaries into the company's efforts to translate ideas of sovereignty into practices of administration from 1757 on. Such complications came to be inscribed in the treaties that the company made with *nawabs* over management of territory and revenue, which detailed the complex distribution of administrative powers between either side: for example, native rulers could "continue in possession" of "all their affairs to be transacted" in their names and be "vested with the administration of all affairs" of provinces, while the company would be "assigned" "the profits" of their particular "Countries"— treaties that were themselves subject to frequent modification, revision, and negotiation.[32] Indeed, whatever agreements the company made with *nawabs* over the collection of revenue, officials recognized that in practice the terms of administration were subject to constant "discussion" and characterized by "much difficulty" in their practical implementation, which in turn "occasion[ed] greater disputes" and "disturbances" over their meaning.[33] On the military question, for example, cultural prejudices and ignorance meant that company units did not easily accommodate native forces. As the military officer John Carnac wrote to the Fort William council in 1764, Mughal cavalry would "never be brought to submit to the ill treatment, they necessarily receive from Gentlemen, wholly unacquainted with their Language, and Customs."[34] The company, therefore, had strategic reasons to encourage officers to attain some knowledge of Indian languages and customs, and from the late 1760s the Court of Directors in London renewed efforts to facilitate this. The army officer, historian, and later company critic Alexander Dow was a beneficiary of this particular enthusiasm. Entering the Bengal army in 1760 as a cadet, Dow slowly ascended the ranks, becoming a captain in 1764. Somehow, he learned Persian, and translated and published several works from the writings of the seventeenth-century Mughal historian Shaikh 'Inayatullah Kanbu in 1768 in an attempt to "shew" English audiences "what the Oriental stile really is."[35] That same year, Dow petitioned the court to reappoint him to the army, stressing that in his term of service, he had "acquired a knowledge of the Persian and Indian Languages." Dow claimed that he was "useful to the Company" because of "the progress he has made in the oriental tongues, and his knowledge of the political state of Hindostan."[36] The court agreed, sending Dow to Bombay in 1769 with instructions to its council that given the "very few" number of "Servants" "acquainted with the Country Languages," officers ought to "avail" themselves of Dow's "abilities whenever it may be necessary to translate from or negotiate in those Languages."[37] The court subsequently expressed its "severe reprehension" and "much weakened" metropolitan "confidence" in the Bombay council in 1771 for what the directors judged as its failure to make proper use of Dow's abilities.[38]

Roughly contemporary with its patronage of Dow, the Court of Directors began to tie the cultivation of linguistically capable servants to the corporation's longstanding investment in the technology of print. It had long orchestrated the publication and circulation of written materials justifying its activities as congruent with the interests of the British state to drum up public and political support for the parliamentary renewal of its charter privileges.[39] In the era of Clive, the company was now open as well to supporting publication projects that would enhance the linguistic capabilities of its servants. Beginning in 1770, the court considered funding linguists and printers who wished to produce an English translation of the Hapsburg orientalist Franciscus à Mesgnien Meninski's *Linguarum Orientalium Turcicae, Arabicae, Persicae Institutiones, seu Grammatica Turcica.* Published in Vienna in 1680, Meninski's work provided a comparative account of Turkish, Persian, and Arabic grammar, thus offering a possible means of comprehending languages of increasing interest to European states and companies as they deepened their territorial and commercial presences in the eastern Mediterranean Sea and the Indian Ocean. On June 21, 1770, the printer William Crichton wrote to the court to request that the company subscribe to his proposed project of publishing a new edition of Meninski's grammar. Crichton stressed the strategic imperative of replacing native interpreters with company officials trained in Indian languages. "The necessity which has too long prevailed of conducting every transaction with the Asiatic princes . . . by the intermediation of an interpreter, is not only below the dignity of British learning, but tedious, indecisive, and dangerous," the proposal stated.[40] The company also received a competing proposal from Archibald Hamilton and George Nicol for printing their own edition of Meninski's text, and the Court of Directors referred both of them to its Committee of Correspondence for deliberation.[41] The committee recommended that the company patronize both proposals in the hopes that together the dictionaries would promote officials' knowledge of Turkish and Persian. The committee also endorsed the production of a Hindustani-English dictionary by the Company Lieutenant John Ferguson on the grounds that such a text would "prove of great Utility in making the Hindostan Tongue easy to the Company's Servants abroad, as well Civil as Military."[42] On August 8, the court authorized a subscription for Hamilton and Nicol's dictionary and encouragement and compensation to Ferguson so that he could work on his Hindustani-English dictionary.[43] Subsequently, in November and December, the court received a proposal from the lawyer and antiquary Sir William Jones soliciting support for the publication of his *Grammar of the Persian Language* as well as for another version of Meninski's *Linguarum*

Orientalium that he was in the midst of coproducing with a fellow lawyer and antiquary, John Richardson.[44] Although the Court of Directors did not support Jones's proposal, Hamilton and Nicol failed to bring out the promised dictionary, and on January 17, 1776, the court demanded that they return the subscription money for "having failed in the performance of their proposals."[45]

Richardson and Jones did ultimately benefit from the corporation's interest in patronizing scholarship to serve the ends of empire. After moving from Edinburgh to London around 1767, Richardson began to study Persian and Arabic. In London, he met Jones, who had acquired a comprehension of Hebrew, Arabic, Greek, Portuguese, and some Persian during study at Oxford where he had been a fellow of University College since 1766. The two lawyers began working together on a translation of a new Persian and Arabic dictionary based on Meninski's. But Jones soon withdrew from the project to concentrate on two others: producing a Persian grammar in English and a commission from King Christian VII of Denmark to translate the *Tarikh-I Jahangusha-yi Nadiri,* a hagiographic biography of the Persian monarch Nader Shah, who waged war against the Mughal Empire from 1739 to 1740, written by his court historiographer Mahdi Khan Astarabadi.[46]

Through these pursuits, Richardson and Jones stressed that imperial government would benefit from cultivating "Indian" knowledge.[47] They believed that a company-state that claimed sovereignty and exercised jurisdiction over Indian peoples needed to train its servants in local languages and customs in order to govern effectively. As Richardson and his brother William explained to Robert Clive in 1771 as they sought his endorsement of their project, "the study of the Court languages of the East is universally considered as an object of great importance to the Hon. East India Company" in light of the company's "present opulence and power." This "opulence and power," the brothers wrote flatteringly, derived from Clive's "superior abilities." Directly tying the imperative of learning languages to the administration of the company's territorial seizures, the brothers emphasized the dictionary's utility not to scholarship but to administration. As they elaborated, "The Hon. Court of Directors, have in their minutes declared that it would be *very serviceable in the correspondence which the Presidencies hold with the Country powers in the East Indies.*"[48] Although this language had not actually appeared in the court's minutes, the idea that linguistic knowledge could be an instrument of rule held sway at a moment when the company was confronting the complexities of implementing territorial sovereignty in India. When John Richardson informed the court in January 1776 that he had completed an "Arabick Grammar" and was "preparing" "a Persian, Arabick and English" dictionary, the company was among those (alongside many of its leading officials acting in a private capacity, including Robert Orme, Nathaniel Smith, Laurence Sulivan, and Warren Hastings) who subscribed to the work to support its publication. The work appeared in two volumes, published in 1777 and 1780 by Oxford, and the second included Richardson's "respectful acknowledgements" to the company for its support.[49]

Like the Richardson brothers, Jones was inclined to focus on articulating the utility of languages for administration as he sought to win company support for his scholarly projects. But Jones also articulated a tension between the local and the metropolitan, one that does not register in the extensive scholarship on his importance to Oriental studies, his service to the company as a member of the Supreme Court of Judicature in Bengal from 1783, or his entanglement with the administration of Governor-General Warren Hastings from the mid-1770s. Moreover, while a significant body of scholarship has examined why company servants from the mid-eighteenth century such as Jones came to be interested in investigating the ancient Indian past as a guide to administration, this development has never been contextualized in terms of the extant role of the archive in imperial governance.[50]

Jones's concern was law, reflective of both his training as a barrister and the issue at the core of the company's administrative dilemma in India after 1765.[51] After defeating the Nawab of Bengal and his French allies at the Battle of Plassey in 1757, Clive had established a "dual system" of government whereby the company as *diwan* assumed control of the Mughal revenue administration. But Clive left judicial administration in the hands of *nawabi* officials, who continued to judge Indians according to Mughal laws and procedures. This system was based on Clive's account of the administrative regime that the Mughals instituted in Bengal after their late sixteenth-century conquest against the Karrani dynasty. "When the Moguls invaded, and became Conquerors of Indostan, they did not attempt to make any Alteration in . . . any of the essential established Laws," Clive believed; rather, as "Conquerors of a civilized, not a savage People" who were "long in possession of a Religion, of a Government, of Laws & Customs," the Mughals (in Clive's view) governed using extant practices of local sovereignty under the supervision of Mughal administrators. Clive sought to do something he conceived to be similar, implementing what came to be known as a dual system of government that enabled the East India Company to collect revenue in Bengal while leaving judicial administration to be executed by Mughal administrators.[52] The contrast between the configuration of Indians in the company's conception of rule in Asia and royal government in America was striking, but the nature of that contrast must be precisely understood. While ideas of American Indian "savagery" and the "civility" of Indians in India animated discourses of comparative ethnology in the mid- and late eighteenth-century pan-European republic of letters, imperial officials thought about difference in other terms. For them, the problem was always one of exercising sovereignty before it was one of establishing hierarchy, and as such the Crown never conceived of itself as a conqueror over American Indians *qua* Indians, whereas the company in Bengal did.

Over the next several years, the dual system came under severe criticism among company officials as it failed to raise expected levels of revenue. One critique rested on defining what it meant to govern over non-English speakers. In the words of an English official, the administration of law under the dual system meant that in "cases which depended on the Mahomedan Law," company officials who did not know Persian, Sanskrit, or Bengali were "obliged to call in the assistance" of Mughal translators and officials to interpret and conduct much of the judicial business—effectively removing the company from the position of exercising authority.[53] Among the most trenchant critics of this reliance on Indian intermediaries was the aforementioned William Jones. Immersed through his legal training and career in an administrative culture in which documents served as an authority upon which constitutional meaning was asserted, Jones recognized the utility of written records to the company-state. In a 1781 letter, Jones invoked the idea that English law was both "partly unwritten" and "partly written." The concept of the "unwritten or common law," Jones wrote, was frequently used to refer in positive terms to the "eminently favourable" rights of individuals "grounded upon immemorial usage," and thus containing "the true spirit of our constitution." The concept of the "written" law, by contrast, was used to refer dismissively to laws "enacted by the legislative power" that expressed "the whims of a few leading men" and thus "unjustifiably altered the form" of the "unwritten" constitution. But Jones explained that it was misleading to refer to the common law as "unwritten" because "the only evidence of it is in writing preserved in the public records, judicial, official, and parliamentary."[54] The meaning of the constitution was to be determined "not by speculation but by the rolls of Parliament and the records of Westminster Hall."[55]

But while archival records of conciliar and legislative decisions were essential sources for governing British subjects, they were inappropriate for governing Indians. In Bengal after the company's receipt of the *diwani,* British documents served purely ornamental, not practical, purposes. "The dullest records of ancient times should be preserved, that they may occasionally be consulted; but they should be deposited in cabinets and archives," Jones wrote in the preface to his translation of the *Tarikh-I Jahangusha-yi Nadiri,* "as the old arms and utensils of the *Romans* are kept in museums for the inspection of the curious, while modern pieces of elegant or useful workmanship are the constant furniture of our apartments, either for our pleasure, our convenience, or our defence."[56] While an English lawyer practicing in England could "wholly and eternally" ignore the study of "Asiatic letters," he explained to the historian Edward Gibbon in 1781, such a study would be fundamental to qualifying an English lawyer as a judge in India.[57] "Any system of *judicature* affecting the natives in Bengal, and not having for its basis the old *Mogul* constitution, would be dangerous and impracticable," Jones reiterated in a proposal for "The Best Practicable System of Judicature for India," which he sent to Edmund Burke in 1784. To that end, Jones advised that "Digests of Hindu and Mahomedan laws should be compiled by chosen . . . Pundits," and "Native interpreters of the respective laws must be duly selected and appointed with such stipends, as will entitle them to respect, and raise them above temptation." Crucially, the actual judging of Indians by Indian laws was to be subject to the oversight of *British* officials because Indians were untrustworthy: "The laws of the natives must be preserved inviolate; but the learning and vigilance of the English judge must be a check upon the native interpreters."[58] But judgment of Indians by British officials was to proceed on the basis of Indian, not English, laws, and this required developing a parallel archive of written precedents—explicitly distinct from those contained in the metropole. Jones reiterated this argument to William Pitt a year later in a letter calling for investment in the enterprise of translating Indian legal texts into English for the use of imperial judges. By using these translations, Jones argued, the company would be able to "check" "the Pundits of the court" and "render" India "a source of great advantage to Great Britain" by placing it on a constitutional foundation of "a good *system of laws*, a *due administration* of them, and a *well-established peace.*"[59] Ruling over Indians could proceed only through the use of Indian sources authoritatively understood by British officials.

For Jones, then, the company's interpretive control of Indian records was vital to exercising jurisdiction over Indians. To facilitate this, he believed that company servants needed to learn native customs and languages. As Jones declared in 1786, the "discharge" of administrative "duty" was now a matter of "the study of Indian laws in their original languages."[60] Seeing like a company-state required looking not from the perspective of its self-generating archive in the metropole but instead from an archive made in the field by expert-servants on the ground: as Jones emphasized in 1789, one could "only attain" "a complete knowledge of India" "in the country itself."[61] The utility of travel and eyewitnessing had, for early modern government, rested in the aspiration to produce administrative knowledge by correlating present observations with the documented wisdom of the past contained in metropolitan repositories. In his comments on company administration, however, Jones severed this relationship between sight and metropolitan record while maintaining the role of the archive in producing political knowledge. In its place, he proposed that non-English speakers be governed in relation to a parallel archive comprising Indian sources authoritatively interpreted by a select class of imperial officials. Language ascended in this new constellation, for (as Jones emphasized) it held the key to understanding and then implementing this ancient Mughal constitution as a technique of rule, and, he believed, the place to learn Indian languages was India proper.[62] Indians in India were to be governed on an evidentiary regime that mirrored the early modern emphasis on precedent understood granularly as textual record but relocated the source of the archive to the imperial field. This formulation dispossessed Indians themselves of interpretive authority over these records. It also sought to challenge the company's London rulers and the authority of its metropolitan archive by positing a rival archive,

constructed by servants in the field out of "native" sources, as the locus of
political knowledge.

Producing Archival Silences

The idea of governing non-British peoples by creating archives of their
cultural materials was never contemplated in the Atlantic world with respect to either of the populations who bore the violent brunt of imperial
policymaking there: Africans and American Indians. Enslaved people fueled the economic growth of the early modern British Empire, yet their
experiences of violent exploitation rarely appear within the records of official government entities. This circumstance sits uncomfortably with another undeniable fact: the trade in enslaved people produced vast amounts
of documentation, with seemingly every transaction that formed a part of
their captivity, transport, and sale generating written records. The Royal
African Company (RAC), which held a monopoly on the trade from 1663,
kept meticulously detailed records—and, as with other early modern corporations, the offices of secretary and bookkeeper were the nodes of its
information management system. In 1663, King Charles II granted a charter
to the Company of Royal Adventurers of England Trading into Africa that
empowered the company with a monopoly over "the buying and selling
Bartering and Exchanging of for and with any Negro Slaves Good wares
and Merchandizes whatsoever to be vended or found" in western Africa.[63]
The company was restructured in 1672 after becoming insolvent, and in
the subsequent charter issued to it that year by Charles II, the body was
organized under the auspices of a Court of Assistants, which supervised its
metropolitan operations through a series of subcommittees and forts along
the western central coast of Atlantic Africa.[64] The company's secretary was
obliged to take an oath that he would "faithfully and truly set downe and
Register all the Acts, Ordinances, and Constitutions" of the RAC's governing body, while preventing "any persons not being Members . . . or Officers of the Company" access to these records "without the consent" of the
RAC's governors. The secretary was to "keep Secrett" all the deliberations
of the court and "not Imbezill any of the books or papers belonging to the
Said Company with which you Shal be intrusted."[65] The bookkeeper was
required to swear that he would "duely and truely, enter into the bookes
of Accounts" "all and every Such Sum and Sums as to your knowledge

shalbe brought in, or disbursed by or for the said Company," while at the same time promising to "not disclose" "the Secretts" of the company nor "Imbezill any of the said Books and Papers belonging to the said Company with which you Shalbe intrusted."[66]

Like the institutions already discussed, the RAC sought to direct the conduct of servants on the ground through the dispatch of written orders that mandated meticulous recordkeeping. Its court issued detailed "Instructions" to ship captains in which it tied every step of the trade in enslaved humans to the production of documentary records. It instructed factors to provide regular information related to the trade in enslaved peoples, to keep logs of all voyages, to keep records of all transactions through a variety of written instruments, and to regularly return such records to the court for review. For example, in a 1686 letter of instructions to Captain Samuel Kempthorne, the RAC made clear that it expected Kempthorne to keep "a booke . . . in which you are to daily enter what Goods you Barter and what you receive for them, Signing the Same every Night for our Satisfaction, in case of your Mortality [during] this voyage." The corporation reiterated that it expected him to "give the Company full advises of your proceedings by all Opportunitys."[67] Independent traders who sought to challenge the RAC's monopoly were no less meticulous in their demands that factors in their employ keep detailed accounts of transactions of sale. For example, Sir Humphry Morice, governor of the Bank of England from 1727 and one of the leading early eighteenth-century English slave traders, required that captains trading in enslaved people on his behalf "send me a copy . . . at first opportunity [of] what Negroes or any Sort of Goods" sold on voyages he sponsored and keep "Receipts" for every transaction, recorded "daily" in a "Book" and "signed by your Self, first, & second Mat[e] & Doctor or so many of them as are present where such Sales are made & such Goods purchased." Morice added that he expected "a Coppy of" these "Book[s] on sheets of paper" to be "transmit[ed] mee from time to time."[68]

When enslaved people rose to the attention of Crown administrative offices such as the Board of Trade, they did so as an aggregate group on whom government legislated and whose exploited status and malignant treatment did not have to be justified via reference to archival documents. In 1708, the board dispatched a circular letter to several governors requesting information about the trade in enslaved people that encapsulated the precise terms in which slavery was conceived institutionally as an object of official knowledge. "It being absolutely necessary that a trade so beneficial to the Kingdome should be carryed on to the greatest advantage," the board wrote, and considering that "the well supplying of the Plantations and Colonies with sufficient numbers of negroes at reasonable prices is in our opinion the chief point to be considered in regard to that trade," the body requested that the governors provide them with the several points of information, which it would then present to Parliament as capturing "an authentick state of that trade": "that number of negroes have been yearly imported directly from Africa into [that government] . . . and at what rate per head they have been sold, distinguishing the numbers that have been imported on account of the Royal African Company, and those which have been imported by separate traders; as likewise the rates at which such negroes have been sold by the Company, and by seperate traders."[69] Government defined the "authentick" information about the enslaved as a matter of price and quantity, turning the lived experience of the enslaved into a mere point of numerical data that it could consider alongside other numerical markers as indexical of the state of imperial political economy. Reduced to aggregate numbers, the enslaved occupied a paradoxical position within the archive of the imperial state: they were "so beneficial to the Kingdome," the Board of Trade acknowledged, yet they figured within the transcripts of government officialdom as objects to be counted or as threats to be countered.

A powerful example of this archival presence is the index compiled by William Popple of the records of early councils of trade inherited by the Board of Trade in 1696 (discussed in chapter 1). By 1696, trading vessels registered in the British Isles had already transported over 300,000 enslaved people out of Africa. The RAC had by that point established a network of forts in west Africa, especially in the Gold Coast spanning the Gulf of Guinea, from which it traded in captured human beings.[70] In one heading of the index, Popple made a "List of Papers Belonging to the African Company" that, having been sent to earlier councils of trade, were now transferred to the archive of the Board of Trade. The listed titles of the papers belie the human suffering and toll of the trade, masking exploitation under the dull language of document description:

"Letter of the Guiny Company to the Plantations"
"Letter from Barbados to the African Company concerning Interlopers and Negros"

"Petition of the African Company about Negros"
"Letter from Mr Proby with a Mapp of the Coast of Africa"
"Merchts: Papers of reasons concerning the African Company"
"Account of Negros"
"Account concerning Negros."[71]

Letters, petitions, papers, and accounts: these were common labels for the records circulated by official bodies. Their use by the Privy Council's clerks with respect to documents about slavery demonstrated how the terms and formulas of institutional archival practices cloaked the brutality of the trade in the language of office. Archival description and classification fabricated extraordinary violence into an ordinary object of administration.

The Privy Council's instructions to officials on how to interact with the RAC reveal how the Crown circumscribed and defined the place of slavery within its informational regime. From the 1670s onward, conciliar bodies tasked with governing trade and plantations consistently instructed governors and other colonial officials that they were to smooth the operation of the RAC's sales of enslaved people in the Americas by ensuring that "payment be duly made and within a competent time" between subjects and the RAC, noting in some of its directives that it was "against reason" that the company would "send good wards to a known bad market."[72] This is a telling expression of the Crown's self-definition of its governing role in relation to the emerging logic of slavery's capitalism. The aim of policy was to ensure the operation of a "good" market in human people—no more and no less—and so its interest in information about slavery was thus about the operation of the market, particularly as it attended the respective trading privileges of the RAC and private traders following the ending of the company's monopoly in 1689. That definition in turn structured the specific information that the Privy Council, beginning in the early eighteenth century, requested from governors: "the number" of enslaved people brought to a given colony, the proportion of the total "supplied" respectively by the RAC and other traders, and "at what rates sold."[73]

Within the imperial constitution, enslaved African and African-descended peoples were conceived of as "Merchantable," and this dehumanizing legal and administrative characterization defined the limits of their presence within the official information order of empire. The status of Indigenous Americans in the official mind of imperial rule was distinctively different because they were not commodified, but nor were they understood in the same way as officials in the East India Company came to regard Indians in India: Native Americans did not grant sovereignty to British rulers. Early promoters of English colonization such as Richard Hakluyt the Younger conceived of a polity in which Native peoples would be converted and disciplined into Protestant rule by colonizers who mastered Indigenous cultures and then communicated English values in Native tongues. The "Defendors of the Faithe" dispatched by the English Crown, Hakluyt believed, had a duty "to inlarge and advaunce" Protestantism by "firste learne[ing] the language of the people nere adjoyninge . . . and by little and little acquainte themselves wth their manner, and so wth discrecion and myldenes distill into their purged myndes the swete and lively liquor of the gospel."[74] This concept of Christian sovereignty tied to learning languages in order to purge Natives of their customs and render them into Protestant believers took official form in the assertions by early English settlers, such as that made by the Company of Providence Island in 1633, that they wished to employ persons "who are acquainted with ye severall natures and Language of ye Indyans" to convert Native peoples into Christians as part of the general project of colonization.[75] It was also an entirely different way of tying knowledge and governance from what officials and writers associated with the East India Company had proposed: to make "Indians" embrace European ways rather than to act as a European surrogate for an Indian sovereign.

In practice, however, Indigenous Americans had a far narrower presence within the governing logics that ultimately came to structure the administration of the British Atlantic. As the English Crown began to place the ruling infrastructure of Atlantic trade and settlement in the mid-1600s under its direct control, the Privy Council confronted the problem of defining the relationship between this emerging imperial constitution and Native Americans. Initially, royal councils of imperial administration issued little guidance on how officials should treat Indians. The Crown assigned colonial governors a consistent set of tasks for relating to Native peoples: to encourage the Indians to trade with the English "rather than to any others of Europe," to maintain friendly relations with Natives, and to keep the Indians in a state of "Submission" by assuring them that the English "will Protect them as Our Subjects, against the French King and his Subjects," especially through the distribution and exchange of "presents" in the form of both manufactured goods and raw consumables such as alcohol, tobacco, and drugs.[76]

But did the words "as Our Subjects" mean that the Privy Council defined American Indians as members of the imperial body politic? The answer was complicated for two reasons: first, because of how territory had come under the administrative hand of the monarch, and second, because the concept of subjecthood was hardly coherent in the early modern British world. As we have seen, English colonization in the Atlantic world was initially a corporate-driven endeavor, and some colonial corporations sought to render Native peoples into subjects of the English monarchy. The Virginia Company construed the behavior of Powhatan leaders during ritual coronation ceremonies in 1608 as evidence that the Indians had voluntarily subjected themselves to the English Crown as "tributaries," existing in a subordinate relationship to the royal sovereign while retaining the ability to be led by one of their own. Once war broke out between the Indians and the English in 1622, the company proclaimed that the Powhatans were infidel "Outlaws of Humanity," *not* under Christian sovereignty any longer because of their rebellion against their presumptive English rulers, and therefore could justifiably be dispossessed of their land through war. The leaders of the Massachusetts Bay Colony asserted that the royal charter granted to them by Charles I in 1629 gave them supreme authority over both Indians and English settlers within the colony's territorial delimits. Such assertions of corporate sovereignty engendered significant resistance from Native peoples over the ensuing decades as war between Indians and English broke out across North America.[77]

By the late seventeenth century, this dynamic was changing in the English Atlantic because of the post-Restoration monarchy's attack on the sovereignty of corporate colonies. As discussed in chapter 1, the Privy Council began to establish a constitutional infrastructure that eventually aspired to resume charters to corporations and proprietors and place administrative powers in the hands of the Crown. While corporations had at times claimed that Indians could be English subjects despite not being members of the corporation's own body politic, royal government did not really agree. As Lisa Ford has observed, "Despite claims to sovereignty and jurisdiction in colonial charters, English colonists exercised jurisdiction over indigenous people in very few cases." Instead, Ford notes, "settler jurisdiction was explicitly defined by British subjecthood rather than territory. It did not comprehend indigenous peoples."[78] Subjecthood in the early modern English world was inseparable from allegiance to the Crown. To be a subject meant to be loyal to the monarch, a relationship of fealty that could transcend territory, blood, and culture, and thereby encompass both the growing number of English people who traveled and settled across the world in this era and the children born to them beyond English borders.[79] With respect to territory over which it claimed sovereignty, the Privy Council sometimes described Native inhabitants as living under its "protection," a tie that implied Indians could, in theory, claim the status of "subject" if they made the requisite declaration of allegiance to the English monarch.[80] This placed Indians in America in a complicated position with respect to the imperial constitution, opening the possibility that they could be under British sovereignty but making that status contingent on demonstrated fealty to the Crown.

The Privy Council's instructions to governors inscribed the hazy nature of its understanding of the Crown's relationship to Native Americans. For the Privy Council, the utility of language learning lay in facilitating the quasi-diplomatic interactions between English and Indian "nations," which could, if they so chose, place themselves under the monarchy's "protection." In establishing a Committee for Foreign Plantations in 1670 to supervise imperial trade and settlement, the Privy Council instructed the appointed members that "in as much as some of the Natives of the s.d Indians may be of great use" to the English, and "if any of the said Indian nations shall at any time desire to put themselves under the protection of Our Government," governors in America should "direct, or employ some persons purposely to learne the languages respectively of them."[81] If Natives put themselves under the "protection" of English sovereignty, the council specified, then it would be necessary for governors to staff their administrations with servants with knowledge of Indian languages and customs.

But Natives were not automatically conceived of as being within the imperial constitution. For a "forreiner or forreiners" "already setled" in territory claimed by the Crown to "enjoy" English "Lawes and priviledges . . . in as full and ample manner as any of his Majesty's naturall born subjects," the council made clear, they would need to have "taken the oath of allegiance to be to all Intents and purposes fully and compleatly naturalized." Only by pledging allegiance to the monarch would they be considered English subjects able to enjoy the attendant protections of English law. Moreover, to be an English subject, a "forreiner" would have to relinquish customary behavior "contrary" to English law, including claims to "any former Law, Act, Ordinance, Usage, or Custom to the Contrary."[82] On this ground, few Native peoples could ever be considered "compleatly naturalized" because few relinquished such claims, or even contemplated doing so. Late seventeenth-century colonial governors and proprietors thus valued language skills among officials as a facilitator of diplomatic interaction with sovereign Indian peoples.[83] As the Lords Proprietors of Carolina instructed one of its servants in 1681, negotiated agreements with Native peoples should be written down and "translated into ye Indian Language, and a Coppy written in that Language signed [&] left with them: And another kept to be read to them every tyme they come amongst us."[84] In a comparable move, the Maryland Assembly in 1689 appointed one Jacob Young, "well known and skilled in the language and customes of the said Indians," to act as interpreter in "the Management" of the colony's relations with Indians.[85] Imperial administration considered the interpreter an intermediary between two distinct sovereignties.

The Privy Council placed these early councils of trade on a permanent establishment when it created the Board of Trade in 1696 as the executive organ tasked with administering colonial matters. But it made no change to the constitutional status of Native peoples at this time. The council's instructions to governors post-1696 continued to emphasize that Native peoples were outside the bounds of imperial jurisdiction, a status that was impervious to the actual ways American Indians and British settlers subsequently interacted. In instructing governors on how to execute the sovereign's will with respect to Indigenous Americans, the Privy Council consistently drew a distinction between "His Majesty's Subjects" and "the Indian natives" who existed under a different sovereign power.[86] American Indians were not constitutionally the same as enslaved Africans, whom the Privy Council declared to be "Merchantable," construing these humans forcibly captured and sold in terms of the distinct legal category of property.[87] Rather, "the Indian natives" were conceived jurisdictionally in terms that grouped them under both a singular nomenclature despite their cultural heterogeneity ("Indians") and located

them outside the boundaries of imperial sovereignty: as "bordering natives";[88] potential parties to agreements and exchanges with the distinct
"English Trade & Nation";[89] agents of potential "Invasion" into English
"country";[90] and "Natives" who could trade with the actual "Subjects"
of the Crown,[91] especially to the exclusion of commercial intercourse
with "any others of Europe."[92] The administrative discourse applied
to Indians who the Crown construed in treaty negotiations as having
submitted to its sovereignty belied their external position with respect
to the imperial body politic. At councils at Albany and Montreal in 1701,
the Iroquois Confederacy, comprising the Mohawk, Seneca, Cayuga,
Oneida, and Onondaga (which the British referred to as the "Five Nations"), agreed to remain neutral in future relations with the contending
French and British Empires, a stance that almost immediately became
impossible to maintain as French-allied Native peoples began encroach-
ing on Iroquois territory.[93] In 1702, the Privy Council instructed Edward Hyde, Lord Cornbury, governor of New York, to "incourage"
the Five Nations to "apply themselves to the English Trade and Nation rather than to any other of Europe," and to "assure them" that the
Crown would "protect them as our Subjects against the French King
and his Subjects," dependent "upon their renewing their Submission
to Our Government."[94] Precisely the same conception applied in the
Caribbean, where governors were ordered to "give all possible Encouragement" to alleged "proposalls" from "the Native Inhabitants" of the
islands conquered or ceded to the British "for submitting themselves
to Us," whereby they would "put themselves under Our protection and
Government" and "renounce any such Dependance on the French,
whether in time of War or peace for ever hereafter."[95] When held out as
a possibility, the treatment of Indigenous Americans as Crown subjects
in the eighteenth-century Atlantic empire was to be limited, conditional,
in need of overt confirmation whenever English protection was actually
claimed, and a matter of gaining and retaining Native alliances against
rival European empires. Rather than expand the boundaries of the constitutional community, government applied definitions of subjecthood in
relation to Indians that made membership in the imperial body politic
incompatible with the retention of customary practices. These definitions shaped what information administrators sought to gather about
Native Americans: since they were defined as external bodies to the im-

perial state, Indigenous peoples were like foreign monarchies and thus engaged diplomatically, not as subjects.

Much recent work theorizing the colonial archive begins with the perceptive observation that nonwhite, non-European voices are often absent in the official transcripts of empire. Applied to the archival epistemology of early modern British imperial order in the Atlantic world, however, the point needs refinement. Information about nonwhite, non-British populations appeared within the archival record in a manner that corresponded to the legal constitutions of these populations as outside the protection of the sovereign. A granular consideration of the imperial archive—not the archive as conceptual scholarly abstraction but the archive as a composite of contextually situated practices and material forms—demonstrates that there was no singular Other against which imperial self-conceptions developed but a variety of them. Not all nonwhite people were construed in the same way in the imperial mind. The fiction of people as property gave rise to a recordkeeping regime that made the experiences of enslaved Africans and their American descendants simultaneously everywhere in the transcripts of imperial rule as people about whom data was collected, and yet nowhere within the regime of archival reasoning through which policy was made and justified. The definition of subjecthood as monarchical fealty led administrators to gather extensive information about the threats or advantages Native American peoples might pose for settler-subjects. But Native peoples themselves were not subject to the laws and policies that imperial rulers justified by making references to records, even as it was Native peoples who bore the violent and destructive consequences of such laws and policies. By contrast, in South Asia, the legitimation and exercise of East India Company rule proceeded not only by administrators' referring to "English" documents—Crown charters, company decrees, official correspondence—to authenticate claims to power and prescriptions of policy but also by the invocation of a growing archive of "Indian" cultural materials that the company at times claimed legitimated its conduct.

The relationship among violence, agency, and epistemology that so much of the inspiring scholarship on the archive, its construction, and its silences has productively aimed to elucidate needs to be understood as contingent on how governing institutions construed the meaning of the political subject. Not all non-English people who interacted with the varieties of imperial rule that emanated from the British Isles in the early modern period were construed in the same way in the minds of rulers—there was no uniform notion of foreignness against which imperial self-conceptions developed but instead a variety of concepts of difference in relation to which administrators brought the same shared epistemology of the archive to bear as they aimed to legitimize projects of rule.

THREE

Contentious Politics

GOVERNING BODIES IN THE early modern British Empire mobilized documents to regulate the conduct of officials, collect information, and substantiate particular policy objects. Because of the institutional power of these techniques and the political value of framing arguments as "authorized" and "proved" by their correspondence to archival records, observers either situated outside or acting outside the formal confines of imperial offices also sought to capitalize on them. The first chapter traced the development of institutional systems of record circulation and archiving in both the Atlantic and Asian contexts of imperial expansion, showing how officials used archival evidence to make, advocate, and enforce policy. This chapter explores the movement of techniques of record manipulation—circulation, citation, and publication—beyond Whitehall and Leadenhall into public debate about empire. A granular understanding of precedent that tied the credibility of arguments to the production of documents as proof in both juridical and administrative practice came to characterize public discourse about political affairs, including those concerning the empire.[1] The archival epistemology not only facilitated the exercise of administration; precisely because there was no separation between politics and administration, actors working beyond the formal confines of state and company availed themselves of the techniques of archival manipulation and the language of documentary proof as they aspired to influence how institutions behaved.

Officially, the sovereign or corporate body controlled the administrative records created under their auspices. Yet, both the self-conceptions of officials and the very practices through which these governing institutions created, circulated, and used records put a consistent pressure on institutional aspirations toward control. Across the early modern European world, administrators often conceived of their official duties as extensions of their personal affairs. The practical consequence of this conceptual porosity was the frequent merging of state papers and private collections of papers, as administrators copied documents or simply removed them from offices for their own use, often while condemning their political opponents for engaging in precisely the same behavior.[2] Protocols that in their letter confined the storage and circulation of administrative records to institutional channels consistently proved leaky in their operations. Those invested in the "political practice" of using documents to make policy claims aspired to both accumulate such records and then construe their meaning as confirmatory of particular policy visions. As England expanded its commercial and territorial power overseas, a growing number of commentators began to apply this style of "thinking about politics" to contentions about matters imperial.[3] Even as the publication of records in the eighteenth century was increasingly done for nonpolemical reasons, the earlier tradition of using records as weapons persisted in the hands of these commentators.[4] These writers were often connected to the administrative world itself and sought to establish their argumentative authority by invoking their knowledge of official "experience," substantiated by references to records presented as secret or otherwise beyond the purview of the public eye and thus revelatory of the hidden machinations of government.

"Authentic Papers"

In a parallel to their circulation of manuscript copies of records within political circles to advance policy views, administrative and political bodies concerned with American affairs sometimes entered the world of print to communicate directly with a public audience. They both made discursive arguments to advance policy priorities and they cited and presented "official" documents as evidence of the wisdom of these policies. The most sustained and consistent way in which this occurred was through the printing of royal proclamations as broadsides or in loyalist newspapers. Just as the Crown organized the printing of proclamations as broadsides (meaning single sheets of text) and then had them circulated by county and town sheriffs domestically, it also did so with respect to affairs of the plantations. These were printed in London by Crown printers, with copies then sent to governors for distribution in the colonies.[5] On a less regular basis, the Board of Trade sometimes printed its reports made in response to conciliar or parliamentary demands, known as "representations," bringing administrative records to a broader view, and on certain occasions it ordered to be printed documents presented before it from colonies.[6] Yet when the circulation of administrative records related to the colonies involved administrators themselves engaged in official business, such movement generally occurred not in print but instead as handwritten documents.

Just as Whitehall administrators emphasized that their policies for governing the American empire were wise because they derived them from the precedents of state papers, commentators on imperial affairs attempting to influence those decisions made a similar argument. Because such state papers were in theory the proprietary possession of the sovereign body under whose auspices they had been created, accessing them could be difficult. Often, writers claimed to have obtained such sources either through or via connections to government service, but in all cases emphasizing the proximity of written documents to eyewitness observations proved crucial to the fashioning of epistemic authority. The culture of English-language historiography that evolved out of Renaissance travel observation now manifested itself in an imperial register. Early American settler writing on the history of conquest and settlement was a prominent site for these expressions, as authors cited and sometimes reproduced official papers to establish that their views were "authentic." The Puritans who produced the first English-language histories of colonization practiced this style of argument.[7] In *A Brief History of the War with the Indians in New-England* (1676), the minister Increase Mather accounted for "the Grounds, Beginning, and Progress of the War," whose "principal Author" he called "Philip, alias Metacomet," by reproducing "information from a good hand," specifically a "Letter" he had received from an English captain fighting "the *Indians*" and written "within the time" of the events described. In addition to peppering his narrative with "good information" he had received from others, Mather reproduced a "Paper" marked "Secret" from the Massachusetts colonial council. He added a postscript in which he transcribed other documents: a "Letter" from a man of "integrity," Governor Edward Winslow of Plymouth, which Mather suggested would satisfy "impartial Judges"; a meeting record of the council that he hoped would "tend to remove Prejudices"; and Philip's "solemn engagement to the English" of 1671 (in which Philip "submitted" to Plymouth's government) on the grounds that "some have thought that if" this document from "the publick Records of the Colonies" "were published, it would farther clear the justice of the War on our part" by establishing Philip as "the Ringleader of all the mischief and misery which hath hapned by this *War.*"[8] Increase's son Cotton was an equally robust practitioner of this style, peppering his history of New England (1702) with quotations "transcrib'd" from the "Manuscript[s]" of many "worthy Author[s]."[9]

Eighteenth-century historians of British conquest and settlement continued to write in this antiquarian mode. Former officials were especially robust practitioners of this style. They leaned heavily on their knowledge of records accessible to them by virtue of their officeholding, grounding their authority on an *arcana imperii* translated into the vernacular of early modern imperial administration. Cadwallader Colden, member of the governor of New York's council, warned that while those "better acquainted with Indian Affairs, may, perhaps find some Mistakes" in *The History of the Five Indian Nations Depending on the Province of New-York in America* (1727), his office "enabled" him "to collect many Materials . . . not to be found any where else," lending his account a particular authority located in the archive.[10] In *The History of the Province of New-York* (1757), William Smith similarly advertised that his appointment by the New York Assembly to review the colony's laws enabled him "to peruse the Minutes of the Council, and the Journals of the general Assembly, from the glorious Revolution, at the Accession of King William, to the Year 1751," as well as many other "Records in the Secretary's Office." "From these authentick Materials, the following Pages were, in a great Measure, compiled," Smith noted, adding that he had also been "supplied" with "useful Papers" from other officials.[11] Such claims to authority based on privileged access to records not available to the reading public infused accounts not only of empire's formation but also of its dissolution. William Gordon explained in his *History of the Rise, Progress, and Establishment, of the Independence of the United States of America* (1788) that having been immediately "struck" in 1776 with the "importance" of the moment, he had "formed an early design of compiling their history, which he made known to the late commander in chief of the American army," who in turn assisted him in "procuring . . . the best materials, whether oral, written, or printed." Gordon's account of his sources would strike any early American historian as highly enviable. The Continental Congress had apparently "favored him with an inspection of such of their records as could with propriety be submitted to the perusal of a private person." He had, moreover, been allowed "a liberal examination" of the papers of key military figures, such as Generals George Washington, Horatio Gates, and Nathanael Greene. "He had the opportunity of acquainting himself with the records of the first settlers in New England," and he had "examined" "near thirty folio manuscript volumes" of the papers of "Massachusett's-bay, from their formation as a company to the close of the war."[12] Although few others could claim access to such prime materials, many eighteenth-century historians of British America, in titles, introductions, prefaces, and footnotes, emphasized that their citations and transcriptions of "authentic documents" and "authentic papers" lent their accounts credibility and authority.[13]

Historical fact, however, was not the only kind considered derivable from "authentic papers": as writers emphasized, such documents also contained definitive knowledge of contemporary commercial and administrative affairs. Excellence in the mercantile arts depended on mastering techniques of collecting, preserving, and interpreting written information. If "the Motions of Trade" could "be observ'd with a strict and careful Eye," the excise commissioner and political economist Charles Davenant wrote in 1699, then "*the true Ballance of Trade*" could be known and "the Wealth" and "Strength" of a state determined.[14] "All Governments, well and wisely constituted, as soon as they began to form themselves into a Politick Existence, have separated from Private Use a certain Proportion of their Wealth, and assign'd it to the Uses of the Publick," Davenant argued in 1700, and good governments were those that had the "Wisdom" to establish "Laws" "to preserve the King's Revenue, by which the Publick was to be supported." English rulers could obtain this wisdom by studying the "matter of the Revenue . . . as far as we can trace [the subject]" in "the best Copies of Records . . . such as have been sign'd and examin'd at the Tower" of London, depository since the thirteenth century of official documents written by royal councilors, "in which," Davenant stressed, "there is no material Error."[15] Policies that would make England wealthy could therefore be developed by comparing observations of current commercial practices made by "strict and careful" eyes with these "authoritative" archival records documenting past practices. Archival records were considered preeminent sources of guidance for the execution of all facets of administration.

Paralleling administrators' assertions that the wisdom required to rule states and empires lay in documentation from the past, these writers believed that the era's commercial and political waters were best navigated by interpreting contemporary predicaments in light of experience. The success of both merchants and governments thus hinged on the proper generation and preservation of written records about the conduct of trade. "*Merchants*" and "*Princes*" had to master "the *Art of Merchandizing* and *Traffique*," the merchant Lewes Roberts explained in 1700. "*The true Mother*" of the relevant "*Knowledge*" lay in the direct "*Experience*" of "*Commodities.*" This "*Experience*" was "best gotten by often viewing" the rules, customs, and practices through which people exchanged commodities and then "committing" these observations "to writing." "The use and custom of noting in this manner," Roberts argued, "will make a man (especially young beginners) more skilful and ready in this knowledge" because writing made the "impressions in a man's mind" necessary to turn him into a talented practitioner and governor of the commercial arts. While a merchant's written observations might initially be "*rude, and undigested,* or . . . *frivolous,*" repeated practice would "both perfecteth skill, and helpeth memory," leading him in time "to a more considerate and judicious observation," the better "marking" of information on paper, and the discernment to distinguish between "*knowledge*" and "misinformation."[16] Several years later, John Oldmixon provided an example of how written observations made by those with firsthand knowledge could in turn inform the advocacy of policy by those at a remove from the ground. The historian began *The British Empire in America* (1708) by confessing to feeling "apprehensive" of "Censures" from readers who he imagined might question whether someone like himself who "never was in *America*" could write a plausible "History of the British *West-Indies.*" But when it came to commenting on the subject of "the *West-India Trade,*" Oldmixon argued that although he personally "never was out of Britain," "there's no part of that Trade, with which he has not been acquainted above twenty years," thus giving him the authority to discuss it. This authority derived from his archive. Oldmixon explained that he had correlated his collection of "*Original* Manuscripts" and "Original Papers" about the colonies, which he claimed to have acquired from former colonial officials as well as from the libraries of metropolitan institutions of knowledge collection such as the Royal Society, with information derived from what he characterized as "Inquiries of Persons who have been on the Spot"—the records, in short, of both travel and administration.[17]

Critics of imperial government questioned policies whose proponents had argued were efficacious because of their grounding in documents. But the critics themselves were politic in their advocacy of different approaches to government, invoking their own preferred documentary authorities as justification for alternative policies.[18] In some cases, it is impossible to tell whether the critics in fact actually had the experience they claimed, underlying that eyewitnessing may best be thought of as first and foremost a rhetorical strategy. An early eighteenth-century example is *An Essay upon the Government of the English Plantations on the Continent of America,* written by an "American" to refute the political economist Charles Davenant. While he may have been a "Man of good Parts," the author wrote, Davenant had "gone beyond his Province . . . on blindfold" in discoursing on the plantations, "having an intire dependance upon the knowledge and integrity of those from whom he received his Informations." Davenant, "being himself unacquainted and very badly informed by others," had "managed his Business very lamely" in his *Discourses on the Publick Revenues, and on the Trade of England* (1698). Indeed, the American continued, Davenant was not the only ignorant metropolitan observer; in fact, the "present Establishment of the Lords Commissioners for Trades and Plantations," the main administrative body tasked with developing policy for imperial commerce, was "Strangers to the Affairs" of the colonies, lacking "certain Information of the true State of the Plantations." Against Davenant and the Board of Trade, the writer proposed to reorient the locus of administrative knowledge from the metropole to the field in order to ensure that the system of producing administrative knowledge would generate "a true Account of the Matter of Fact." Deploying the language of observation characteristic of early modern travel writing, the American proposed that a Crown servant be "commissionated" "to travel through all the Colonies on the Continent," with powers to "fit in the Councils of every Colony where he comes" and "have free access to all Records, Council-Books, Publick Accounts, and all other Books and Papers relating to the Government, or any Office of Trust or Profit." The provincial archive, not the metropolitan archive, ought to be the source of administrative knowledge, and its holdings ought to be complemented by "a Scheme of material and pertinent Queries" sent to officials in the colonies themselves. The answers from these officials were to be correlated not against metropolitan "Instructions" drafted by the board (which, as chapter 1 demonstrated, was the practice of imperial government). Instead, they were to be assessed against other "true and impartial Relation[s] of the Constitutions and Transactions" by "the Agents of every Colony residing in *England*," who notably were appointed by and corresponded directly with the colonial assemblies. The board and its archive played no role in this "Scheme"; rather, the records generated by the legislative parts of the imperial constitution were posited as the best source of policy knowledge.[19] The archive thus framed the discourse in which political contestation around imperial policy occurred: disputes about *which* archive mattered revealed a shared, underlying commitment to the idea that policy positions had to be grounded in archival records to be considered authoritative. As we will see, a similar discourse later played out with respect to Bengal.

In the decades that followed the publication of *An Essay upon the Government* and Oldmixon's *British Empire in America,* written records continued to be widely regarded as generative authorities for making descriptive and prescriptive claims about the administration of empire. Both historical understanding and policy knowledge were understood to involve correlating observation with authoritative records, and research into "authentick Manuscripts," "publick Papers," and "Collection[s] of Books" was seen as requisite for understanding the development of empire over time.[20] At the same time, discerning the present state of the empire's government and economy continued to be understood as involving the study of documents. Thus, when debating the balance of trade between Britain and France in 1713–1714, Tory polemicists such as Davenant and Daniel Defoe and Whig writers such as Oldmixon strategized to discredit each other by invoking the "clear Documents" and "authentick Vouchers" that proved the "Fact[s]" of political economy favorable to their respective positions.[21] "Trade is the Foundation of Wealth, and Wealth of Power," Defoe wrote subsequently in 1728, echoing the earlier discussion, and it was through the "Correspondence" of the "Merchant" that "the whole Nation" was "rais'd" to glory. The "Grounds of Calculation" for determining this greatness lay in the critical data— "the Quantities and Value of any Trade or Exportation"—recorded in "the Custom-House Books."[22] To "know the real state and usefulness of trade, with regard to the body of the nation," one writer similarly argued in 1759, it was necessary to examine archival documents—specifically "the books of the custom-house" themselves "and not . . . transcripts or printed papers" nor "printed bills of entry." But if writers such as Davenant could valorize copies of official records as authentic sources of political economic knowledge, then why were "transcripts" here denigrated as unreliable in favor of original records? The reason lay in the distinction between the purported disinterestedness of the official and the potential self-interest of the merchant. Although a servant of government could be expected to act honestly, not so a merchant, who might seek to dangle "a sum of money" in order to "induce the compositor to depart from his copy, and lessen or increase the quantity, as may best suit the merchant's advantage."[23]

This concept of the commercial and jurisdictional constitution of empire as knowable through the experience contained in reliable archival records reached a descriptive apogee in the prerevolutionary British Atlantic in Adam Anderson's *An Historical and Chronological Deduction of the Origin of Commerce* (1764). It was to "the instrumentality of Commerce alone" that the greatness of the British Empire was "peculiarly indebted," Anderson, a trustee of the colony of Georgia, declared. But the nature of that commercial greatness could not be known through "the so-called Science of political Arithmetic," whose "Position" (promulgated by the "once famous" but now apparently less authoritative "Sir William Petty") had been "effectually exploded" by "dear-bought Experience." Instead, Anderson invoked the authority of the royal historiographer Thomas Rymer's "grand Collection of Records," known as the *Foedera,* a succession of volumes containing transcriptions of diplomatic and commercial treaties and arrangements between England and other states that had begun to be published in 1704. Anderson proclaimed himself "indebted" to this collection of state papers for both "Facts" about "the great commercial interests of the British Empire" and "the Rectification of sundry Mistakes" made by "less authentic" writers. Crucial sources also lay in the scholarship of antiquarians who had "collected" numeric and descriptive information contained in manuscript records, "digesting and methodizing" these quantitative and qualitative facts into a readable form.[24] For Anderson, as for Davenant, Oldmixon, and Defoe, historical truth and political economic truth were interlinked by a common foundation in administrative records.

But whereas the author of *An Essay upon the Government of the English Plantations* elevated the records in the colonies over the archive in the imperial capital, subsequent practitioners of the archival style tended to emphasize the particular value of metropolitan records, especially those of the Board of Trade. In past times, "when our Board of Trade and Plantations, which should be stiled the Council of Commerce, has been composed of men versed in the commercial art, and capable of communicating all due information to the superior officers of state," Thomas Mortimer argued in *The Elements of Commerce* (1772), "Great Britain has ever rose superior to all other maritime powers, and has extended her commerce and national credit to the remotest parts of the globe." According to Mortimer, the board's "attainment of commercial knowledge" through communication and "information," and its deployment of this "political wisdom" in "a glorious administration of the public affairs of the state," determined the empire's success.[25] However, access restrictions made it difficult for those interested in using the papers to elucidate the contours of imperial history and advise on policy to actually know the archive's contents. Modeling the proprietary status of the State Paper Office as the sovereign's possession, the board's commercial archive was controlled exclusively by the monarch's delegated administrators. Consequently, and perhaps paradoxically, discourse about imperial commerce and politics largely proceeded without reference to the specific holdings of the archive even as writers such as Mortimer invoked their value—except on occasions when government officials deployed the records of state in more public-facing ways to substantiate and advance legislative or political goals. The loyalist historian Jonathan Boucher captured the situation perfectly when he wrote in 1797 that a truly "complete vindication" of the British government's conduct during the imperial period required "a fair, clear, and full exposition of facts, supported by authentic documents," to which "none but men in office, or those to whom they give permission, can have access."[26] The potential of official records as instruments that could substantiate historical and policy claims remained a widely shared epistemic value throughout the eighteenth century, independent of whether such records could actually be accessed by those who invoked their authority.

Defending and Debating the East India Company

This style of argumentation also characterized debate about British involvement in Asia.[27] As with debate over imperial policy in the Atlantic world, particular claims about Indian affairs and the efficacy of the East India Company's administration were advanced on the basis of their supposed grounding in "authentic" documentation. The first chapter showed how the company itself practiced this style of reasoning—for example, in relation to its efforts to circulate an account of the Amboyna affair authenticated by reference to records. Both the company's defenders and critics made similar moves in the debates that raged around its conduct, monopoly, and charter in the seventeenth and eighteenth centuries.

The East India Company invoked and sometimes published its records to advance its political interests, construing documents as proof of the prudence of these interests and their congruence with those of the state itself. In the early 1600s, the Anglican clergyman and editor Samuel Purchas was perhaps the most notable participant in these efforts. In his self-described capacity as the company's "Orator and Patron," Purchas construed records on terms favorable to the corporation by printing its 1600 charter in 1625, an endeavor in which he was supported by the company itself, which granted him access to its journals in part to combat criticism of its monopoly advanced by Robert Kayll in his 1615 pamphlet *The Defence of Trade*.[28] Another strategy, seen in Josiah Child's famous 1681 defense of the company's monopoly and its contiguity with the interests of the "nation," was to deflate the power of the royal grant itself against charges that "the Company have half the known World in their Charter, and that's too much for any Company." For Child, the company's charter was not only not as exclusive as its critics claimed but also included "no more" powers than had been granted to "all the *East-India* Companies in Christendom," and confirmed that the company was not a self-interested monopoly but instead "a Company of all . . . of the Kings Subjects."[29] In this way, the company inflated and deflated the importance of its founding document depending on the political situation.

The charter was not the only text the East India Company published and invoked to advance its interests. The corporation also strategically endeavored to print otherwise secret administrative correspondence—a strategy especially evident in its late seventeenth-century conflicts with the Dutch East India Company (VOC), a war conducted using not only gunpowder and ships but also the weapons of pamphlets and records. In 1687, for example, a pamphlet entitled *A Justification of the Directors of the Netherlands East-India Company* appeared in London, a translation (ostensibly done "for the Satisfaction of all such as are Impartial Judges of the Matters now in dispute between the two Companies") of a defense the Dutch VOC gave to the States General of its military attacks on English factories at Bantam in 1682. Transcriptions of several "official" documents were appended to the pamphlet, including an "Extract out of the Register of the Resolutions of the High and Mighty Lords, the States General of the *United Netherlands*" and a "Memorial of the Marquis of Albiville Exhibited the 1st of August, 1687," implied as further substantiation for the claims advanced.[30] A response to this pamphlet proposing *An Impartial Vindication of the English East-India Company, from the Unjust and Slanderous Imputations Cast upon Them* soon appeared in which the author dismissed the rival text as "a tedious Rhapsody of Fictitious, Fallacious Inferences and Arguments" whose claims could be refuted by "expos[ing] to publick View" "true Copies of those Original Papers" "which will give sufficient Light and Confutation" on the "willful mistakes" of the other pamphlet. To that end, the author of *An Impartial Vindication* appended over two hundred pages of transcriptions of a variety of administrative records from the English East India Company's archives—letters sent to it from the VOC, an "Extract out of the Consultation Books received" from the English company's factors at Bantam, accounts, affidavits, and diplomatic correspondence, all of which demonstrated the "Coherence," "Verity," and "Proof" of the argument.[31]

After 1688, the company widened its targets to include enemies closer to home. It found itself subjected to attacks by Parliament emanating from the corporation's institutional and ideological connections to the Crown and growing challenges to its commercial monopoly from within the British Isles. Again, the company made recourse to the archival epistemology to make its case in public, selecting and printing records as vindication. Such a tactic can be seen in its answer to the complaints of the brothers and merchants Samuel and George White after Samuel's ship *Satisfaction* was seized by the Bombay Admiralty Court in 1687 for challenging the company's privileges by trading under the flag of the Kingdom of Siam.[32] In his critiques of the company, Samuel White published a pamphlet offering a "true account" and "faithful Relation" of what had passed based on recounting his eyewitness experiences.[33] The company's defenders countered by invoking their own papers against White. For example, Francis Davenport, who had served the company at Siam, published *An Historical Abstract of Mr. Samuel White, His Management of Affairs* refuting White's account based on evidence "collected out of the said Davenports own Private Memoirs," including "a True Copy of the Original" letters exchanged among White, Davenport, and the company, and further authenticated by Davenport's relation to White "in Quality of [a] Secretary."[34]

The practice of justifying or critiquing policy by appealing to authentic records was also prevalent in debates *within* company administration—a strategy that, as Robert Travers has noted, grew particularly prevalent among company servants after the corporation's military victory of 1757, as different factions strived to present "so-called authentic documents culled from official records of the Company as a means of disseminating a preferred interpretation of events."[35] A 1764 pamphlet entitled *An Address to the Proprietors of East-India Stock,* in which a company servant criticized the conduct of Henry Vansittart, governor of Fort William between 1760 and 1764, demonstrates how the archival style of argument infused debate over policy. "From the Papers communicated to us at the late General Court," the author wrote, it was clear that Robert Clive, Vansittart's predecessor, had "left the Company's Affairs at Bengal in a very happy situation in January 1760." But Vansittart, a "Governor" in "Want of Experience" arriving "from a distant Settlement" and "unacquainted with the Scene he was to engage in," governed in "a total Deviation from those wise Maxims, by which Lord Clive acquired so much Honour to himself and to this Nation." As proof, the author ended the pamphlet with an "Appendix" consisting of two documents from the company's records: a treaty made by Vansittart with Mir Jafar Ali Khan, *soubah* of Bengal, and then a transcription of "Mr. Vansittart's Minute acknowledging the Errors of the Treaty."[36]

In these ways, the company's critics proved as adept at mobilizing records against the corporation's policies and practices as the corporation itself was in invoking the archive in its own defense. These practices were not confined to works printed in the metropole. Document leakage and reprinting accompanied the introduction of newspaper printing into Company Bengal by James Augustus Hicky, who established the first press in the territory in 1777 and whose newspaper, *Hicky's Bengal Gazette*, published from 1780 to 1782, operated as an outlet for Calcutta's free merchant community, often in rivalry with the *India Gazette*, published under the auspices of the governor Warren Hastings.[37] Hicky's paper exemplified the politic discourse of disclosing elite political maneuverings through the printing of unflattering anecdotes about Hastings and his allies and "Inteligence Extraordinary from Leaden Hall Street, on India affairs."[38] Indeed, such a tactic was fundamental to the political strategies of the company's most famous late eighteenth-century critics: Philip Francis and Edmund Burke.[39] Both were intimately familiar with the worlds of administrative information by the time that they turned against the company. Francis had initially served in Crown government as a clerk in the War Office between 1762 and 1772, and then the company as a member of the Supreme Council of India from 1774. In the latter office, Francis became a critic of the company's governor-general Warren Hastings and eventually of a broader array of late eighteenth-century political norms. Burke was the New York colonial legislature's London agent during the 1770s, in which he appeared before administrative bodies like the Board of Trade, shuffling paper as he advocated on behalf of the interests of his client.[40] While the impact of these experiences on Francis's and Burke's thought was complex, prior service meant that they argued from a position of intimacy with the administrative practices they subjected to critique.

In his attacks on company government, which fomented with especial force in the late 1760s and 1770s, Francis, in the words of Robert Travers, "drew on a powerful stream of British oppositionist ideology concerned with the erosion of public virtue and constitutional rights through executive abuses," indicting the corporation's leadership and especially Hastings using many of the discourses of radical and Whig political thought simultaneously being invoked by American colonists on the other side of the world *contra* Parliament and Crown.[41] But there was an important divergence in their rhetoric about the evidentiary basis of this constitutionalism. Whereas in the Atlantic world, those who invoked the "ancient constitution" increasingly insisted during the 1760s and 1770s on disentangling its basis from documents and emphasizing that its legitimacy anteceded writing, the company's critics continued to speak in the vernacular of the archive, disputing Hastings on the basis of what they had "collected from the records," not claiming (as American radicals increasingly did) that the archive was an inadequate ground of political knowledge.[42] Indeed, like other opponents of the company in this period such as the surgeon John Zephaniah Holwell, Francis compiled, circulated, and published records as well as parliamentary speeches in order to indict company administration and advance visions of reform, often working in collaboration with political allies.[43] He understood this work as having crucial stakes for politics because of the distinctive temporality of written documents. "Wide is the Difference between a Speech spoke & a Speech written," he wrote to his friend Sir Gilbert Elliot in 1788 as they worked together to edit one of Elliot's speeches for publication, for while "he, who speaks currently, with tolerable Matter, tho' loose and incorrect, may carry his point and Escape Criticism," "woe be to him, if he trust the same Discourse to paper," since "by the written Speech You will be judged, both now and hereafter."[44]

Francis sought to shape those judgments in a favorable direction (especially when they concerned his personal conduct in office) by strategically circulating records advantageous to his reputation. Such a strategy can be seen in his behavior following his pistol duel with Hastings in August 1780. Two months later, Francis wrote from Calcutta to the Court of Directors to preempt the arrival of "Accounts You will receive" of the standoff, a subject that he "presume[d] would attract some Degree of" their "Attention." The details of the event (which ended with Hastings shooting and injuring Francis) ought to be "accurately stated," Francis wrote, since they concerned both "the Company's Interest" and "my Honour and Reputation." "The only fair, and impartial method of bringing them forward is by laying before You, as I now do, authentic Extracts of such of our Proceedings, as have a Relation to them, without Narrative or Comment." To that end, he appended a "List" of the "Papers" he had enclosed with the letter, documents that he presented as an "impartial" vindication of his claims.[45] Hastings, for his part, was no less aggressive in defending his conduct and imputing blame to Francis by circulating his own papers to leading politicians such as Lord North, documents that Hastings described as containing "justification of my Conduct & a minute Explanation of the measures which have been objected to me." While Hastings explained that he "lamented the length of these papers," he "venture[d] to promise that these will present you with a connected & just state of Facts."[46]

In policy debates, Francis also deployed this argumentative style to push his reform proposals forward. In 1782, he "laid before the public" a set of "Papers" which he believed "ought to be interesting to the nation at large," for these papers would "establish and explain" "facts and principles" that would justify the wisdom of the plan of revenue reform that he distilled in the pamphlet's opening pages. Through "the labour of collecting" and publishing, he hoped that the "information and materials" would "contribute to the introduction of a more benevolent, and therefore of a wiser, system than that, which has hitherto prevailed in the ordering and management of the territorial Revenues." Francis printed Hastings's and Richard Barwell's April 1775 plan of revenue reform followed by his own counterproposal. Francis "annexed" a supplementary set of "Papers," including accounts, extracts from letters from administrators in Bengal, and copies of his debates with Hastings over revenue reform. Whereas Hastings had defended his plan of revenue collection as grounded in the study of "ancient" Indian sources, Francis disputed not simply the content of Hastings's proposals but also their evidentiary validity because of their presumed lack of correspondence with an authoritative archival record. Hastings's "assertations" were "not easily" "proved in a country, where successive revolutions have for the most part destroyed the records of the Government," Francis countered. Indeed, he insinuated that Hastings had simply fabricated his evidence, since the "disorders and confusion" of Indian history, "in which all laws and regulations perish, seldom leave any direct evidence of their having existed." "*My* information obliges me to deny every one of the facts asserted by the Governor-General," Francis retorted. Whereas he accused Hastings of having "formed" his plans "on conjecture" and "without the inspection" of records, Francis asserted that his own were drawn from "experience" located in documentary "materials" that would "enable" the "reduc[tion]" of "conjecture to an accuracy."[47]

Edmund Burke was perhaps even more audacious in how he shifted his relationship to the archive in response to the vicissitudes of imperial politics. Prior government service had rendered Burke, like Francis, intimately familiar with the inner workings of administration by the time he emerged as one of its most prolific critics. As the London agent for the

New York colonial legislature in the early 1770s, he had appeared before the Board of Trade to lobby on behalf of the assembly's interests.[48] But as he turned from participant in executive administration to parliamentary opponent of a Crown-centric approach to imperial rule in the late 1770s, Burke directed his ire at the archives of the state. Proposing a bill in 1780 to eliminate the Board of Trade, Burke ridiculed the organization as "an academy of Belles Lettres" whose archive of "2,300 volumes in folio" offered less insight into imperial affairs than "the small volume of common sense, the ideas already traced out, and registered in the volume of his brain." William Eden, who had served as undersecretary of state to Lord North, countered Burke by stressing that the board's archive, full of "much important and interesting information," testified to "the utility of the establishment."[49]

When Burke believed administrative documents might advance his purposes, however, he invoked their authority against his political enemies. This strategy can be seen most dramatically by considering his shift from dismissing the value of official records with respect to the Board of Trade to energetically embracing their utility when he helmed the parliamentary attack on Hastings during the late 1780s and early 1790s for corrupt conduct in the administration of Bengal. Burke knew that both Hastings and the East India Company were selectively curating what records they made available to parliamentary investigators in the hopes of derailing the prosecution. Writing to Henry Dundas in 1787, Burke criticized "the prevarication used by Hastings with regard to his correspondence, distinguishing it into official & not official, according to what may best suit his purposes in producing or withholding it." "This is a distinction neither founded on reason, or in the fundamental Instructions given by the Court of Directors in consequence of the Regulating Act of 1773, in which no such distinction is made," Burke complained. The act was "precise & universal" in declaring that "every correspondence" related to the company's "affairs & Interests" could legitimately be accessed by Parliament. But the company had "adopted [Hastings's] distinction" in an effort to thwart investigation, only putting forward Hastings's "official correspondence when they know at least as well as I do that his correspondence have been carried on by private agents" such as the governor-general's political allies. "He ought to be forced to produce his Letter Books," Burke contended. Indeed, Burke was keenly aware that the documents provided by the company and Hastings gave a partial, interested view of the evidence, which Burke believed could only be rendered complete through recourse to the archive itself. "I never look into the accounts laid before us without finding that nothing can be done without being actually at the India House, or having the Books at the House," for without such direct access to the company's records, Burke concluded, "every document produced [by the East India Company] raises new matter for just suspicion."[50]

In his attack on Crown administration in the Atlantic world, Burke had criticized the "contrivance" of imperial government that documents could bridge oceanic distance, warning the House of Commons in March 1775 that "letters of office" and "instructions" "do not make your government." The "three thousand miles of ocean" separating London and the American colonies rendered metropolitan commands ineffectual: "Seas roll, and months pass, between the order and the execution; and the want of a speedy explanation of a single point is enough to defeat [a] whole system." Instead of the "dead instruments" of administrative documents, Burke argued that it was "the spirit of the English Constitution which, infused through the mighty mass, pervades, feeds, unites, invigorates, vivifies every part of the Empire, even down to the minutest member."[51]

In prosecuting Hastings, however, Burke blurred constitutionality with the materiality of records. "Government to be preserved in authority and respect, ought to be acknowledged to be *true* in its declarations, and authentic in its acts," he argued in April 1789. An "office" was at an "End" "if upon any pretence whatsoever you admit a false Entry" into its recordkeeping—indeed, "the administration of a publick Revenue requires exact records and clear accounts," he emphasized. Documentation here was indexical of imperial constitutionality and, equally, of unconstitutional behavior, since "Mr. Hastings's conduct" could be known via "testimony recorded in the Company's Books and authentic documents taken from the public offices." Moreover, Burke suggested Hastings's repeated "violent transgression of the Company's orders" was a core argument for conviction—an elevation of the letter of documentation that Burke had disavowed in the context of the American war. While records were not necessarily definitive proof—"for as we know that witnesses may be perjured, and as we know that documents can be forged"—they could be rendered useful sources of information if measured against "testimony" about "the circumstances of the Country" and "the Characters of the persons" under scrutiny.[52]

Burke's prosecution strategy centered on invoking these records against Hastings and his defenders. This included disputes about trial procedure, seen in a detailed report on the rules governing evidence in the trial that Burke prepared between March and April 1794 in conjunction with the impeachment managers' lawyer, Richard Troward. Here, Burke defended the rules of procedure in the trial by grounding them in documentary precedents. Against the charge from Hastings's lawyers that the trial was being conducted unfairly, Burke contended that the prosecutors had "neglected no Means of Research, which might afford them Information concerning . . . Rules of Proceeding, and of Evidence," and had "examined carefully the Rolls and Journals of the House of Lords" in conjunction with other documents. On the substantive allegations against Hastings, Burke cited "Office Document[s] of [Hastings's] own Department, concerning himself, and kept by Officers of his own, and by himself transmitted . . . to the Court of Directors" as "Proof . . . in the record" of the "Charge made against him."[53]

At the same time, Burke assailed the governor-general's own efforts to marshal documents as evidence in his defense. Hastings claimed that the cost of copying records from India House in preparation for the trial had led him to bankruptcy. Burke disputed this, since "he had been at the India House and desired the proper person to tell him what it had cost Mr. Hastings . . . he was told, *not one farthing*."[54] Hastings also resorted to character witnesses who had traveled to Bengal; Burke proclaimed himself "astonished" that someone "who was in possession of all the Records, in possession of all the Registers with the power of consulting all the Lawyers, with all the means of information that in that Country could be had, should at your Bar have recourse to the whole rabble of Travellers to prove the nature of his government." Hastings patronized Orientalist scholars who had translated Mughal records into English, and then invoked their results in his defense by arguing that he had acted in accordance with precedents drawn from the administrative records of earlier Indian governments. Burke retorted that he had "asked of persons the best conversant with the Arabic and Oriental language" to read these works and that his authorities reported that "none of the conquerors ever claimed such a power as Mr. Hastings' had." Indeed,

Burke argued, Hastings had "made up" "a volume and code of arbitrary power" that was "not supported" even by the documentary sources whose translation Hastings had patronized.[55] "Mr. Hastings probably never read those books . . . he is not borne out by these books, either in the total spirit of them or in any passage of them, in any one act that he has done," Burke contended.[56]

Burke also accused Hastings of violating protocols for the conduct of official writing by carrying on a "clandestine correspondence" with confidants, one "not appearing in the Company's records . . . not appearing in any way to which the Commons could have access," and "unknown" to the company's directors and councilors. During the trial, Burke endeavored to "produce" these documents "as a heavy aggravation of our charge and a proof" of Hastings's "wicked" "rebellion."[57] Burke had only learned of their existence in an "oblique manner," via an "anonymous Letter" that tipped him off to Hastings's circumvention of protocols of administrative correspondence.[58] Now, Burke made these documents central to his exposition—specifically "a trunk" of "records of the Governor General and Council of Bengal" kept by Captain Jonathan Scott, Hastings's Persian translator, which Burke charged Hastings and his allies with trying to keep "completely hid" from the Bengal council and using as an archive of document manipulation: a "trunk into which they put what they please, take out what they please, suppress what they please or thrust in whatever will answer their purpose," and which therefore constituted "the real and true channel of intelligence" about the company's activities. "There is nothing [that] will speak for [Hastings's] conduct like the records," Burke emphasized. These records, which Burke subjected to meticulous examination in the remainder of his speeches during the trial, revealed "the whole machinery" of Hastings's "business" of acting "contrary to the orders of the Court of Directors." Such "Letter[s] lets you into the whole of it completely," Burke emphasized.[59] Documents could be invoked to fit the ends of politics—indeed, as Burke's skepticism of records as indexical of constitutionality in America and his subsequent mobilization of records against Hastings demonstrated, the construal of the meaning and even relevance of administrative records to fit such ends was fundamental to politic behavior.

Despite Burke's efforts, Hastings was acquitted in 1795, seven years after the trial began. Over its duration, the proceedings inspired a considerable discursive output by both Hastings's supporters and detractors that exposed the complex attitudes toward empire which circulated within late eighteenth-century British society.[60] Commentators also noted the role of the archive within the trial. In 1788, the poet and former Bengal army officer Ralph Broome published a series of rhyming commentaries on Hastings's impeachment in a London periodical, *The World*. Subsequently appearing as a pamphlet entitled *The Letters of Simpkin the Second, Poetic Recorder, of All the Proceedings, upon the Trial, of Warren Hastings, Esq. in Westminster Hall*, Broome sought to defend Hastings by satirizing the "scurrilous BURKE" as an intemperate, hotheaded fool whose speeches were full of oratorical bluster but little substance. Broome was especially critical of how Burke and the other prosecutors used administrative records to forge their case. Burke "drew" his arguments "from the Company's records" that he claimed were "incontestably true," Broome noted. Yet, the invocation of "such *bundles of papers*" demonstrated the obvious ("a *charter was read,* by show friendly assistance, It was prov'd that the *Company has an existence*") and inspired boredom:

> Many PAPERS . . . were read by the CLERKS,
> Whose dryness was moisten'd by EDMUND's remarks:
> "By reading these documents, 'tis my intent,
> "Of the *soot of* CORRUPTIONS to give you *the scent.*
> "The scent of CORRUPTION is lasting and strong;
> "If we follow our notes, we cannot go wrong."
> The sniffing and snuffing BURKE follow'd the track
> Of corruption, like BRAWLER, *the head of the pack;*
> But in spite of this hunt and the musical cry
> Of BRAWLER, the sport grew insipid and dry.
> By the Ladies the Court was but thinly attended,
> And *the* CLERKS seem'd asleep ere the business was ended.

Perhaps Broome's ridicule of the "not entertaining" "business" of "document reading" would have appealed to the earlier version of Burke who, at the end of the American Revolution, had dismissed the Board of Trade's archive and the "contrivance" of locating the constitutional bonds of empire in paper and parchment.[61] In the context of the Hastings trial, however, both the practice and rhetoric of the archive proved useful to Burke and other opponents of the East India Company, which in turn placed

Burke on the receiving end of attacks similar to the ones he had once made against document-centric political arguments.

The administrative archive, then, was central not simply to the everyday workings of imperial government. The archive also formed both a set of practices of document creation, interpretation, and manipulation and provided a vocabulary—composed of words like "records" and "papers"—in which political contestation occurred. The archive was as liable to invocation as it was to denigration, depending on the circumstances in which actors found themselves. As the territorial and demographic composition of British imperial sovereignty began to transform in the 1760s, 1770s, and 1780s, another position within this discourse over records developed: that the archives requisite for the conduct of imperial government were not British or English at all but instead those of the other peoples over whom empire had asserted sovereignty through conquest.

FOUR

Records of Conquest

AT THE END OF THE SEVEN YEARS' WAR in 1763, imperial administrative bodies in the Atlantic world and South Asia alike again faced a common predicament of expansionary late medieval and early modern states: governing "extended polities" where the scale of territorial holdings, the physical distances between ruler and ruled, and the limitations of central fiscal capacity raised the specter of negotiation with conquered subjects as a strategy to avert the disintegration of the polity.[1] In Bengal, the East India Company grappled with the exercise of Mughal offices to which it had succeeded as *diwan,* while in the Atlantic world the Crown contended with the problem in relation to its territorial acquisition of the former French colony of Quebec, inhabited by a large population of French-speaking Catholics. Moreover, in both contexts, imperial government encountered the challenge of administering in relation to people with distinctive linguistic and cultural traditions whose experiences were not contained in the metropolitan archives used to govern over British subjects.

Guidance might have come from Edward Coke's decision in *Calvin's Case* (1608), in which he defined non-Christians as the "perpetual enemies" of Christian princes, who could conquer and subordinate them to confessionally correct constitutional rule. But in the subsequent century and a half, the reality of imperial conquest—especially its dependence on alliances with non-Christian peoples in both North America and Asia to achieve success—saw Coke's account subsumed by a recognition, pronounced in both the theory and practice of administration, of the legitimacy of cross-confessional cooperation in the service of the ambitions of power. Equally important was an increasing recognition within administrative circles that the conquest of non-Christian peoples did not inherently result in the abrogation of their "native" laws.[2] Writing in 1764 with respect to Quebec, William Murray, 1st Earl of Mansfield, and chief justice of the King's Bench, dismissed the idea that the "laws, and customs, and forms of judicature" of a conquered people could be "abolished" merely by conquest. Such an act had no precedent, he argued, for "the history of the world don't furnish an instance of so rash and unjust an act by any conqueror whatsoever: much less by the Crown of England, which has always left to the conquered their own laws and usages, with a change only so far as the sovereignty was concerned." "The fundamental maxims are, that a country conquered keeps her own laws, 'till the conqueror expressly gives new," he emphasized.[3]

Yet, Mansfield introduced three complications into this seemingly straightforward formulation. First, he invoked Ireland as an example where a more radical alteration of customary law had occurred over "a great length of time," enabled in part by the existence of "a pale of separation between the conquerors and conquered." Second, he dismissed as absurd the idea of "a man *sans aveu,* without knowing a syllable" of a conquered people's "language or laws" acting under "an English title of magistracy" and trying to administer English laws "inexplicable, and unexecutable" by the local customary usages. Third, Mansfield emphasized the profound tie between archival documents and the knowability of constitutional authority. The "origin" of constitutional powers such as "the power of [colonies] to tax themselves and raise money" "can only be found" in records: in the case of "Charter and Proprietary Governments," these were "Letters Patent"; in the case of "the King's Government," the relevant documents were "the King's Commission, and Instructions to the Governors of an early date, which may be found at the [Privy] Council Office or the Board of Trade."[4] Mansfield's statement raised a question: if a conqueror was to execute the laws of a conquered people, what was the archive through which it was to know what these laws were?

In the aftermath of the Seven Years' War, administrators answered this question in the vocabulary of early modern statecraft—namely, they claimed the existence of an archive composed of non-English language documents out of which governing protocols could be devised and authenticated by British officials. These archives were in no sense "vernacular." Rather, British administrators looked for elite and administrative corpora within other linguistic and cultural contexts that they deemed similar to the records of the Crown and East India Company offices. Through rhetorical conceits, concrete textual productions, and institutional formations, these administrators then analogized the form, content, and structure of such records to those which metropolitan bodies had drawn on to govern English-speaking subjects and servants. In the American context, analogy worked to bolster the extant authority of monarchical rule. But the backlash against the empire during the American Revolution generated new vocabularies for thinking about the relationship between government and document—ones that led to a seismic rupture between early modern and modern statecraft in the Atlantic world.

Quebec and the Problem of Custom

The 1763 Treaty of Paris placed the British as sovereign over territories including Quebec, formerly under French control and populated with settlers who differed from their new rulers in both their linguistic (French) and confessional (Catholic) attachments. The Crown pursued a number of strategies in order to integrate these peoples into projects of rule, based on article 20 of the treaty, which stated that as the French ceded "the sovereignty, property, possession, and all rights" to the British Crown, the British would "grant the inhabitants" of the ceded territories "the liberty of the Catholick religion" "as far as the laws of Great Britain permit."[5] With respect to Quebec, the Privy Council allowed for the preservation of existing laws based on the same principle that had long operated in colonial legal culture: non-repugnancy. In its commission to its appointed governor, James Murray, the council specified that laws not "repugnant" to those prevailing in England were to remain in force.[6] However, there was no clear agreement about which of these French laws ought to persist, nor about how far English law, especially acts of Parliament targeting Catholics, ought to apply. Courts in Quebec continued to refer to French laws and customs alongside English ones.[7] In 1767, the Privy Council sought to resolve the problem by commissioning a report from Francis Maseres, who had been appointed attorney general for Quebec.[8]

In his report, produced in 1769, Maseres characterized Quebec as a territory in which the conqueror had already changed the laws of the conquered and imposed those of England in their place. According to him, the Royal Proclamation of 1763, through which George III had defined the terms of jurisdiction for the ceded territories in the Atlantic world, "introduced" "the laws of England" into Quebec. The "intention" of the Crown had been "to assimilate the laws and civil government of it to those of the other American colonies and provinces which are under your Majesty's immediate government, and not to continue the municipal law and customs by which the conquered people had heretofore been governed," Maseres wrote. But he identified a problem: communication. Because the "royal proclamation" and the "commission to General Murray" had "never been published . . . in the French language," Maseres wrote, "the greatest part of your Majesty's new subjects remain ignorant" of the change. Consequently, these "new subjects" "imagine[d]" "that their ancient laws and usages are in many points still in force." This situation introduced "uncertainty" into the administration of Quebec, he continued, and specifically confusion about "the legal continuance of the ancient laws and customs that were observed here in the time of the French government." Some of the resulting "inconveniences" were logistical (specifically, that it made the system expensive and slow to administer). But Maseres was primarily concerned that the population's continued "respect for the wisdom of the parliament of Paris, and the excellence of the French government" undermined British sovereignty, for Quebec's inhabitants continued to maintain a "reverence for those edicts, reports, and other law-books, and for the authority of the French king who made the edicts, and for the parliament of Paris that has made the decisions reported in the books of reports."[9]

To counteract the credence given to these legal archives, Maseres proposed replacing the textual authorities on which French administrators had relied with ones that would allow British officials to promulgate laws while gesturing toward the traditions of the conquered. The task of "settling the laws of this province," he argued, required "making a code of all the laws by which it shall be governed for the future," one "in a great measure be taken from the laws of England" and only in a limited sense respectful of the "ancient laws and customs" of the French. Governing Quebec according to this code would protect "English judges" from being "puzzled and misled by artful French lawyers, partially citing and misrepresenting and misapplying the doctrines and cases contained in the French law books." Archival disorganization encouraged political disorder, he warned, for "as long as the French laws and customs subsist at large without being reduced into a code, so that the several French law-books, books of reports, and edicts of the French king at the books of authority upon the subject, to which recourse must be had continually in the decision of points of law," the inhabitants of Quebec would harbor "a secret wish" "to return to their subjection to the French king." But if the Quebec inhabitants could "continue to enjoy the most important of their ancient laws and customs under a new name," specifically "the stamp" of the British Crown, they would be reconciled to their new sovereigns while being less liable to be swayed by French authority. British rule would in this way be extended in a manner that gained the acquiescence of the conquered population. Any administrative settlement of Quebec that required "a general reference to the French law-books that contain it" to proceed would undermine royal power. According to Maseres, the preferable method would be one in which "the law of England become the general law" of Quebec, with "an exception of some particular subjects" where "the ancient customs of the country" were left to prevail on British terms. Specifically, he argued, the Crown ought to make "an ordinance or proclamation" that should "describe" which of these customs were to continue so that they could be known "without any reference to the law-books in which they were formerly contained." This work of administrative interpretation would "cut off all connection, in the minds of the Canadians, with the French laws, lawyers, and judges, and the government under which they were maintained."[10] In Maseres's vision, the former archive was to be completely supplanted by an imperial project of textual codification and promulgation of its interpretation of the "ancient laws and customs" of the French Canadians.

Maseres's proposal was rejected by the royal governor of Quebec, Guy Carleton, who produced his own report that same year in conjunction with William Hey, chief justice of the province. In disagreement with Maseres, Carleton and Hey suggested that the archive of extant French law retained authority and utility. Yet, like Maseres, they also wished to conform it to an imperial interpretation, and also like Maseres, they envisioned that this interpretation should be codified and manifested in a tangible set of precedents to which lawyers and administrators could refer. The "former Laws" of Quebec, "whether derived from the Custom of Paris, the King's Edicts, or Governor and Intendant's Ordonnances," with the exception of French criminal law and laws of trade, ought to be "deemed the Law of the Province," they argued. "Experience" showed that "a thorough Change of the Laws and Customs of a settled Province" would be "a Work of great Time" and "slow and gentle means." This necessarily required reference to "French Law Books of Authority, and Decisions of the Parliament of Paris," but only until the Crown's law officers could produce their own authoritative written accounts of such laws, after which "neither French Law Books, or the Decisions of the Parliament of Paris may be any more heared of."[11] Even though Carleton and Hey proposed a somewhat different vision of how Quebec should be governed, they shared with Maseres a belief that ruling over the sovereign's subjects-by-conquest required constructing an archive of textual authorities out of their documentary heritage, in parallel to the kind of constellation of records used to govern over the sovereign's subjects-by-birth.

In 1772, the solicitor general Alexander Wedderburn produced his own opinion on the question. "Canada is a conquered country," he declared at the outset of his report, which raised a question: "Can it therefore be said that by the right of conquest the conqueror may impose such laws as he pleases?" The answer required drawing a distinction between "power & right." While it was "certainly in the power of a conqueror to dispose" of existing laws, "in more civilized nations," "when subjects & not slaves are the fruits of victory," "no other right can be founded on conquest but that of regulating the political and civil government of the country." The conquered people were to be allowed "the enjoyment of their property and . . . all the privileges not inconsistent with the security of the conquest." Wedderburn did not propose replacing the French legal archive with an Anglophone one, as Maseres had, nor did he follow Carleton and Hey in envisioning administering based on a Crown interpretation of French legal records. But in his own way, he sought to limit the power of non-English authority. Rather than letting "orders from England" determine the laws of "a distant province," Wedderburn argued, it would be better to accommodate the "many local interests of police, of commerce, and of political economy . . . acquainted with the affairs, and immediately interested in the prosperity of a colony" by creating a local assembly "entrusted" with "the power of making laws." This assembly ought to be given only relatively general "rules" for legislating and otherwise draw on "their knowledge of local circumstances" in "form[ing] the necessary detail for executing" laws. Canada was "not in the condition of a new settled country, where the invention of a legislator may exercise itself in forming systems," Wedderburn wrote. Instead, Canada had "been long inhabited by men attached to their own customs," and it would be "improper" to unilaterally "transfer to that country" the whole of English law. He thus sought to empower political elites on the ground to use their local knowledge to craft appropriate laws for Quebec.[12]

For all the specific differences among the positions staked out by Maseres, Carleton and Hey, and Wedderburn, their proposals shared three characteristics. First, all understood "law" not as an abstraction but as intimately tied to its manifestation in written records. They understood that disciplining these records through possession, control, and interpretation was fundamental to effective rule, even though they differed on exactly how that process was to occur. Second, all aimed to produce a version of customary law that enhanced the authority of the British Crown while reducing the interpretive power of French jurists. Third, their projects of translating the written laws of the French Empire into a British administrative vernacular were aimed at bolstering, not undermining, the power of metropolitan authority. While these officials disagreed about exactly how that translation was to occur, all conceived of the customary archive of French records as an extension of the kind of political wisdom produced out of the records of the imperial state. In the case of Quebec, territorial conquest and the integration of non-British subjects into the compass of empire served to bolster both metropolitan authority and reduce the power of native interpreters. In the Atlantic world, the metropolitan archive became more, not less, authoritative as a result of conquest over non-British people.

The Quebec Act, passed by Parliament in October 1774, codified this constellation of authority into law. The act empowered "all his Majesty's *Canadian* Subjects within the Province of *Quebec*" to continue to "hold and enjoy their Property and Possessions, together with all Customs and Usages" in so far as these remained consistent with "their Allegiance to His Majesty, and Subjection to the Crown and Parliament of Great Britain." Although the act allowed the inhabitants of Quebec to apply to "the Laws of *Canada,* and not to the Laws of *England*" in matters related to property and "civil rights," the legislation also instructed royally appointed jurists to resolve such disputes, locating the power to define the meaning of "the Laws and Customs of *Canada*" in the hands of the Crown's officers. Moreover, the statute established that because "the Criminal Law of *England*" had been "sensibly felt by the Inhabitants, from an Experience of more than Nine Years," criminal disputes were to be judged in terms of English, not Canadian, laws. Finally, the act demanded that conciliar decisions be "regularly transmitted" to London for review by the Privy Council, which retained the prerogative to "disallow" them.[13]

The instructions issued in January 1775 by the Privy Council to Guy Carleton in his capacity as Quebec's newly appointed governor elaborated the procedures through which this administrative arrangement was to unfold on the ground. Here, the Crown made its ultimate controlling power clear. Carleton was informed that "no Ordinance touching Religion" or "respecting private property" was to "take effect" "until Our Royal Will and Pleasure is known." He was bound by the familiar requirement imposed on royal governors that all "Ordinances" passed in the province be "transmitted" to the Privy Council via "One of our Principal Secretaries of State," with "Duplicates" sent to "Our Commissioners for Trade and Plantations." Carleton was to ensure that these laws were "abstracted in the Margents" "with very full and particular Observations" as to whether the said ordinance "is introductive to a new Law or does repeal" an existing one. Carleton was also to "transmit" "fair Copies of the Journals of the proceedings" of the provincial council for review. The Privy Council continued with a set of detailed provisions regarding the administration of civil and criminal law. Stating that "a proper Mode of administring Civil and Criminal Justice through the whole Extent of Our Province, according to the Principles declared" in the Quebec Act, "demand the greatest care." The council affirmed that, consistent with "the said Act of Parliament," "our Canadian Subjects should have the benefit and use of their own Laws, Usages, and Customs in all Controversies respecting" property. To realize this, however, the Privy Council gave its appointees the power of "framing" the relevant "Ordinances" and determining "whether the Laws of England may not be, if not altogether, at least in part the Rule for the decision." The process of appeal specified in the instructions was also centered in metropolitan authority. The appellate court of the province dealing with civil matters was to consist of the Crown-appointed "Governor and Council," whose "Judgement" was to be "final in all cases not exceeding the Value of £500 sterling." In cases involving higher values, all appeals were to go directly "to Us in Our Privy Council."[14] While "Canadian Subjects" were to be granted the use of their own "Laws, Usages, and Customs" in property disputes, the power of defining what these were lay in the hands of officials constrained by royal instructions and accountable to the Crown.

Quebec's integration into the imperial body politic in this way served to significantly undermine the archive of French legal authorities while elevating the civil wisdom of the Crown. The 1791 parliamentary legislation commonly known as the Constitutional Act, which lasted as the governing arrangement for Canada until the 1840 Act of Union, cemented this power configuration by constraining the ability of French Canadians to exercise legislative autonomy. Formulated entirely on the basis of information from colonial and metropolitan officials "with scarcely any input from Quebec-Loyalist, merchant, seigneur, or *habitant*" (in the words of one analyst), the act served to enhance the power of the governor and his council under Crown appointment over provincial legislative institutions.[15] Specifically, the act gave the royal governor the power to appoint the assembly's speaker and make lifelong appointments to the provincial council and tied eligibility for those appointments to a person's possession of hereditary titles, which "His Majesty . . . shall think proper to confer upon any Subject of the Crown of Great Britain." Indeed, while the act allowed occupants of legislative assemblies to swear their required oaths "in the English or French Language," the statement had the same end irrespective of the language in which it was spoken: subjects made a declaration of "true Allegiance to his Majesty, King George, as lawful Sovereign of the Kingdom of Great Britain, and of these Provinces dependant on and belonging to the said Kingdom."[16] Conquest over non-English speakers in the British Atlantic saw the enhancement of metropolitan authority and its archival apparatus.

Imperial Backlash and Constitutional Reimaginings

In the mid-1770s, an intense debate about the Quebec Act erupted across the British Empire. A central point of contention was the power granted to the Crown to determine the administrative constitution of the province. Defenders of the act invoked the language of Mansfield, positing themselves as engaged in an act of constitutional restoration based on "translating" French law into English terms. This, they emphasized, placed the ascension of British rule on deeply rooted historical precedent. Referencing "a thousand instances of the same kind" "upon record," the

Scottish writer James Macpherson wrote in defense of the Quebec Act
that there was "no maxim in the Law of England more generally known
or less controverted than, That in conquered or ceded countries, which
have already laws of their own, such laws remain in full force, till they are
altered and changed by the Sovereign."[17] "There is a distinction to be
made between the law of France, and the government of France," emphasized Thomas Lord Lyttelton; whatever the constitution of the latter, the
former was "not despotic" but rather "originated in freedom." It would
be "a glorious and happy revolution" if one could "restore" France's
"ancient laws free from the control of power"—and such an opportunity
lay in Quebec, he emphasized.[18]

For the Quebec Act's transatlantic critics, however, these terms
caused alarm. They agreed that the act "restored" "the ancient laws of
Canada," but for them these formed "a despotic constitution" of French
"arbitrary power" and "Popish Religion," as Alexander Hamilton, then a
student at King's College in New York, warned in 1775. Even worse, Hamilton continued, these "ancient laws" were now "liable to such variations
and additions, as shall be deemed necessary, by the Governor and council,
and as both the one and the other are to be appointed by the King." This
made "the King absolute, in Canada" even as the act's language aimed
to "conciliate the minds of the Canadians."[19] In the act, Hamilton saw
danger, "the oppressive designs of administration against the other parts
of the empire" made manifest.[20]

In his political thought, these considerations dovetailed with a
more general skepticism of the idea that constitutional authority needed
to be founded on the kind of documentary referentiality predominant in
the practice of imperial governance itself. In an effort to refute Samuel
Seabury's arguments in defense of the imperial constitution, Hamilton
offered an extended analysis of several of the charters granted for the establishment of the American colonies. He quoted extensively from several seventeenth-century charters, including those granted to the Virginia
Company, to the Calverts of Maryland, to Connecticut, to Massachusetts,
and to Carolina, among others, all of which in Hamilton's reading proved
"the absolute non-existence of that parliamentary supremacy" claimed
by Seabury. But after making this "pretty general survey of the American
charters," Hamilton pivoted to a somewhat different argument. Addressing the circumstances of his adopted New York, Hamilton admitted that

the colony "has no Charter." Yet, Hamilton wrote, there was "no need" to assert New York's "claim to liberty" by making reference to a charter, for that claim rested not on the documentary authority of the sovereign but instead on "the sacred rights of mankind," which were "not to be rummaged for, among old parchments, or musty records," but instead were "written, as with a sun beam, in the whole *volume* of human nature, by the hand of the divinity itself; and can never be erased or obscured by mortal power."[21] The "volume of human nature," rather than "old parchments" and "musty records," were the source of legitimate governing authority.

Hamilton was not alone in distinguishing political authority from its engrafting in the kinds of documents upon which imperial government grounded its sovereignty. By the mid-1770s, critics of the imperial constitution in the north Atlantic were invoking a language of political justification purged of reference to the authority of an archive of parchment and paper. This project involved, in part, the excavation of the historically grounded "principles" of an ancient "English" constitution that, they emphasized, antedated the invention of writing, such that the integrity and purchase of such principles was not contingent on their written expression or their codification in official documents. Patriot writers juxtaposed the inferior written remembrancers of parliamentary legislation and Crown decree to the superior activity or exercise of these ancient principles, whose precedential significance, they argued, transcended inscriptive media. "Our Saxon forefathers established their government in Britain, before the transactions of mankind were recorded in writing," the author of a 1776 pamphlet published in Philadelphia explained, and "the principles of their government" were knowable not with reference to "records" (only a "few" of which were "remaining") but instead through "the actual exercise of their rights."[22] In the north Atlantic outposts of the British Empire, it had become possible to conceive of "Right" as being at once "prior to all written Records" and "co-eval with, and essential to the very existence, of this Constitution," as a patriot sympathizer in London observed in 1776.[23]

The Quebec Act demonstrated that in extending empire over non-English-speaking peoples in the Atlantic world, the Crown justified its activities using the same epistemics that had undergirded its projection of power over the preceding century and a half: claims to authority based on reference to written records. The project of colonization in Quebec was in this sense an eminently early modern one in which the archive of conquest was integrated into an archive of rule, a process that in this particular context augmented monarchical authority. But in the American state that emerged from revolution and war against the British Empire, "constitution" came to mean "single documents," and among political elites of this new republic, there was ambiguity over whether these documents needed reference to other governmental records in order to have constitutional significance. Indeed, whether the preeminent governing document of the new United States—the federal Constitution—even had a fixed meaning remained a matter of considerable contestation in the early American republic. So too did the question of how that meaning was to be known: through the plain text of the words in the Constitution? By comparing the Constitution to other texts?[24] Some politicians claimed that such a meaning could be derived from the consultation of "historical" texts that, they contended, provided authoritative insight into what the Constitution meant. At the same time, a seemingly contrary position also emerged in national political discourses: that the features that distinguished the American constitutional order from that of the British Empire was that in the former, no such archival references were necessary to determine what was constitutional because the singular document had a clear meaning on its own. "In the construction of other Constitutions, some formed by mere charters of privilege, others arising from practice, we find the historian and the commentator obliged, in the support of theory, to resort to records unintelligible, from a change of names and of manners, or to the uncertain lights of mere tradition," stated the Maryland representative William Vans Murray in 1796. "But, in construing our Constitution, in ascertaining the metes and bounds of its various grants of power," Murray continued, "the explicitness of the instrument itself" and the continued participation in political life of its drafters who had "seen the Constitution from its cradle" and thus "have the most perfect knowledge of it," rendered reference to such records unnecessary to determine its meaning.[25]

Yet, whatever the differences among early U.S. political elites over how constitutional meaning should be determined, they shared a common commitment to a vision of sovereignty that entirely excluded the possibility that Native Americans might be able to exist within it while retaining some version of their customary practices of governance. At both the federal and state levels, U.S. officials neither attempted to accommodate some

version of Native custom within the compass of American sovereignty
nor in any substantive way respect Native sovereignty. Instead, the U.S.
government sought the violent submission of First Peoples to its own sovereignty through war and forced their subjection to "American" cultural
modalities, including through the imposition of the English language on
Native communities and active efforts to dissuade or eradicate the use of
Indigenous languages and cultural practices.[26] As the next chapter explores, the project of integrating an archive of conquest into an archive of
rule unfolded differently in East India Company Bengal, not generating a
different vocabulary for thinking about the relationship between inscrip-
tion and constitutional authority but instead deploying an early modern
one in an imperial scene. In the context of imperial South Asia, administrators acted both to legitimate their own decision-making by reference
to non-English-language records and to undermine the metropolitan archive as a governing instrument. Their project was as much an exercise
in neutering existing institutions as it was an attempt to construct new
ones—justified discursively and executed practically in the early modern
episteme of archival government.

Dueling Systems

IN THE ENGLISH ATLANTIC WORLD, companies at times attempted to place Indians under their sovereignty. They proved unsuccessful. In 1608, for example, the Virginia Company sought to make Powhatan into a vassal of King James I by staging a coronation ceremony at the village of Werowocomoco on the banks of the river that the Powhatans called Pamunkey and the English named after the Duke of York. According to the eyewitness Captain John Smith, who thought the ceremony foolish, the English tried to subordinate an Indian to English sovereignty by placing a crown on his head. Powhatan, however, resisted, an act Smith attributed to Powhatan "neither knowing the majesty nor meaning of a Crowne."[1] Over a century later in Bengal, an imperial project proceeded by a very different, indeed inverse strategy: the English East India Company placed itself under the sovereignty of an Indian ruler. In 1757, at the Mughal city of Alinagar, which the British called Calcutta, Robert Clive, military commander of the company army, and Admiral Charles Watson of the Royal Navy signed a treaty with Siraj ud-daula, *nawab* of Bengal, which led to Clive's eventually being declared a Mughal officeholder with the title "Sabit Jang Bahadur" ("The Firm in War").[2]

These two events occurred in vastly and incomparably different contexts. Yet, both were efforts to determine where non-Europeans fit in relation to forms of European sovereignty, and in both cases the drawn-out processes of resolving this problem unfolded in terms of an archival epistemology. As this book has shown, in the years following Powhatan's failed coronation, English and then British officials ultimately came to regard North American Indians as external to the imperial body politic. When imperial government integrated non-English speakers in the Atlantic world into the compass of subjecthood, as in the case of Quebec, administrators sought to govern them in terms of the archival epistemology, envisioning some set of documentary precedents as the legitimating basis for rule. The East India Company over the course of the late seventeenth and early eighteenth

centuries pursued a different approach. The corporation gradually impli-
cated itself into Indian society by co-opting what they perceived to be the
vocabularies, customs, and categories of Mughal administration in order
to facilitate the exercise of sovereignty. Here, the epistemics of archival
governance proceeded in a manner that induced significant internal conflict within imperial administration.

Shortly after signing the Treaty of Alinagar, Clive requested that
the Court of Directors send "five young gentlemen" and "annually two
others" to the company's factory at Basra on the Persian Gulf "to study
the Persian tongue and nothing else." "When qualified to be of use" to
the company in India, Clive continued, these gentlemen should be dispatched eastward, where the employment of such "Europeans perfected
in the true and genuine Persian speech and literature" at the corporation's Indian establishments would result in "many future advantages"
to "the Company's affairs."[3] Accustoming Indians to Anglophone norms
of government and rule was foolish, Clive argued. "Every Gentleman
who has been in India will I am sure agree with me in asserting that
the People of Indostan, the Gentoos, would rather suffer Death than an
Alteration in their Laws, Customs, & Religion," he wrote in an undated
memo. If such an alteration were attempted, he predicted that Indians
would "fly from us & take Refuge in remote parts of the Country," leaving "Provinces depopulated, & uncultivated" and thus the company's
potential "Revenues . . . Prosperity & Commerce . . . in that moment
annihilated."[4] The increasingly closer imbrication of the company into
Indian society thus raised a dilemma: how was the corporation to successfully rule over and extract revenue from a population whose "Laws,
Customs, & Religion" were entirely unlike those of Britain? As administrator, was the East India Company to inhabit the offices of a polity
whose linguistic and cultural traditions were entirely outside the experience of its new imperial rulers?

Navigating what Clive later described as this "nice and difficult
System of Politics" in which the company's "Interests" were inseparably
"connected" with those of "surrounding Powers" embroiled the corporation in a series of predicaments associated with exercising sovereignty
over non-English-speaking peoples.[5] The company sought to both understand and administer the systems of rule over which it gained control
from the *nawabs* and to bring these systems, which had developed on

cultural and historical protocols entirely alien from European patterns, under its administration. Three aspects of administration were particularly urgent. First, how was the company to exercise the revenue privileges that inhered in the Mughal offices it came to occupy? Second, how was the company to maintain order using a hybrid army that was composed of British, continental European, and Indian troops? Finally, and encasing the other two problems, there was the issue of determining the laws by which the company should govern Indians and how they should be implemented.[6]

The company's challenge bore a structural affinity to that confronted by the Crown with respect to Canada. Whereas negotiating with settler-colonial elites could proceed through reference to a shared framework of language, law, and custom, the practical framework for governing with respect to non-English speakers, whether French or Bengali, was less clear even with the broad guidance provided by jurists such as Edward Coke and Lord Mansfield. Yet, upon closer inspection, the company's challenge was also distinctive in several respects. In Quebec, the Crown confronted the question of what ought to be done with the legacy of French law and administration, but it was not in itself succeeding to French administrative offices. By contrast, the company's status as both *zamindar* from 1698 and eventually as *diwan* from 1765 meant that it actually inhabited Mughal administrative offices and was empowered to exercise the associated duties of collecting taxes as well as adjudicating revenue, land, and criminal disputes using Mughal courts and laws. At the same time, it sought to transform the organization and administration of these offices in order to establish control over them and maximize its revenue. Company administrators reached for the same solution that Crown officials had with respect to Quebec: they sought to assert the existence of an archive of "native" records analogous to those of metropolitan offices that could, in turn, be used to govern non-English-speaking subjects. In both Quebec and Bengal, imperial officials determined the composition of this native archive. In South Asia, however, administrators with extensive experience of India itself opposed this native archive to metropolitan archival authorities. They asserted that this archive of the field was at once analogous to official archives in Britain in form while at the same time superior to London authorities as a guide for ruling non-English speakers.

An Archive of Indian Authorities

This tension between archival authorities most dramatically manifested itself in the political thought and practices of Warren Hastings, eventually governor-general of India. When Hastings set sail from England to Madras on March 26, 1769, several months after the East India Company appointed him as a member of the council at its settlement of Fort St. George, he had already spent fifteen years in India in service to the corporation. As a writer at Calcutta from 1750, he had helped administer the corporation's thriving trade, especially in cotton and silk, in relation to Mughal authority constituted in the person of the *nawab* of Bengal; witnessed Clive's victory at Plassey in 1757; and served both as the company's representative at the court of the *nawab* and on the corporation's Bengal Council between 1758 and 1764, where he was an ally of the company's governor, Henry Vansittart.

After Vansittart resigned in 1764, Hastings returned to Britain. He spent the next several years promoting the idea within metropolitan learned and political circles that cultivating knowledge of South Asian cultures was essential to both the company's political success and British power. Illustrative of these efforts was his 1766 publication entitled *A Proposal for Establishing a Professorship of the Persian Language in the University of Oxford.* Using the distinctive early modern idiom of "manners," Hastings argued that the study of Persian ought to be "introduce[d]" "into our Seminaries of Learning." "By familiarizing ourselves to a general inspection of the manners of the various inhabitants of the earth; by a frequent observation of the effects which climate, habit, superstition, and other adventitious causes are capable of producing upon the minds and hearts of men," he wrote, "we shall accustom ourselves not only to revere their virtues, but even to view their errors with indulgence," an effect that would "open our minds" and increase feelings of "benevolence . . . for the whole race of mankind." While most of the world did not offer "any useful acquisitions" to European knowledge, "the Asiatics" were an exception, "since from them we derive the first seeds of all the knowledge which we have carried to so much higher a degree of perfection." Citing the European debt to Arabic medicine, chemistry, and mathematics; to Asian silk and cotton manufacture; and to Indian architecture and mechanics, he stressed that there was much Europeans could still learn from the "eastern nations" and then improve with Europeans' superior abilities. Such learning involved the application of techniques of archival reading to non-European cultural objects. Hastings was especially interested in the possibility of deriving knowledge from the Persians, for "there is a large collection of manuscripts in the Persic language in the University of Oxford" that, though currently regarded as "merely . . . useless curiosities," "might be made subservient to the most useful purposes" if "placed under the charge of some person skilled in that Language, and capable of selecting such materials as may any way contribute to the instruction or entertainment of the world."[7]

Establishing a professorship at Oxford whose holder would study and publicize the materials from these manuscripts would advance the interests of both the company and the nation, Hastings contended. The Persian language was "not only spoken in all the courts of Indostan, but is used in all their public records, in writing letters, and in the transactions of state." As a consequence of "the interests which this country has lately acquired in the political, as well as the commercial affairs of Indostan," administrators' knowledge of Persian was "an object of national concern," which could "promote" these interests:

> The great and rich possessions of the East-India company in that part of the world make it of the most consequence to them to have persons in their service well instructed in the Persic Language, which might easily be made a part of their education at home, and save a great deal of labour and time, which are frequently and ineffectually bestowed upon it abroad, for want of a proper method, and from the difficulty of application and retention in minds too young for voluntary restraint, and yet past that period in life when the memory is most susceptible of lasting impressions.

While such knowledge might have been considered "superfluous" "whilst the affairs of the East-India company were confined merely to commerce," Hastings wrote,

> at this time, when the servants of the company exercise the rights of sovereignty over a rich and extensive country, surely something more than a bare proficiency in writing and merchant accounts; a more liberal exercise of the understanding; a preparatory knowl-

edge of the principles of government, and especially of our own
constitution; some acquaintance with men and manners, are necessary to enable them to fill the parts of magistrates and legislators,
and to discharge the difficult offices of government, at such a distance from those from whom they derive their powers, that every
little error in their conduct may be productive of dangerous and
fatal consequences.[8]

Emphasizing the insufficiency of scribal and accounting skills to the administration of this new situation and the comparative necessity of language to the exercise of office, Hastings here envisioned a break between
the existing knowledge regime of imperial government in both its royal
and corporate guises where such activities had reigned supreme. Moreover, by invoking the "distance" between the metropole where officials
"derive their powers" and the world of "offices" in which they actually had
to exercise them, Hastings gestured toward where he believed the center
of administrative knowledge production ought to be located. The expertise of the field—especially language—was essential as a form of official
knowledge for the company-state, and it could be derived by studying the
manuscript heritage of a subject people.

Hastings's circle of confidants and admirers echoed his arguments
using a similar characterization of rupture. "You ask, my Friend, what
kind of Education I would recommend for a young Gentleman 9 or
10 years old intended for the East Indies," wrote David Anderson, Hastings's Persian translator, to a correspondent in 1770. A "very common
but mistaken notion," Anderson continued, held that "a Knowledge of the
various Branches requisite for forming a Merchant was the Chief Quali-
fication necessary for a Company Servant." In fact, he advised, "experience has since taught me that a man may be a valuable & useful servant to
the Company without understanding Marchants Accounts."[9] "It is new,"
Samuel Johnson wrote in an oft-quoted letter to Hastings in 1781, "for
a Governor of Bengal to patronize learning."[10] Scholars have tended to
take Johnson at face value, characterizing the period following Hastings's
appointment as governor-general of Bengal as an age of fracture between
governing styles, indeed of "the birth and development of a colonial bureaucracy."[11] But Hastings was neither a bureaucrat nor an innovator; instead, he was an official who deployed the constellation of vocabularies

and practices associated with the archival style to enhance his position.[12] Like administrators before him, Hastings located the experience necessary for exercising office in archival records, particularly those records which he controlled. For this reason, his description of the collection of Persian texts at Oxford was revealing. He analogized these texts to European equivalents by describing them as "manuscripts" that, as with the exegesis of Western manuscripts by scholarly experts, could be rendered "useful" if put into the hands of someone with the requisite linguistic knowledge and hermeneutical skill of selection.

When Hastings proposed the establishment of the Oxford professorship, the East India Company was in the midst of trying to "co-opt and manipulate the hierarchies and routines of power established under the Mughals and the *nawabs*" in order to enhance its own revenue. As Robert Travers has shown, the corporation proceeded by mounting an "ideological critique" of extant Indian rule as corrupt, a strategic response to its own declining revenue and rendered more urgent by the collapse of its stock price in 1769. That critique focused especially on Indian landholders who exercised privileges to collect taxes by virtue of holding titles such as *zamindars* and *taluqdars*.[13] Johnson's own rhetoric of break likely emanated from a desire to flatter Hastings, since in the same 1781 letter he sought the governor-general's support for a translation of Ludovico Ariosto's poetry by the company official John Hoole.[14] Hastings's invocation in 1766 of the Persians as a polite, learned people with a manuscript heritage served to analogize an Eastern to a Western textual culture. Several scholars have recently pointed to the way analogizing between cultural traditions structured the reception of both Islam and Hinduism within erudite eighteenth-century European circles.[15] In the milieu of Hastings's office, the ends served by analogy were increasingly the articulation of a style of administration meant to facilitate rule over conquered non-English-speaking peoples on the same terms of archival governance, while at the same time defanging both the precedential authority of metropolitan archives and the competing power of Indian officeholders.

Hastings's return to India as a member of the Fort St. George council in 1769 coincided with a burgeoning discourse of disgruntlement among company officials who complained that insufficient information was undermining revenue collection and judicial administration. In June 1769, the Court of Directors wrote to company servants to emphasize that while they had "no view to prejudice the Rights of the Zemindars who hold certain Districts by Inheritance," the servants were to "propose Terms" for the collection of revenue based on their "Knowledge" of its "real State," which would "in process of time" yield the company "a certain increase" in its profits.[16] Replying to the court in August 1769, Harry Verelst, the company's governor at Bengal since 1767, noted that the company's "Accounts of particular districts" were "imperfect," and "an explicit Knowledge of them" "likely to prove" "useful." Developing a program for gaining that knowledge in response to the court's request, Verelst reported that he had sought to compile "a Work . . . that might serve as a standing Record of all material Transactions since the Grant of the Dewanny." The text was to contain "a summary History of each district, the form of it's Constitution, the Nature of it's Soil & productions, the Succession of it's Zemindars, the Connections & Revolutions in their Families & the Changes which have happened in it from time to time." However, Verelst described himself as being "interrupted" in these efforts by the requirements of travel, which put him at "distance from the Records of Government," making it difficult for him to make "those frequent References which are requisite" to these "established Authorities" from which "authentick Facts" and "Knowledge of the State of the Country" could be derived. To remedy the problem, he proposed that "persons be appointed on the part of the Company . . . to act jointly with the Servants of the Nabob, & to take Copies of all papers whatever." It was now time, he argued, for the construction of a robust repository of Mughal administrative records under the control of the company, whose servants could then use them as a source of knowledge. "We now take an intimate part in the Welfare of these provinces," he argued, "& I apprehend in Our Circumstances those monuments of the progress of Government which must abound in serviceable Material ought not to be neglected, or suffered to remain in a State of Obscurity & perpetual danger of being lost, or mutilated."[17] Archival authorities were the grounds on which plans were to be generated.

To this end, Verelst drafted a set of "Instructions" that directed company servants to collect records, adapting the vernacular of archival governance to local conditions; the instructions were subsequently approved by the Bengal council, which reiterated that the project was an endeavor of making "an authentic Record to refer to on every occasion

as an established authority."[18] Verelst subsequently published these instructions in 1772 as one of several "papers" constitutive of "proofs" of
his conduct, which he posited against the "misconstruction" of company administration by critics such as William Bolts and Alexander
Dow. According to Verelst, servants were to "collect . . . the form of the
ancient constitution" of Bengal by seizing Mughal land records, specifically "a complete Hustabood, or rent-roll, with the number of Begahs,
or measures of land, contained in each district, according to the original surveys and measurements, and the method in which they were laid
out and appropriated." From such "informations" "derived from genuine authorities, and confirmed by an accurate inspection of your own,"
he argued, officials could then construct general rules "for how far the
wealth and prosperity" of the province "may be augmented." Without
recourse to an archive on the English model, company administrators
risked being undermined by the duplicity of Indians. Proposing rules
for judicial administration, he warned that "the want of regular registers" "has encouraged the natural propensity of the judge to bribery and
fraud . . . whereas, whilst a reference to records is always open, he must
live in perpetual fear of detection." He suggested that "registers . . . be
lodged in the principal Cutcherry [court] of the province, and an authenticated copy transmitted to Murshed-abad," where the superior court of
the *nawab* sat. Where records might be "destroyed or mutilated," administrators were to make "reference" to an analogous form of "experience,"
namely "living authorities" such as "men of the best understanding and
longest experience in the district," out of whom company servants were
to use their own "judgment . . . in extracting the truth, and distinguishing between the private bias of individuals and the real state of facts."
Turning to "the regulation of commerce," Verelst advised the servants "to
obtain a sight or copies" of accounts to check the accuracy of *zemindary*
collecting and to facilitate "the introduction of fair dealing, and the dissolution of clandestine compacts of particular sets of men, intended to
rob the manufacturer of his due." The enabling condition of constructing
and then deploying this archive was the servants' linguistic knowledge:
"Versed as you are in the language, depend on none, where you yourself can possibly hear and determine," he emphasized.[19] As governor of
Bengal in 1772 and then as governor-general from 1774 to 1785, Hastings
built on Verelst's directives, enhancing the effort to build an archive of

administration out of Indian materials. More aggressively than Verelst, Hastings conceptualized such materials as part of an archive of governing experience that he posited as superior to the metropolitan archives of the company-state and eventually the state itself.

Hastings's Archival Politics

In September 1769, soon after arriving back in India, Hastings sought advice from Thomas Motte, an English free merchant trading in Bengal, on the definition of the Persian term *zamindar,* a subject about which the Court of Directors had sought advice several months earlier. Citing Motte's "great Experience in Zemidarree Matters," Hastings asked him to "answer some Enquiries" about the nature of the "hereditary right" and "legal Forms of the Mogul Government."[20] In the following months, Hastings made similar requests to officials and private traders traveling through the company's territories, encouraging these experienced observers to supply him with "any . . . particularities of the Country through which you may pass, or of the people which may fall under your Observation, whenever you have a leisure half hour."[21] As Hastings's efforts at information-gathering continued, he came to describe Indian politics as elaborate, intricate, and heterogeneous. In an October 1770 letter discussing regulations being developed by the Fort St. George council on judicial administration, Hastings noted, for example, that procedures for resolving caste disputes in the Carnatic region "would be of no service in Bengal, where the usages, & the cast[e]s themselves are totally different." He understood that "the Shaster" (the Sanskrit term *Śāstra,* referring generally to sacred texts) "is their Law for all their Casts," and was referred to by "competent Judges to decide in all Cases." Hastings expressed his hope of imminently obtaining a copy such that it might be referred to in the Mughal courts now under the company's administration.[22] He was soon (perhaps pedantically) correcting his colleagues for their failure to accurately analogize Mughal offices to European ones using the terms Hastings deemed correct.[23]

By the late 1760s, many other company servants were similarly invoking their on-the-ground knowledge of Indian culture as the legitimating basis for their plans for the reform of the government of Bengal. Debate over these plans occurred within this shared epistemic vocabulary as authors advanced what one writer described as "reflections" aimed at improving the company's fortunes "for the benefit of all his Majesty's subjects," which, far from being "the fruits of empty speculation," were "drawn from the result" of "practice" during "long residence in India."[24] Quoting extensively from the company's correspondence to substantiate his views, for example, the former governor of West Florida and member of Parliament George Johnstone in 1771 presented a "Plan of Government for Bengal," "opinions" that, he stressed, "merit[ed]" "weight" because of "the experience of the system he presumes to combat."[25] In the course of a pamphlet attacking Johnstone published the next year, the sometimes company servant Alexander Dalrymple moved to denigrate metropolitan experience, contending that "it was impossible for the Commerce of the Company to be extended or improved by any Ideas thrown out, or resolutions formed in a General Court." "Commerce so distant must depend on so many concurrent circumstances that the utmost attention; and the most ample information only, can give a probability of Success to any new undertaking, or even to carry on the old branches in the manner most advantageous," he wrote.[26]

Hastings tapped into this discursive stance of invoking superior "experience," which he located in records either under his observation or produced by those whom he considered legitimate authorities. He mobilized this experience against a similar target as that attacked by other company servants who had worked in South Asia: metropolitan administration. But Hastings critiqued from a more powerful position, one of conciliar authority that allowed him access to a robust archive of local records and Indian-language documents which dwarfed the written evidentiary record available to most of these other servants. Neither Crown officials nor the Court of Directors could solve the problems plaguing the company's administration, Hastings argued, which were especially pronounced in the aftermath of a crash in the value of the company's stock in 1769 and the great famine that swept through Bengal between 1769 and 1770. Amid a tide of criticism and calls for greater oversight of the company's activities, Hastings asserted his own expertise. A government "under the protection of the Crown," he wrote in 1770, "must of necessity become a dependency of the Crown, I mean no longer the Company's but the King's government."[27] In fact, Hastings wrote the next year, the company's metropolitan leadership was complicit in enabling the state's growing authority over the corporation, and he warned that the directors would concede both "ample Power . . . to control the Company's Servants" and "the Rights & Authority of the Company to the Crown."[28] Insofar as the company's rule in Bengal was now "a scene of Ruin & Confusion," rife with "Famine" and "the incessant Drain of Money," Hastings principally blamed metropolitan authorities: the directors, whom he alleged had "fomented" "Disputes" among officials, and "the King's Ministers," whom he accused of having "added to some dangerous Evils in our political system here" and "weakened the Hands of this Government."[29]

In Hastings's view, company rule in Bengal ought to proceed based on written authorities from the field rather than via direction from Leadenhall and Whitehall. The "Novelty" and "Importance" of "our Records" "deserve the attention of our superiors," Hastings wrote to company servant Robert Holt in early February 1771.[30] For "a Knowledge of the Facts," Hastings advised turning to "the Transactions" and "Military Consultations" of his own government, which, though in the form of "scattered materials," provided an accurate account of "the present State & prospect of our Affairs."[31] Appointments to the company's offices in Bengal, he noted to the company official Laurence Sulivan on another occasion while objecting to the court's choice of a secretary, ought to be made from among "Men of Abilities" "acquainted at the same time with" the knowledge requisite to the duties of the office. The "Accountant's Office," Hastings elaborated, ought always to be "supplied from England," for the position "requires talents of a particular Kind with much practice, & ought to be as little exposed to change as possible." In the case of a secretary, however, the requisite experience was of "all the official Forms" of Mughal government, "which Kind of Knowledge a Man from England cannot well possess" but which was "of the greatest Utility in the dispatch of Business."[32] "Observation" by servants on the ground, not "speculation" and "ministerial interference," ought to guide the company's "Affairs of Bengal," he reiterated.[33]

An ideological pillar of Hastings's push against both Crown and court authority was his projection that his system of generating political knowledge constituted a break from the company's earlier practices of rule and was better suited to governing a political configuration that he also projected as having been fundamentally transformed by its recent territorial acquisitions. "There was a Time when very moderate abilities joined to integrity were sufficient to have administered the most weighty affairs of the British Settlements in India with Credit & Success," he wrote to Lord Shelburne in 1771, "but Talents of a different kind are now become necessary to support a system which is ready to fall to Pieces by the counter action of its parts, and which must fall soon unless it be presided by the timely Interposition of some Superior Power." "The Company's System has within these few years undergone a total change," he continued, "from a merely Commercial Body . . . into a Military & Territorial Power, to which their Commerce is but a Secondary concern." "Yet," Hastings noted, "the Principles, Regulations, & Laws which were originally Instituted for their Government continue the Same, nor has one Step of any Consequence been taken for improving their new System, for reducing the vast Materials of which it is composed into Order or combining the great Powers which lie Scattered over the different Parts of India into one solid consistent plan." Here, Hastings was arguing not only for "an established union" among the company's presidencies at Bengal, Madras, and Bombay under his own supervision but also for "a general, as well as a particular Plan of Government better adopted to the present Interests & Possessions of the Nation in India than that which was originally framed for the Encouragement of their Commerce, & the Police of their little Factories." This plan was to be formed not on the grounds on which the company's government was "originally Instituted" but instead on the "vast Materials" collected from the imperial field.[34] Hastings's case for a rupture between the pre- and post-Plassey administrative order was thus rendered in the episteme of early modern archival government. The archival "Materials" from which administration was to be justified was not that of the metropole but rather those which Hastings and his allies had located in India itself.

By mid-1772, Hastings had decried the state of the company's government by comparing it to a disordered archive. "The new Government of the Company consists of a confused Heap of indigested Materials, as wild as the chaos itself," he wrote in July. The company decision-making process was to "adopt a plan upon conjecture, try, execute, add, & deduct from it, till it is brought into a perfect state," he lamented. Hastings proposed that the "first step to be taken" in the reform of the *diwan* was seizing records, specifically "the Bengal Accounts"; second, "abstracting" and "rendering" the documents into codified, general instructions for revenue collection; and finally, "calling for the papers" of Mughal revenue officers "and comparing them with the Abstracts."[35] He described himself as having formed such an opinion on "the Subject of the Affairs of Bengal" "from Observation" rather than "Speculation."[36] The company's status as *diwan* meant that it had jurisdiction over revenue disputes, Hastings explained, and he advised that "a separate Register" of complaints be kept "both in Bengalee & in English."[37]

Elevating the guiding power of Mughal records reorganized on the same protocols of collection, abstracting, and comparison that characterized the institutional culture of metropolitan recordkeeping, Hastings contested the latter's epistemic relevance to the company's administration. For him, it was instead the Indian archive—reconstituted according to the classifying logic of the metropolitan—out of which administrative knowledge should be produced. He made the case for divergence using a rhetoric of analogy. "The extent of Bengal and its possible resources are equal to those of most states in Europe," Hastings emphasized to the Court of Directors in 1773, but its "difficulties are greater" because it lacked a "regular constitution." Addressing the court, Hastings insisted that the grounds for forming such a "regular constitution" did not lie in the "ancient Charters" of the company, "framed" as they were "for the Jurisdiction of your trading Settlements, the sales of your Exports, and the provision of your annual Investment." "I need not observe," he emphasized, "how incompetent these must prove for the Government of a great Kingdom, and for the preservation of its riches from private violence and embezzlement." Echoing his 1772 disparagement of the company's government as a "Heap of indigested Materials," Hastings expressed his hope that the court would soon organize the administration by sending "Instructions for establishing a System of Law and Policy" which would address "the well known infirmities in our Constitution." Yet, in the interim, Hastings emphasized that he would exert his own authority to frame a reformed system for securing "the future Prosperity, and even the being of the Company, and of the National Interests." "The Distant and slow interposition of the Supreme Power which is lodged in your Hands cannot apply the Remedies to the Disorders which may arise in your State," he wrote to the directors. "A principle of Vigor, Activity and decision must rest somewhere in a Body of Men," and "its Efficacy" risked being "lost by being too much divided."[38] Rather than Leadenhall, the cogitative power of the company-state ought to be vested in the field and institutionalized in an office held by Hastings himself.

Hastings's proposed solution was "not to introduce fresh Innovations" into the government of Bengal but "to restore the Government of the Country to its first principles," based on an account of "the original Constitution of the Mogul Government."[39] He juxtaposed his project against the reformist criticisms launched against East India Company administration in Bengal by officials such as William Bolts and Alexander Dow. Both Bolts and Dow had substantiated their critiques by making references to official papers, but Hastings was unconvinced. "I detest both Bolts's performance and Dowe's," he wrote to Laurence Sulivan in November 1772, calling Bolts "a medley [of] nonsense, as well as falsehood" and Dow "grossly deficient in the knowledge of the Revenue, Forms of Office and Justice, and in many other points respecting Bengal." He continued by expressing his "hope" that "the Court of Directors do not form their Judgement of the Conduct & Character of their Servants from such Evidence." Moreover, he emphasized that his judicial reforms were "simple, and adapted to the Customs and understandings of the People." Any metropolitan proposals should be "superadded" to his own "and built on our ground work." "It will grieve me to see the structure which we have raised, destroyed to make room for any which can be formed in England;—But more especially for any that shall subject the Natives of Bengal to the Laws of England, or make them amenable to Our Courts or Forms of Justice," he continued.[40] "I am sorry the House of Commons should think of Establishing Laws for this Country, ignorant as they are of the Laws in being, of the Manner and Customs of the Inhabitants, or of the form of Government," he wrote with respect to the proposed Regulating Act of 1773. "I hope the Act will not take place, or should it, everything we have done will be destroyed, and my labour will prove like the Toil of Sysiphus," he continued.[41] "The Company's Interests have suffered already by the many innovations which have been introduced into the Administration of the Revenue," which in turn "becomes rooted to the Constitution" and thus permanently corrupting, he noted to Sulivan in March 1774. The end of this was justification of his own position, since, Hastings argued, in "whatever System be adopted, extraordinary Powers must be given to the Governor to enable him to support the Principles on which it is founded, and these Powers must extend in an equal Degree to every other Part of his General Authority."[42]

The Regulating Act, passed in Parliament in June 1773, established a government for imperial India organized around the offices of a governor-general and a four-member council, headquartered at Fort William, whose decisions were to be made by simple majority vote, inhibiting Hastings's veto power. The act named the four councilors as John Clavering, George Monson, Richard Barwell, and Philip Francis; established a Supreme Court of Judicature under Crown letters patent; and required that the governor-general and Council transmit all rules and regulations to the Secretary of State for the Crown to evaluate and, if deemed necessary, disallow.[43] To Hastings, reform made the project of elevating an Indian archive of authorities, constructed and interpreted through the specific lens of his own cadre of loyal servants, against those of the records controlled by both state and company more urgent.

This context of political contestation is crucial for understanding Hastings's strategic appeal that year to Lord Mansfield against metropolitan legal promulgation for India. Disputing the charge that "written Laws are totally unknown to the Hindoos or original Inhabitants of Indostan," Hastings contended that "they have been in possession of laws, which have continued unchanged, from the remotest Antiquity," the "Protection" of which "it would be a Grievance to deprive" them. He presented Mansfield with "a Specimen of the Laws themselves," which he explained had resulted from Hastings's own efforts to administer Bengal by making "no essential Change" to "the ancient Constitution of the Province" and instead restoring it "to its original Principles." To execute this restoration, Hastings explained that he had invited *pandits* "to form a Compilation of the Hindoo Laws with the best Authority which could be obtained." "This Code they have written in their own Language, the Shanscrit," he noted, and under his supervision, these had now been translated into Persian "and from that into English," specimens of which he now sent to Mansfield. Hastings was at pains "to vouch for the Fidelity" of these "translations," "such Parts of it as I have compared with the Persian Copy having been found literally exact" and which were "close and genuine Transcripts from the Original." Presenting these laws, "as well defined, as that of most States in Europe," Hastings expressed his hope that Mansfield would use the text "toward the legal Accomplishment of a new System which shall found the Authority in Bengal on its ancient Laws, and serve to point out the way to rule this People with Ease and Moderation according to their own Ideas,

Manners, and Prejudices."[44] In a letter to the Court of Directors dated a few days later, sent alongside "a specimen" of the code, Hastings echoed the rhetoric of archival analogy aimed at displacing the authority of the metropolitan. Suggesting that the work contained "nothing hurtful to the Authority of Government, or to the Interests of Society" and was "consonant to the Ideas, Manners, and Inclinations of the People for whose Use it is intended," Hastings "presumed" that "on these Grounds [the code] will be preferable to any which even a superior Wisdom could substitute in its Room." The code, he hoped, would "afford at least a proof that the People of this County do not require our Aid to furnish them with a Rule for their Conduct, or a Standard for their Property."[45]

Here, Hastings's analogy between a subject peoples' textual heritage and that of European states served to bolster the authority of customary records *against* those of the company's metropolitan archives. Even "the Evils of a divided and contested Rule" emanating from Hastings's enmity with the other members of the Fort William council, especially Philip Francis, outweighed the prospect of "leaving the Company's affairs in Hands certainly not qualified by Experience to Conduct them."[46] For Hastings, "whatever advantages" servants with "higher Connections" to metropolitan authorities might enjoy, "their want of local Knowledge" would "disqualify them for the Exercise of Powers which they have assumed." By contrast, he sought to advance those servants connected to him, whom he claimed "possess a very complete Knowledge of every Branch of the Company's Affairs in this Country."[47] The particular "Understanding" garnered from "knowledge of the Persian Language" and the "Insight" derived from "daily access to the Records" generated by administration on the ground "afforded" these officials "the most effectual Opportunities of instructing" themselves "in the Secret and most important Transactions of the Government."[48] To be sure, this kind of laudatory invocation of "local Knowledge" was strategic. Hastings was simultaneously circulating copies of his own official company records within metropolitan circles in the hopes that such "materials" would "convince" the political establishment that he had "in no way merited the malevolent attacks which have been made on my reputation by the new Members of the new Council."[49] He was also circumventing Leadenhall's communication channels with the Crown by sending company records privately to Lord North in the hopes of "establishing a direct Connexion between the

Crown and the Indian Powers," mediated through Hastings and his allies at the expense of the Court of Directors.[50] When the company's official correspondence served his ends, Hastings was politic about invoking the relevant documents in his defense. At the same time, when the circulation of such records threatened his reputation, he was keen to dissuade powerful figures from giving them credibility by dismissing them as "filled with personal Attacks" against him merely because he had tried "to support the great and valuable Interests of the Nation in this remote and difficult Branch of its Empire."[51]

These sentiments took the form of concrete textual output in late 1775 and 1776 as Hastings sought to turn the code, which he had presented a specimen of to Mansfield, into an accessible collection made out of records that he analogized to those regularly consulted by metropolitan officials for governing wisdom. Hastings sent the completed code, compiled by company official Nathaniel Brassey Halhed, to London in August 1775. Describing Halhed's text as one that "opens a new and ample Field of Knowledge on a Subject equally curious and interesting," he asked his confidant Edward Wheler to present the work to the Court of Directors in the hopes of receiving their "Patronage," or at least their approval for Hastings to publish the translation at his own expense.[52] The circulation of the text formed a core component of Hastings's project to sway the opinion of metropolitan officials in his favor and against his rivals on the company's Bengal council, namely John Clavering, George Monson, and Philip Francis, by "lay[ing] before the Court of Directors" "a true Account of the late Proceedings of the Majority of the [Fort William] Council, of which no one in England can be so well informed."[53] By presenting the court with the evidence of "recent Experience" of "the true state" of Bengal, compiled from the testimony of company servants whose "knowledge of the Persian Language" and "daily access to the Records of the Council" had "furnished" them with "the most effectual Opportunities of instructing [them]selves in the Secret and most important Transactions of the Government," Hastings claimed that he was engaged in a project of "restoring Peace and Order to a whole Nation."[54]

To bolster his reputation, Hastings sent Halhed's work to prominent members of the metropolitan political and literary establishment, seeking their patronage and endorsement for a project of codification that Hastings could then wield against his rivals, whom he derided as a

"Government [which] has proceeded on Principles diametrically oppo-
site to mine."[55] In doing so, Hastings sought to cast the work in a variety
of idioms that might appeal to the particular person whose support was
being solicited. To the Tory essayist and lexicographer Samuel Johnson,
Hastings described the "Compilation" as not only an effort "to assist the
Courts of Justice in their Decisions" but also one that, if made available to
Western audiences, would "free the Inhabitants" of India from the charge
of "Ignorance and Barbarism" "undeservedly cast upon them" by the "too
precipitate Information" about the East currently circulating in Europe.[56]
Writing to the jurist Mansfield, Hastings analogized the code to the common law by describing it as "a Performance which bears an affinity to that
Department over which Your Lordship presides, and which treats of the
Science of Jurisprudence in which you have so eminent a share and so
consummate a knowledge."[57] Halhed's production was merely a "Translation, with a preface and Introduction of the Pundits, or original Compilers," one Hastings offered to Mansfield alongside a "plan which I have
drawn up and sent . . . to the Court of Directors . . . of additional Regulations proposed for the Administration of Justice in these Provinces,"
which he believed would "be found compatible with the indispensable
Principles of the English Law," namely that "neither the Laws, Usages nor
Inclinations of the people of this Country will be injured by the Introduction of it." Hastings further recommended two "amply qualified" people,
both "Masters of the Persian Language," whom Mansfield could consult
to "satisfy" any further interest he might have on Bengal judicial affairs:
Hastings's own confidants, George Vansittart, whom Hastings described
as holding "great Experience" and "Extensive Knowledge of the Company's Interests in these Provinces," and Alexander Elliot, whom Hastings
claimed was "peculiarly qualified to answer any Enquiries which your
Lordship may have occasion to make upon the Subject" of the proposed
judicial reforms because Elliot "had charge of the Records of the Superior
Courts of Civil & Criminal Justice, and was the first Person appointed
to the Office of Superintendant of the Khalsa Records." Hastings similarly urged Mansfield to confer with Hastings's confidant and the chief
justice of the Supreme Court at Fort William, Elijah Impey, who "on all
Occasions" had demonstrated in his rulings the ability "to Support the
Authority of Government, and temper the Law of England with the Laws,
Religious Customs, and manners of the Natives."[58] For "ample Informa-

tion" on the company's affairs, Hastings emphasized to Laurence Sulivan, the best archive was found among his own allies, such as Halhed, Impey, Elliot, and Vansittart, "who [contain] all that is worth consulting of all our Records."[59] To the Court of Directors, Hastings noted that Halhed's work had been done "with great ability, diligence, and fidelity" from a Persian original "under the immediate inspection of the Pundits or Compilers of this Work," who had refused to make "any alterations" to the text.[60] Receiving Halhed's translation, however, the court noted that while they could not "pretend to judge of the Accuracy of the Work," they believed he ought to be given "all suitable encouragement" but did not fund the project.[61]

The appearance of Halhed's *A Code of Gentoo Laws* in 1776 under Hastings's patronage brought this archive of local knowledge, pitched as the formal equivalent to metropolitan archival authority yet contextually superior as a guide to governing, into tangible, printed form. Significantly, the full title—*A Code of Gentoo Laws; or, Ordinations of the Pundits, from a Persian Translation, Made from the Original, Written in the Shanscrit Language*—posited the work neither as a composition nor interpretation authored by Halhed but instead (echoing how Hastings had presented the text to Mansfield) as a "translation" of an "original": an exact rendering from one language into another of a codified group of laws drawn from what Halhed described in the text itself as "Records of . . . unfathomable Antiquity." Hastings and Halhed began the work by reproducing letters they had sent to the Court of Directors in which they emphasized that *A Code of Gentoo Laws* was "undertaken under the immediate Inspection of the Pundits or Compilers of this Work." In a lengthy introduction, Halhed described the documents presented in the text as a corrective to extant European ideas of India. Against "conjectural Doctrines . . . circulated by the Learned and Ingenious of Europe" on the nature of Hindu law, Halhed posited the work as offering "the real Appellations of the Country and of the Inhabitants of Hindostan" as "denominated in the ancient Writings of the Natives," excerpts of which he reproduced using the "Alphabets" of Sanskrit and Bengali. "The Hindoos [as] well as the Chinese" both had "an Antiquity infinitely more remote than is authorized by the Belief of the rest of Mankind," and had been "acquainted with Letters from the very earliest." Moreover, the archive of ancient Hinduism, like that of ancient China, was perfect, given that "their Annals have never been disturbed or destroyed by any known Revolution." *A Code of*

Gentoo Laws bore a "striking Likeness" to "the Laws of Moses" as well as "many other Parts of the Holy Scriptures," Halhed wrote. Even if "no Part of these Laws be thought worthy of adoption into the System of a British Government in Asia," they nevertheless "deserve the Consideration of the Politician, the Judge, the Divine, and the Philosopher." Following this introduction, he included a set of apparatuses that made explicit the authorities on which the text's authenticity rested, including a list of the "Names of the Bramins, Who compiled this Work," glossaries of Sanskrit terms with English equivalents, and "A List of the Books From whence" the code was "compiled."[62]

Scholarship treats *A Code of Gentoo Laws* as a notable contribution to the Orientalist study of Hinduism, as an intervention into the political disputes within the Bengal council in favor of Hastings's belief "that English officials proficient in Indian languages were the foundation of legitimate and effective imperial rule in Bengal," and as part of an administrative effort to excavate a form of "ancient" Mughal constitutionalism as the guiding framework for the contemporary governance of Bengal by the company.[63] But the significance of *A Code of Gentoo Laws* cannot be fully understood unless the work is also contextualized in relation to the politics of archival governance. In a move comparable to the codification project envisioned by Crown lawyers with respect to Quebec, discussed in chapter 4, Hastings and Halhed envisioned replacing a corpus of administrative texts written in the language of the ruled with an archive of authorities rendered out of that native archive on the epistemic and formal terms of metropolitan records. In the profoundly different spaces of Company Bengal and Crown Quebec, plans of ruling over non-English speakers proceeded based on analogizing the form, purpose, and utility of learned native administrative texts to British imperial records. Furthermore, the intention behind both projects was to supplant the power of native interpreters by empowering imperial administrators to read the native archive in the language of the Crown and company. In both situations, the epistemics of early modern archival governance were brought to bear on the administrative problem of executing sovereignty over people with distinctive cultural traditions. In the context of Bengal, however, the archive of conquest was also intended by Hastings as a rival to the company's metropolitan records, an effort to supplant the experience derivable from the records contained in Leadenhall Street with the experience that could be garnered out of a documentary heritage on hermeneutical terms defined by Hastings and his confidants.

Halhed's code was one of several projects in which Hastings and his coterie engaged from the late 1770s to craft an authoritative archive for governing in relation to Indian subjects. These projects came to encompass (among other endeavors) support for translations of other Hindu as well as Islamic texts by company servants such as Charles Wilkins; the orchestration of an expedition by the official George Bogle to investigate the government, laws, and religion of Tibet; patronage of other servants such as William Davy and Jonathan Scott, who sought to write works on the history of the Mughal Empire; support for the founding of the Bengal Asiatic Society; endorsement of the founding of an "Oriental Museum" at India House, where the company's Asiatic collections could be displayed; the establishment of a *madrasa* at Calcutta where Islamic legal scholars known as *maulavis* could offer instruction; and the botanical introduction of new plants such as cinnamon into company territory.

Hastings's support for these projects is well known and has been perceptively interpreted as an expression of his efforts to conciliate Indians and British people together through cultural interchange, the extension of Enlightenment discourses of commerce and civility into company political thought, and as part of his strategy of legitimating the idea of governing according to an imagined "ancient Mughal" constitution as a means of subverting metropolitan political authority.[64] But they also need to be contextualized in terms of the archival epistemology of imperial political contestation. To be sure, the Court of Directors expressed support for many of these projects. They encouraged Bogle's expedition to Tibet and understood it as an endeavor that "may contribute to extend our commerce, enlarge Our Interests," and "add respect to the English Name."[65] Moreover, the court backed the establishment of the company's museum and library at Leadenhall Street in 1801 under the supervision of Hastings's confidant Charles Wilkins. Both the establishment of the institution and the appointment of Wilkins were strongly urged by Hastings, who stressed that support for Wilkins would help "in the formation of a new and untried system intended for the purpose of ingrafting the science of India on the pursuits of the Company" and "add the acquisition of knowledge . . . to the power, the riches and the glory which [the company's] acts have already so largely contributed to the British Empire and Name."[66]

But Hastings conceived of these projects as rivals to metropolitan archival discipline. He justified the superiority of his preferred authorities in two ways. First, he emphasized that India was too remote and complicated a scene of rule for London-based guidance to be effectual. "The Dominion exercised by the British Empire in India is fraught with many radical and incurable Defects, besides those to which all Human Institutions are liable," he wrote in 1777. These "Defects" emanated from "the Distance of [the empire's] Scene of Operations, the impossibility of furnishing it at all Times with those Aids which it requires from home, and the Difficulty of reconciling its primary Exigencies with those which in all States ought to be the place of every other concern, the Interests of the People who are subjected to its Authority."[67] The necessary "Aids" through which metropolitan officials could bridge this "Distance" were codifications of documents prepared by or under the supervision of Hastings himself, which he promised Laurence Sulivan would give "a succinct and comprehensive View of our political State, which you will with difficulty collect from our general Letters, and the diffuse Materials of our Consultations." It was necessary to refer not only to the archive produced in the imperial field; it was also, Hastings emphasized, essential that this archive be read on the terms of its authoritative interpreter—Hastings himself. "While you form your Judgement on my political Conduct," he continued, Sulivan ought to bear in mind that compared to Hastings himself, "no Man in England or in India has more studied the political state of India, and of its different powers, nor has possessed equal opportunities of knowing it."[68]

The oppositional character of Hastings's knowledge projects was also entwined with a second discourse of justification: his perception that the Court of Directors favored his opponents on the Bengal council, or in his words, the court's zeal for "joining the Cry against me for Corruption and rapacity." Just as he denigrated his opponents on the council as ignorant "strangers to the Country, to the Politicks, to the language of Indostan," and equally "unversed in the Revenue or Business of the Company," he worried about the company's metropolitan leadership falling under the sway of the malicious and poorly informed.[69] As the "Company's Affairs" came to be "managed by Persons equally ignorant and indifferent about their Interests," he posited "the degree of Knowledge, which I may be allowed to attribute to myself from long Experience" as what "may help to save [the company] from those dangers toward which

the current of Party and Faction is now carrying them."[70] This meant elevating the experience of his loyal supporters against those officials sent
from Britain and their Indian allies.

Hastings expressed this sentiment in his response to complaints
made against him in 1775 by Muhammad Reza Khan, the Mughal official
who had assisted the East India Company since 1765 in administering revenue collection under the grant of the *diwani* but whom Hastings had removed from office in 1772.[71] Disputing Khan's charges, Hastings conceded
that one accusation was "closer to Truth," namely, "that which related
to the Exclusion of the old and experienced Muttaseddes [Mughal revenue officers] from Employment or Confidence, and the Trusts reposed
in the servants of English Gentlemen." Hastings expressed his agreement
that the company had mistakenly displaced these "old and experienced"
Indian officials and instead "entrusted" "young and inexperienced" "Englishmen" who were "totally ignorant of the Languages of the Country"
"with the Management of the Collections." Hastings argued that he had
sought to reform the system by giving "a fixed Authority to the Experienced and professional Muttaseddes" but blamed Khan for obstructing
him. "I much fear," Hastings wrote, that as "the Old Muttaseddes die away,
and there is no encouragement for young Proficients," "the Collections
will be exposed to all the worst Consequences of Ignorance, Caprice, &
the Rapacity of temporary Power, for the Court of Directors by prohibit-
ing the Removal of any of their Servants from their Employments without
a criminal Charge formally brought against them, & proved by a Judicial
Process, have unfortunately taken off the Check which Government before possessed over this kind of Influence."[72] Learning of a "Motion in the
Court of Directors for an Address to his Majesty for removing me from
the Government of Bengal," Hastings defended his conduct as "having
been actuated by no other Motive than the good of the Company."[73] As
he engaged in "writing Volumes by every Dispatch for the Vindication of
my Character from the most illiberal and unjust attacks which have been
made upon it," he also mobilized his own set of authorities in his defense,
which he believed proved "the disinterested Motives" out of which he
had "departed from the rigid Lines" of the court's "Instructions."[74] "The
"experience I possess," he emphasized, "would enable me at the Head of
a consistent & cordial Administration to increase and secure the lasting
Prosperity of the Company" in India.[75]

The political practice of maneuvering documentary authorities was
thus fundamental to Hastings's defense against his opponents on the Bengal supreme council, especially Philip Francis and John Clavering. Hastings was especially eager to enlist his allies in London as surrogates who
could publish and circulate records that would vindicate his decisions.
These included long narrative justifications of his conduct, which Hastings hoped his confidants would "shew . . . to my confidential Friends"
along with their own annotations and explanations ("be yourself the
Commentator, for it will want One"), presumably made in the governor-
general's favor.[76] By placing his preferred "Facts and Documents" before
audiences both public and private, Hastings hoped that they "will judge
of the weight which is to be given to them, & of the Conclusions which
ought to be drawn from them."[77] Such papers, he thought, would counteract what he suspected were the efforts of his opponents to act similarly.
Sending copies of his papers to two allies in London, Hastings instructed
that the records should be published in order to counteract what he
suspected were efforts by Clavering to send defamatory papers to Lord
North. If Hastings's own "Papers" were made "public," he explained, they
would "shew how little Delicacy or regard to Truth and Decency has been
observed by my Adversaries in their attempts to ruin my Reputation and
to compass their own Ends."[78]

Indeed, Hastings described the meetings of the Bengal council as
a scene of disputation via writing. When Francis "writes long Minutes
against me, I must reply to them," a task that occupied "all my Time
out of Council," Hastings explained, while "in Council" the "Business"
was regularly "wholly suspended though we have sat together for Six
Hours at a Stretch, while each Member occupied the Secretary by Turns
in dictating long Minutes of Controversy." He further asked his allies in
London to "publish" refutations of any of Francis's documents that had
"made" "Appearance" in the metropolitan press.[79] This mobilization of
records in defense of his conduct involved precision and accuracy but
also discretion. Instructing his ally Jonathan Scott "to publish any of the
Transactions of this Government, the Knowledge & clear Explanation
of which shall be necessary to the Vindication of my Character from any
attempts made to depreciate it," Hastings advised Scott "to use the greatest Caution that no Assertion, opinion or argument escape you for which
you have not a sure Warrant either in the Papers of your own Possession,

or in those which are or may be in the Hands of Mr Sulivan, or in your own Knowledge." At the same time, Hastings expressed his preference "that you will put your own Name with the Declaration of my Authority to every such Publication." He also asked Scott to compile a collection of records for the governor-general to use in the future, instructing Scott to "put into your immediate Possession Copies of all our Proceedings in a regular series. . . . These & all other papers which I may hereafter have occasion to send to you, you will be so good to keep apart, properly labelled & return to me whenever we meet, if in England, as I may have occasion to imploy them hereafter."[80]

Hastings subsequently employed Scott and his other confidants in "scholarly" endeavors in the 1780s, which, like his presentation of Halhed's *A Code of Gentoo Laws,* also constituted an effort to deploy a particular archive of preferred authorities against the recorded precedents relied on by his opponents. With the exception of his pistol duel with Francis in August 1780 on the outskirts of Calcutta (which left Francis wounded but not incapacitated), Hastings's weapons of choice were documents. His strategy involved orchestrating the publication of narrative accounts of his administration for public view in conjunction with his ally Charles Wilkins, whom Hastings had placed in charge of the company's printing press at Calcutta. Through the dissemination of "official" papers, Hastings aimed to construe a favorable explanation of events. This politic behavior can be seen, for example, in the texts that Hastings sought to disseminate in the aftermath of a 1781 battle between the company's forces and the *raja* of Benares, Chait Singh, who refused to make revenue payments demanded by Hastings. In a prefatory note, Hastings described one of these publications, printed by Wilkins in Calcutta in 1782, as "sheets written to guard the minds of my superiors against the suspicions to which all great political movements are liable, especially such as pass at a distance from observation." In an appendix to the narrative, Hastings included "papers which contain my transactions," arranged "in the proper order of their dates in the narrative," and "official letters, and other papers, which form a connected series of the events and proceedings recorded in the narrative" itself.[81] In another of these texts, published contemporaneously in London, Hastings offered a "narrative" interspersed with transcriptions of relevant copies of "material papers" "for the satisfaction of such as shall have more patience or leisure to look into them."[82]

142 DUELING SYSTEMS

What scholars treat as Hastings's paradigmatic statement on the intertwined nature of empire and knowledge needs to be understood primarily as an instantiation of politic behavior and only secondarily as an expression of his sentiments about "Oriental" learning and Enlightenment commerce. A shift in the constitution of company administration had forced Hastings to make the argument for his preferred documentary authorities as the basis of governance not just to the corporation's directors but also to the Crown. Parliament's passage of the India Act in July 1784, which would come to serve as a long-lasting constitutional framework for the imperial governance of India, established a Board of Control under the power of the royal sovereign's prime minister and Privy Council. This board was empowered to exercise supervisory authority relating to any issues of "the civil or military government or revenues" of India, displacing the company's shareholders from influence on Indian issues and consigning the Court of Directors to power only over matters of the corporation's commercial affairs and official appointments. At the head of the Board of Control, William Pitt placed a strong supporter and confidant, the Scottish politician Henry Dundas.[83]

On December 16, 1784, the company's packet boat *Surprise* left Bengal bound for Limerick in Ireland, where it arrived slightly less than four months later, on April 9; eight days later, the letters on board were delivered to East India House on Leadenhall Street. The conveyance contained several documents of varying dates written by Hastings, which he at some point noted in a "List."[84] Among these was a letter dated October 4, 1784, from Benares, which Hastings described in the list as "To Nathaniel Smith Esq.r with a Copy of the Gheeta & its Notes." The "Gheeta" referred to a translation of the Bhagavad-Gita undertaken by Charles Wilkins, a copy of which Hastings now dispatched to London. In another letter in the packet, Hastings explained the meaning of these texts to his confidant Jonathan Scott. The letter to Smith with Wilkins's translation had "began in Play," Hastings wrote, but "is also Business," indeed "the Effect & part of a System which I long since laid down, & supported, for reconciling the People of England to the Natives of Hindostan, & the Company to their Servants."[85] His "motive," he explained in a further letter to Scott, was "three fold": literary taste, the salvaging of his reputation "in the last moment of my political Existence" "by reconciling the Company & the People of England to the Natives of India under their

Subjection," and finally the restoration of the reputation of company officials in India, "whose Characters have been most grossly falsified even in
those Places where they ought to have had the strictest Measure of Justice
dealt to them."[86] In Hastings's view, it was not the metropolitan archive of
the company but rather this system—comprising texts, institutions, and
expert interpreters whom he had personally cultivated and supported—
which was to legitimate and guide company rule over Indians.

Wilkins subsequently printed Hastings's letter to Scott as the first
of several prefatory apparatuses to his translation of the Bhagavad-Gita,
published in London under the company's patronage in 1785.[87] Addressing Nathaniel Smith, then chair of the company, as "the first member
of the first commercial body, not only of the present age, but of all the
known generations of mankind," Hastings described the work as "an offering to the public" of "a very curious specimen of the Literature, the
Mythology, and Morality of the ancient Hindoos" "written upwards of
four thousand years ago by . . . a learned Bramin," whose "merit" lay in
having "reduced the gross and scattered tenets of" the Hindu "faith into a
scientific and allegorical system." Mirroring his dismissal of metropolitan
records as authoritative guides to governing the company-state in favor
of "local" experience, Hastings rejected European literary hermeneutics
as an appropriate method for interpreting the work. "I should exclude,
in estimating the merit of such a production, all the rules drawn from the
ancient or modern literature of Europe" "as by no means applicable to
the language, sentiments, manners, or morality appertaining to a system
of society with which we have been for ages unconnected, and of an antiquity preceding even the first efforts of civilization in our own quarter of
the glove," Hastings asserted. At the same time, by emphasizing the ancient character of Hindu textual heritage, he placed this native archive on
a temporal foundation equivalent to that invoked in the rhetoric of ancient
constitutionalism. Even as he insisted on the difference between Europe
and India, Hastings also sought to produce analogy by investing Wilkins's
Bhagavad-Gita with the same degree of textual authority that European
audiences were familiar with from their more proximate experience of bib-
lical exegesis. The Bhagavad-Gita had emerged from the milieu of "the
Brāhamans," Hastings explained, whose role within Hinduism was "to
perform a kind of spiritual discipline, not, I believe, unknown to some of
the religious orders of Christians in the Romish Church."[88]

This authority inhered as well in "the Translator," Wilkins, whom Hastings cast in the letter to Smith as possessed of the requisite experience for having "united to an early and successful attainment of the Persian and Bengal languages, the study of the Sănskrĕĕt." Wilkins had "profitably applied" his knowledge to "many official purposes" of "your government" as a company servant; now, these were brought into a public view through the medium of the text.[89] Hastings urged the court to encourage further "studies" such as Wilkins's—indeed, Hastings wrote that he viewed such "cultivation of language and science" as "a duty appertaining to my office." It was in this context that Hastings then asserted the utility of the archive of the field to the exercise of territorial sovereignty:

> Every accumulation of knowledge, and especially such as is obtained by social communication with people over whom we exercise a dominion founded on the right of conquest, is useful to the state: it is the gain of humanity: in the specific instance which I have stated, it attracts and conciliates distant affections; it lessens the weight of the chain by which the natives are held in subjection; and it imprints on the hearts of our own countrymen the sense and obligation of benevolence. Even in England, this effect of it is greatly wanting. It is not very long since the inhabitants of India were considered by many, as creatures scarce elevated above the degree of savage life; nor, I fear, is that prejudice yet wholly eradicated, though surely abated. Every instance which brings their real character home to observation will impress us with a more generous sense of feeling for their natural rights, and teach us to estimate them by the measure of our own. But such instances can only be obtained in their writings: and these will survive when the British dominion in India shall have long ceased to exist, and when the sources which it once yielded of wealth and power are lost to remembrance.[90]

While Hastings wrote that "every accumulation of knowledge" was "useful to the state," he was in fact elevating not literally "every" kind of knowledge but rather a particular one: "only" those "writings" obtained from "social communication with people over whom" the company exercised sovereignty derived from "conquest." If these documents were read "in England," administrators would gain an "observation" of the true grounds on which Indians were supposed to be known as well as governed. Reading Hastings's classic statement of the value of knowledge to the state makes clear that he was using the epistemics of politic experience to mobilize his preferred documentary authorities in defense of his reputation and against those of his opponents.

The Bhagavad-Gita was not the only work that Hastings sent to London. Also on board the *Surprise* were what he described as "10 Copies of the 2d. Volume of the Ayin Aikbarry"—a reference to a translation undertaken by the company servant Francis Gladwin, begun in the mid-1770s, of the *Ain-i Akbari,* a sixteenth-century work documenting the administrative history of the reign of the Mughal Empire under the Emperor Akbar, which had been prepared by the Mughal court historiographer Abu'l Fazl ibn Mubarak.[91] Gladwin had previously received the financial support of the Court of Directors in 1777 for producing a comparative vocabulary of Indian languages, which appeared in 1780.[92] Four years after the publication of Gladwin's vocabulary, Hastings was now urging the court to support the publication of Gladwin's translation, invoking the necessity of "Encouragement" for "every undertaking which has for its end the promotion and extension of Eastern literature, as well in regard to the use its Advancement may be of to the persons employed in your Service."[93] Hastings was similarly enthusiastic about recommending the court's support for publishing another work, a translation of the Hedaya, a key text of Islamic law composed by the twelfth-century Muslim jurist Burhan al-Din al-Marghinani, prepared by company officials James Anderson and Charles Hamilton. Describing his work, Hamilton echoed the terms in which Hastings and Halhed had presented *A Code of Gentoo Laws*—as a textual authority equivalent to metropolitan archives in its antiquity and form yet superior to them as the precedential grounds best fitted to governing Indians. After "a wonderful revolution threw the government" of Bengal into "the hands of the English," "the British government," being "little acquainted with the *forms,* and still less with the elementary *principles,* of the native administration of justice in their newly acquired territories," decided to make "few innovations" in the administration but instead to appoint its "servants to superintend and decide" over Mughal courts. But, Hamilton continued, "the gentlemen who were appointed to superintend the proceedings of the courts" had "no opportunity of studying the languages in which the laws are written" and thus were "constrained" by "the advice of" "ill informed" "native officers" "generally open to corruption." Therefore, it was necessary to form "certain rule[s]" on which judgment could proceed that were derived from "a direct appeal to the *Mussulman* or *Hindoo* authority on the ground of which they were to decide." Just as Halhed had made such a "compilation" for "the *Hindoo* laws" "under the inspection of the most learned *Pundits,*" now Hamilton presented an equivalent for "the *Mussulman law,* called the HEDAYA, or *Guide,* a work held in high estimation among the people of that persuasion" which had been made through a comparable process of company servants' supervising native experts, in this case "the principal *Mohammedan* professors in Bengal." The "*Mohammedan* LAW" was "the sole standard of criminal, and in a great measure of civil jurisprudence throughout our dominions in INDIA," Hamilton wrote, and those "who are responsible for the proper administration of public justice, should possess the means of consulting the principles on which the decisions of the *Mussulman* courts are founded." Indeed, he continued, "it would perhaps be neither prudent nor possible hastily to introduce any other system" into India.[94]

Hastings justified his patronage of these projects on the grounds that they were valuable aids to the work of administration. The "Expence" of their production was justified, he wrote in 1784 to the Court of Directors, because "while the Mahomedan Law is allowed to be the Standard of the criminal Jurisprudence of your Dominion, under the Control and Inspection of your English Servants," it was "indispensably necessary" that the English-speaking "judges of the Courts should have a more familiar Guide for their Proceedings than the Books of the Arabic Tongue, of which few have opportunities of attaining a competent Knowledge." It was "necessary," Hastings emphasized to the court, "that your Servants should possess the Means of consulting the principles on which those Judgments are founded which in their Ultimate Resort, and in extraordinary Cases, may fall within their immediate Cognizance, and of the Laws of which they are the Protectors."[95]

Taken together, the patronage of Halhed's code, the Bhagavad-Gita, the *Ain-i-Akbari,* and the Hedaya constituted an effort by Hastings to build an archive of authorities that he posited as at once analogous to those of the state and company in their power to guide the administration of rule over Indians, yet at the same time superior to metropolitan archival wisdom because it was built out of native texts. As chapter 3 demonstrated, during Hastings's trial, his opponents sought to invoke records that they argued indicted his conduct while seeking to undermine the authority of the records Hastings and the company advanced in his defense. The company provisioned many of these records out of its own archive in response to demands from both sides, with Edmund Burke and his allies regularly calling for copies of papers from the company's records pertaining to the conduct of Hastings and his allies. Flurries of orders from the House of Commons demanding that the Court of Directors "lay before" parliamentary investigators "all such informations" they required saw the directors order the corporation's clerks to prepare copies and abstracts of records to be sent in response.[96] To that end, the court itself demanded that Hastings and his allies "send . . . all such Correspondence, papers, & Documents" as required by the investigators.[97] Hastings himself was no less diligent in pushing back; he sent his own requests to the court, which it granted, for "recourse to the Company's records and authenticated Copies of such Extracts thereof as he may require for Evidence in his defence."[98] Yet, the trial seemed to heighten his own sentiments that his strongest defense came from the testimony of his Indian allies, whom he deemed "best appertained to pronounce upon my real Character, according to their several relations or Concerns with the Government of Bengal during the Periods in which I held an efficient Share in its Powers."[99] Hastings sought to collect these "authentic Testimonies of the native Inhabitants . . . respecting my Conduct towards them," regarding these Indian testimonies as more authoritative "than any [that] could be offered here [in England]" by the company "respecting my Conduct."[100]

Hastings was indeed acquitted in 1795, and even as he retreated from company office in the aftermath of the trial, he continued to advocate for a vision of governance based on rule via a native archive. In 1812, Hastings wrote a long letter to Francis Rawdon-Hastings, Earl of Moira, who had recently been appointed to the office of governor-general. Hastings reiterated his conception of administrative knowledge as emanating from the archive of the field. Administration, he advised, ought to proceed based on "an attention to the native inhabitants, a reference to their customs, a discriminate observance of their relative ranks in society, a search after such as are capable of affording useful information in matters concerning the internal interest of the Country, and a frequent communication with them." As the definitive source of what Moira needed to know, Hastings recommended to the earl's "perusal and study" "a book, entitled Ayeen Akbery," "comprising a statistical history of the Empire of India under the reign of its first founder, the Emperor Akber." "It is an admirable compilation of all that it can be essentially useful to know of the natural and political state, its internal confirmation and official management," he wrote of Gladwin's translation of the *Ain-i Akbari,* and "a perfect model for that species of composition." Whatever authorities Moira ultimately relied on, Hastings argued, they ought to be from India itself. "Your Lordship," he continued, "will better know by inquiry of a native informant, than of any European, whether any, and what articles of taxation bear hard upon the people." Indeed, Hastings argued that it was "incumbent upon every foreign Government to consult the constitution, customs and habits of the governed people, before they enact any novel institutions, which may trespass upon those relations."[101]

In his letter to Moira, Hastings invoked the name of one of his successors, Charles Cornwallis, as one "which I can never remember but with veneration."[102] An influential scholarship has conceptualized Hastings and Cornwallis as embodying opposed visions of governance—with Hastings embracing an "Orientalist" mindset open to the embrace of Indian institutions and Cornwallis embodying an "Anglicist" one that, in the words of one influential interpreter, "chose alien solutions to Indian culture problems" based on an "anti-Hastings philosophy of administration" and a desire to impose Western concepts of rule onto Indians.[103] In recent years, this distinction has come under significant critique from scholars who have argued that in fact, "there was little difference . . . between Hastings the Orientalist and Cornwallis the Anglicist about extending the legal and punitive claims of the state," and that Cornwallis actually used the strategies of patronage to attempt to continue Hastings's arrangement of governing.[104]

Yet, all of these interpretations miss what was indeed a significant change in the constitution of governance in the closing decades of the eighteenth century. It was one to which Cornwallis, and ultimately all administrators, were forced to respond: a shift in the meaning of "office" itself and in the expectations that had structured its exercise in the early modern period. In response to domestic critiques of government expenditure, Lord North in March 1780 established a set of commissions to examine public accounts and the conduct of administration. These "Commissioners appointed to Examine, Take and State the Public Accounts of the Kingdom" produced fifteen reports between 1780 and 1787 that included a consequential redefinition of "office."[105] An office was no longer to be understood as a position granted by a sovereign body that rendered the occupant accountable to an internal hierarchy of authority—whether a Privy Council or a Court of Directors. Instead, the commissioners defined an "Officer" as "a Trustee for the Public" who was "bound to husband the Public Money committed to his charge with as much Frugality as if it were his own," and "ought not to be permitted, by any Management or Contrivance to carve out for himself an Interest in the Execution of a public Trust."[106] In another report, the commissioners expanded on how this definition of office should shape government archival practices. While it had been the practice of officers of government "when they went out of Office, to take with them the Books and Papers that relate" to their activities, as if such "Books and Papers" were "their own private Property," this behavior was no longer acceptable. "An Officer appointed to a Public Trust" inhabited "an Office created for the Use of . . . the Public." This meant that "all these Official Books and Papers" "should be considered as the Property of the Public, and as such left and deposited" in the office itself "for the Use and Information of Posterity."[107] This recommendation aimed squarely at the porosity between "official" and "private" papers that, as we have seen, enabled the early modern politics of archival contestation.

The commissioners made other recommendations that bore on the practices of official recordkeeping—including, significantly, the language in which such records were to be kept. In one report, they referred to a 1731 act that, in an effort to remedy the "many and great mischiefs" arising "from proceedings in courts of justice being in an unknown language," required that "all proceedings in courts of justice within that part of Great Britain called England, and in the court of exchequer in Scotland, shall be in the English language."[108] The commissioners noted that as promulgated, the act was "not to extend to the Court of the Receipt of His Majesty's Exchequer," but they disagreed. All official records ought to be kept in English: "The Use of the *English* Language" would "save the Time and Trouble of" Officers and remove "Mystery and Obscurity" from public proceedings, which were supposed to be "intelligible to all." The "Learning" contained in official records was not, they emphasized, "in Danger of being lost" because "the Bent of the Antiquarian, and the Interest of the

Keeper of Records will preserve it."[109] The claim that such "official records" contained "Learning" echoed the basic principle of early modern archival administration. But the commissioners rendered the point of preserving such learning toward a radically new end: not the maintenance of politic experience in the hands of the sovereign and his officers but instead "Learning" that "should be intelligible to all" and, as the commissioners wrote in another part of the report, directed toward "the Public Good." "The Principle which gives Existence to, and governs every public Office, is the Benefit of the State," the commissioners wrote in another part of the report. "Government requires that various Branches of Business should be transacted, and Persons must be found to transact them," and such public officers served in the interests of "the Good of the Community."[110]

Cornwallis embraced many of the commissioners' principles in his shaping of new protocols of governance for Indian administration in the late 1780s and early 1790s.[111] In the process, he articulated his own account of the relationship between government and records, one that broke even more radically than the commissioners had from an early modern conception of the place of archives in administration. Government was not to proceed by mastering control of an archive of manuscript sources accessible to an administrative elite. Rather, effective government required *overcoming* the manuscript form and secretive nature of the archive entirely, and replacing the archive as a source of policy knowledge with printed, non-manuscript texts that everyone could access and read. "When we first obtained possession of [Bengal]," Cornwallis wrote in 1793, "we found no written laws, except as are contained in the Mahomedan and Hindoo code." These codes, while "still in force," were "in many respects inapplicable to the internal Government of the country." Their status as manuscript and document was an obstacle government needed to *overcome* in order to rule effectively. "Our regulations are now partly in manuscript, and partly printed on detached papers, and drawn without any particular form," he argued. This made reference to them "extremely difficult"; hence, "all regulations now in force, that relate in any respect to the rights or property of the people, or the administration of justice . . . should be collected, and be printed and bound up in a separate volume."[112]

If office was a public trust, not a service to a sovereign, then the documentary information on which it operated needed to be rendered toward public view. For Cornwallis, this meant shifting the material form of government information from manuscript to print. This sentiment came to be embodied in a complementary development at the end of the eighteenth century: the establishment of a parliamentary commission in 1800 tasked with "the arrangement, Preservation, and more convenient use" of the "public Records of the Kingdom." This commission was to arrange and methodize the records contained in government "Offices and Repositories" on the grounds that doing so "would be beneficial to the Public Service." Indeed, the commission was also to determine which of "the more antient and valuable amongst" these records "should be printed" to greater facilitate public use. The commissioners were also given "full Power and Authority to cause all" "officers" of the state "to bring and produce" all "Rolls, Records, Books, and Papers or other writings belonging to the said offices or Repositories" that may have been in their private "Custody."[113] The commission engaged in many of the same kinds of practices of recordkeeping that administrators had been doing from the beginning of the early modern period—arranging, making calendars, transcribing, and making catalogues, all to help serve the ends of government. But now, rather than aimed at facilitating the exercise of "office," these feats of organization were to be directed toward the end of "Public Service."

What guidance records conceptualized under such protocols might provide officials in the execution of their offices was unclear. As the next chapter shows, at least some administrators in government during the early nineteenth century articulated visions of official papers as valuable sources of governing wisdom in a manner that embraced the terms and practices of early modern political discourse. Even in 1840, government archivists were framing the purpose of archiving official records as "the preservation and defence" of the sovereigns' "rights and prerogatives," as well as "the dignity" of the "Imperial Crown."[114] But by the early nineteenth century, such sentiments were beginning to be dwarfed by a discourse that presented "state papers" not as a source of wisdom for governance but as of historical interest. This discourse disentangled the epistemic authority of political knowledge from a connection to written records. It came to be possible to claim, as a government commission devoted to publishing such records proclaimed in 1831, that "State Papers" documenting the past (in this case, any "relating to the period antecedent to the accession of

George the third") were "*exclusively* valuable as materials for history—&
that therefore it would be highly adviseable, that they should be deposited" and stored in a manner so "they would be generally accessible to
the public."[115] Such a severance of history from administration pointed
to a regime of government that was distinctively different from the early
modern world of Hastings and others invested in the archival style. The
terms of political debate had clearly shifted—the archive no longer provided either the institutional referent point or epistemological vocabulary
in which to think and argue about the contours of government.

In place of the archival style, new ideas of government information ascended, characterized by a belief in the existence of general rules,
especially in the realm of political economy, that governed how people
behaved and that did not require reference to the documentary information of the past in order to be known. Indeed, such general rules could be
applied to governing everyone, no matter what their cultural or linguistic
traditions, and this assumption led to the rise of new forms of data collection that were geared toward helping government make universalizing
comparisons across space.[116] Documents were no less important to this
world than they had been to the early modern one. But in this constellation, a diminishing number of people thought of the archive as a governing
instrument—and for this reason, what emerged in the British Empire in
the early decades of the nineteenth century was a distinctively modern
political enterprise.

From State Papers to Public Records

IN 1839, THE HISTORIAN Patrick Fraser Tytler complained to the home secretary Lord John Russell about the difficulty of accessing records held in the State Paper Office. There was something "evil," Tytler argued, about a world in which "the State have turned Publishers and Historians, instead of leaving that task to the activity and enterprise of literary men,—and facilitating their labours by a free communication of their manuscript stores."[1] In Tytler's opinion, government was supposed to maintain archives so "literary men" could use them, not sequester records as their privileged source of policy, or even historical, wisdom. In fact, Tytler asserted, the state was not a historian. Such an attitude toward the relationship between government and scholarship overlapped with a growing conception in early nineteenth-century Britain that access to government archives should be widened to the public, not restricted to government officials. Indeed, a growing discourse emphasized that archives of old administrative records should not be the exclusive province of officials because historical records were irrelevant to making policy. A telling expression of this sentiment came in an 1851 article in the *Gentleman's Magazine* on the subject of "The Accessibility of Our Historical Materials." Writing with specific reference to the State Paper Office, the author contended that the consultation and use of the records contained therein should not be subjected to restrictions. While "English history may be guessed at . . . from other sources," the author contended, "it can never be written without access to the materials in the State Paper Office." Still, the author complained about the restrictive conditions of access, under which "no one, without the permission of a Secretary of State, and then for only some definite purpose fully explained to the Secretary of State beforehand," could gain permission to read the documents in the office. The author contrasted these terms of access with those that pertained at the British Museum, where a researcher "chooses to pursue his course of inquiry in his own way," with free access to any "materials" desired. But a researcher visiting the State

Paper Office found themself "under an entirely different system" in which they were restricted to viewing only those documents which the Secretary of State had given explicit permission and "cannot see anything or obtain anything without inquiry and explanation." Such distinct access policies, the author conceded, might be defended by arguing that "public detriment may arise" from exposing such papers "to prying eyes" given their utility for policymaking. It was precisely this claim of utility that the author disputed. Old papers were irrelevant to guiding present policy decisions: they could assert "with perfect certainty that a diplomatic correspondence of Henry VIII. or Elizabeth (although it may operate by way of historical illustration) can have no possible practical bearing upon public or private business of the present day." "To subject papers whose *only* use is that of being materials for history" to such restrictions was "ridiculous," the author concluded.[2]

Indeed, over the course of the early nineteenth century, access to government records had gradually liberalized, though evidently not to the degree that the 1851 writer deemed sufficient. One wonders whether the writer was satisfied by the decision of government a year later to allow "literary men" access to records without payment of fees, or the transfer of records from the State Paper Office to the Public Record Office in the 1850s, where they could be consulted without prior approval of government officials.[3] These mid-nineteenth-century developments that enabled unrestricted access to historical government records emerged in the context of a transformation in the nature of politics itself. The effect of this transformation was to exclude the practices of archival governance from the definition of what it meant to produce political knowledge. Crucially, this attitudinal change did little to assuage the appetite of governing institutions for gathering and controlling information. Instead, it allowed governing institutions to at once expand public access to a past now conceptualized to have limited relevance to policymaking while continuing to restrict public knowledge about present-day government activities.

The careers of two officials—George Chalmers and John Bruce— encapsulate how the power of archival reasoning began to fade as a form of political knowledge in the context of these shifts in the meaning of the political. Both Chalmers and Bruce were quintessential practitioners of the early modern political style of invoking archival records to substantiate policy claims; their practices and methods would have been familiar to the officials this book has examined. Yet, as they deployed familiar techniques of archival politics at the turn of the nineteenth century, both found that their efforts generated decreasing interest from institutional and public audiences.

Inventing the "Science" of Political Economy

"In order to write even a paragraph in a newspaper on finance," the Scottish banker Walter Boyd observed in the early 1810s, it was conventionally understood "that the author should be possessed of certain *data,* certain authentic documents upon which his reasonings may rest." Boyd admitted, however, that he "possessed . . . no authentic documents." Yet, he still insisted that he could reason about "the finances of Great Britain." As Boyd explained, "the finances of the kingdom" were governed by "principles" whose existence was not contingent on their written expression. Once known, these principles could be used in lieu of records to generate knowledge for policymaking. Even if numerical data continued to be written down on paper, records merely recorded the workings of such principles, which operated to shape political and economic relations like laws of motion shaped the physical world, entirely independent from their description in language.[4] During the early nineteenth century, a language of exactitude characterized by a lexicon of "principles," "science," "fact," and "mechanics" came to be attached to nonarchival methods of political reasoning. Indeed, producing knowledge about politics and political economy came to be widely understood as involving the search for principles that were "not the offspring of legislative enactments." Instead, these principles were "part of the original constitution and of the physical world." Therefore, the method for discerning them was through a "science" of "fact and experiment," comparable to how physicists derived "mechanical principles" about the operation of the universe.[5]

Boyd was writing at an inflection point between two worlds: one in which "data" and "authentic documents" had been synonymous and seen as the fundamental grounds of political economic reasoning, and an emerging world in which the finances of a state could be reasoned about without reference to such documents. Straddling between these two worlds was the figure of George Chalmers, whose career in office and in public life encapsulated the shift. Born in northern Scotland and baptized in 1742,

Chalmers studied law at the University of Aberdeen before embarking for Maryland in 1763.[6] Chalmers spent the next several years practicing law in Annapolis and Baltimore in a number of different courts, as well as before the governor, council, and House of Burgesses.[7] Like administrators, lawyers in eighteenth-century Britain and its empire privileged the authority of written evidence—in the form of court records, published compilations of laws, and administrative documents contained in archives—as the source of factual knowledge.[8] Transcribed and circulated in manuscript or privately printed form, such documents were especially important with respect to the American colonies given the irregularity of official printing of statutes.[9] Chalmers applied these archival methods to the analysis of commercial history. As he wrote in 1780, "abundant intelligence on every subject" related to British America was to "be found" in the "Archives" of the imperial state, and "every topic" related to its "genuine history" was knowable based on what "the State papers demonstrate."[10] Although his Aberdeen origins might suggest ties to a Scottish Enlightenment culture concerned with tracing the historical evolution of manners and commerce in order to develop a philosophical science of society, Chalmers's interest, like that of other officials examined in this book, centered instead on harnessing documentary precedents to both validate and generate specific political stances and policies.[11]

That said, Chalmers's claim in 1780 to know the contents of the state archives was odd, since he had not yet held an office that would have enabled him to access them. His access was instead a product of the fortuitous alignment of his political advocacy and the interests of metropolitan administration. Vocal in defending imperial prerogative as a polemical writer and speaker in Maryland during the late 1760s and early 1770s, Chalmers fled to England in 1775 to escape the rising anti-imperial sentiment. There, he endeared himself to pro-imperial officials by publicly defending ministerial policy. In early 1780, as Chalmers was preparing a history of the imperial crisis, he applied to George Germain, secretary of state, and William Knox, undersecretary of state for the American department, for access to government records contained in the State Paper Office, which he hoped to use as research materials. Knox was particularly interested in the use and publication of state papers to advance political views, and during the same period he was actively collecting government documents as he performed his official duties, copying or taking them from state archives into his personal possession.[12] Recognizing that Chalmers's antipathy to the colonists made him useful to the government, Germain and Knox granted him use of the records in March 1780, instructing clerks in the State Paper Office to give Chalmers "access to such papers . . . as relate to the said Colonies & to permit him to make Extracts of such as he shall judge proper for his purpose."[13] Chalmers prepared transcripts and took notes from these documents for his own use and in some cases removed the documents themselves, compiling in the process a massive personal archive of state papers.[14]

Chalmers used these records in terms of the archival epistemology this book has examined. As we have seen, so many political writers, officials, and administrative institutions across the early modern British Empire drew on the language of documents and the techniques of archival practices to advance particular political arguments. So too did Chalmers in the late eighteenth century. He sent Germain transcriptions of documents he had "discovered" in the Paper Office that officials "might possibly wish to see" as guides.[15] He lobbied officials to advance specific policy goals, such as authenticating loyalist claims for compensation and assistance from the government, whose wisdom he authorized with reference to documents "found in the Plantation office."[16] He also articulated and defended this method of argument as an authoritative way to reason about political and economic matters. "From the days of Elizabeth to the present . . . a twelvemonth has scarcely passed away, in which a treatise has not been published, either by ignorance, by good-intentions, or design, bewailing the loss of our commerce, and the ruin of the state," Chalmers noted in his 1782 work, *An Estimate of the Comparative Strength of Britain during the Present and Four Preceding Reigns; and of the Losses of Her Trade from Every War Since the Revolution.* But these accounts were erroneous, he argued, for they were based on "delusive speculation," not "accurate research." His account of the history of commerce, by contrast, derived from "documents" he had "collected" that "authenticated" with "unvarnished evidence" that the "losses" to British commerce as a result of imperial warfare were merely "temporary." In Chalmers's view, archival records added "the authority of experience to the decisions of judgment."[17]

Like his early modern predecessors, Chalmers believed knowledge of political economy also lay in written records. As he explained in the preface to *Opinions of Eminent Lawyers, on Various Points of English Ju-risprudence, Chiefly Concerning the Colonies, Fisheries, and Commerce, of Great Britain* (1814), the subject of imperial commerce comprised a quar-tet of topics: "manufactures set up abroad," "the acts of navigation," "mis-cellaneous matters of trade," and the circulation of currency. In his view, each of these topics was ultimately a problem of "jurisdiction," meaning a question of determining how the powers of the sovereign-in-council and the sovereign-in-Parliament to enforce "*the laws of England*" "over the transatlantic colonies" manifested themselves in each context. For Chal-mers, deriving that knowledge of jurisdiction required reading the records "collected, and digested, from the originals, in the Board of Trade, and other depositories." The facts of empire as a space of exchange, law, and politics were to be known through official archives.[18]

By the time the *Estimate* appeared, however, the institutional ar-rangement of imperial government was changing from its earlier configu-ration in ways that bore on the status of official archives. In the immediate moment, these changes benefited Chalmers's projects. But in the longer term, the institutional changes were followed by epistemological ones that marked the waning appeal of archival methods among administrators. In 1783, in the aftermath of the American war, the Privy Council dissolved the Board of Trade and shifted both responsibility for administering com-mercial affairs and control of the records of the old board to a new Com-mittee of Trade.[19] The *Estimate* caught the attention of Charles Jenkinson, president of the committee, who invited Chalmers to testify before the body in 1784 as an expert on Maryland's role in imperial trade, and asked him for papers on the historical export statistics from Scotland to the West Indies.[20] In 1786, Jenkinson appointed Chalmers as the committee's chief clerk, entrusting him with control of the accumulated records of imperial government.[21] Now Chalmers had direct access to official archives, which earlier writers who shared his confidence in the power of records to sup-ply commercial knowledge had not enjoyed.

As both a polemicist and an administrator in William Pitt's govern-mental machine from the mid-1780s, Chalmers worked in parallel to other officials who also brought early modern practices to bear on policymak-ing and political debates in these years. Yet, these figures confronted an environment in which there was a shrinking audience who shared their as-sumptions that claims about policy required references to archival records in order to be considered authentic. The reception of Chalmers's own writings illustrated how these doubts about the utility of records manifested themselves with respect to political economy. One line of critique leveled against his *Estimate,* for example, contested Chalmers's claims about the power of mercantile records as a source of fact. As a reviewer wrote in 1787, Chalmers had "in general, relied on custom-house entries, as the source of his principal facts," but the nature of such records "do not authorize that confidence which he has all along placed in them." As the reviewer explained, merchants frequently reported numbers that were "far above the truth" when "no duties were charged on certain articles exported," while "if, at another period, a high duty should be demanded on exporting the same articles, care would not only be taken not to over-rate them, but pains would be bestowed to enter them as much under value as possible." Hence, the reviewer argued, "no reliance should be had on customhouse entries," which were "more likely to mislead than to direct the judgement."[22]

To be sure, these gradual changes did not cause practitioners of the archival style to vanish from government overnight. But as administrators and politicians showed less interest in their techniques, Chalmers and his fellow early moderns invested in using their privileged access to records to pursue projects directed at audiences beyond policymaking circles. Although Chalmers remained chief clerk at the Privy Council's trade committee during the early nineteenth century, the administrative leadership did not make significant use of his archival research. Nevertheless, he continued to draw on the records to indulge projects that he understood as both historical and intimately connected to the practice of politics. In some cases, this meant the politics of present-day policymaking. In 1814, for example, Chalmers published a two-volume transcription of eighteenth-century royal legal opinions concerning the colonies that he based on his transcriptions of records from various government collections. By collating and publishing these documents (which otherwise lay "separated" and "obscured" "in different depositories"), Chalmers intended for them to serve as guiding "rays of knowledge" for contemporary British officials "setting out" to "execute" their service to the empire.[23] In other instances, Chalmers located the stakes in the politics of historical interpretation, as with his hagiographic *Life of Mary, Queen of Scots,* in which he defended Mary as "innocent of the crimes . . . imputed to her" based on the evidence of "new documents" drawn from "state papers" whose unimpeachable authority allowed for "many old falshoods" to be "detected" and "many new truths" "established" in their place.[24] Chalmers's intervention into the controversy over the authorship of the *Letters of Junius,* a series of radical pamphlets critical of George III pseudonymously published between 1769 and 1772, also evinced the melding of the archival and the programmatic: since Junius advocated "anarchical violence" against the monarchy, Chalmers argued, determining the author's true identity was a question of *"political importance"* and required the collection and review of "documents."[25]

But a dwindling number of audiences shared this understanding of the political. By the early nineteenth century, for example, commercial affairs were increasingly thought to be intelligible through reading publicly available parliamentary legislation, rather than through researching handwritten records housed in restricted state archives. In 1772, the political economic writer Thomas Mortimer had defended the Board of Trade's archive-centric "political wisdom," but in 1801 he argued that while an archival approach to commercial governance might have been "well adapted to the infant state of our trade," it was "by no means suited to the present extensive commerce of Great Britain." Instead, the knowledge required to govern a mature imperial economy lay in the compilation of a single, "digested," "complete mercantile code, or body of commercial laws"—replacing the plethora of letters, reports, account books, and scraps of paper that Chalmers and his predecessors at the Board of Trade had sifted through to find authorities for their policy proposals.[26]

Although the past remained a valid source for deriving economic fact, the relevant form of historical knowledge was no longer understood to reside either exclusively or even primarily in old official records. In the 1810s, Chalmers was still insisting that government "documents" provided "facts," "facts" constituted "Experience," and "Experience" in turn provided "certainty" about matters of *"commerce."*[27] Other writers on political economy invoked the wisdom of history, but they had a different understanding of "Experience." The "whole business of political economy" was "to study the causes which have thus cooperated to enrich and civilize a nation," the writer Jane Haldimand Marcet observed in 1816. However, Marcet elaborated, although this "science" was "essentially founded upon history," it was "not the history of sovereigns, of wars, and of intrigues" but instead that of "arts," "discoveries," and "civilization"—subjects not clearly knowable through archives whose function was to preserve the documentation of these sovereigns' activities.[28] Within government itself, in fact, a so-called "information revolution" in the early nineteenth century saw quantitative data become increasingly disaggregated from the archive, collected as documentation of current conditions in both national and imperial space by an expanding army of officials. Administrative investments shifted from the development of policy based on detailed research into old documents and came to focus instead on ruling through what Sir John Sinclair described in 1793 as both a "science" and "a *new* branch of politics" that promised to illuminate "the real state" of a country's "commerce" in present time: statistics. Whereas history could still be found in archives, policy knowledge would be generated not from reading state papers but by reasoning in terms of both this new "statistical philosophy" and less-granular understandings of the past.[29]

The Last Early Modernist

This ascendant understanding of policy as no longer contingent on correspondence to documentary precedents contained in archives dovetailed with another attitudinal shift: the idea that state papers lacked relevance to policymaking and therefore should be considered public records that public audiences could access freely. Patrick Fraser Tytler's 1839 argument, cited at the outset of this chapter—namely, that the state should facilitate the work of historians but was not itself a historian—came to be shared by officials themselves. An early modern political epistemology that understood historical scholarship and precedent-centered statecraft as overlapping pursuits gave way to a modern one that conceived of government as the facilitator of the work of historians but treated archival methods as irrelevant to the work of government. This shift is demonstrated in the biography of John Bruce, another official and archivist whose career bore similarities with that of Chalmers. At the end of the eighteenth century, Bruce continued the practices of early modern documentary governance and in the process imagined how this archival epistemology might be applied in ways that disciplined the archive of the East India Company under the control of the state. But Bruce's methodological and epistemological commitments, like Chalmers's, found dwindling purchase within both Crown and company circles.

Bruce's ambitions focused initially on academia. Entering the University of Edinburgh in 1764, he rapidly ascended its ranks and achieved the chair of logic and metaphysics a decade later.[30] As a student, he had become acquainted with Henry Dundas while both were members of a debating club called the Speculative Society.[31] Dundas convinced Bruce to take a leave from his position between 1786 and 1788 to travel the continent as tutor to Dundas's son Robert. When the younger Dundas matriculated to Emmanuel College, Cambridge, to complete his education, Bruce sought Henry Dundas's assistance in reentering the Edinburgh professorship. However, in Bruce's absence, the Edinburgh professorship had been filled by another without his official resignation, angering Bruce. Compounding Bruce's frustration was the hostile reception of his 1786 work *Elements of the Science of Ethics,* which had been lambasted for its "impropriety of expression," "provincial idiom," and Bruce's "haste" and "negligence" in a review orchestrated by academic rivals.[32]

Bruce turned to Henry Dundas for assistance. Leveraging his influence within the East India Company's administration, Dundas offered Bruce a role involving the use of the company's archive—specifically to continue the longstanding political practices of using documents to substantiate preordained policy arguments, and to extend the power of the Crown's administration over company affairs. As this book has shown, for several decades, government ministries had sought to intervene into company affairs and supervise the contents of its official documents. A key moment in this pattern was the passage of the 1784 India Act, which established a Board of Control composed of privy councilors and the secretaries of state—including Henry Dundas—which aimed to extend ministerial control over the governance of British India. Upon ascending to membership on the Board of Control in 1784, Dundas sought to exert control over the company's records. He immediately ordered the board's solicitor, Francis Russell, to "be much at the India House collecting materials for" the body's "information."[33] Over the mid-1780s, Dundas continued this practice of dispatching the board's secretaries and clerks to collect records from the company's archive for his review.[34] With the charter granting the East India Company a monopoly on the trade to India set to expire in 1793, Dundas asked Bruce to prepare a work, drawn from official documents that he provided, which would argue for the alignment between the corporation's interests and those of the British imperial state based on the authority of records, hopefully convincing Parliament to renew the corporation's privileges. On September 6, 1789, Bruce updated Dundas on "the Business at the India Board, which you had assigned me," to devise a "Plan for forming a History of British Affairs in the East Indies" "prepared from the Materials furnished by Mr. Dundas." This planned work would encompass three parts: the first, a "History of the Events which explain the State of the British Affairs in the East Indies" from the establishment of British territorial power in Bengal to the present; the second, a "History of the East India Company" from its origins to the present; and the third, a survey of the plans "suggested for the Government of India, after the Charter of the Company, shall have expired." As Bruce indicated, the projected "History" would survey possible forms of government for India after the expiration of the company's charter and demonstrate that the continued system of monopoly government was best in keeping with the tradition of company rule.[35] Bruce was thus to substantiate these already decided on policy positions with the evidence of archival records. In an accompanying letter, Bruce explained both his method of labor and progress on this project. Having received Dundas's approval for the "outline" of the history as well as access to the company's records, Bruce was now "at work, ten hours every day" giving the proposed "Contents the form of historical detail, with proper references to authorities" drawn from these "papers." Once this had been completed, he would "give to the whole" work "that Copiousness of Matter, and simplicity of Style" to facilitate its use by Dundas.[36]

Bruce elaborated on the specific written records he required for the composition of this history in a 1791 memo addressed to William Cabell, then Henry Dundas's private secretary. While Bruce reported being "nearly" "in possession of Materials . . . which will fully answer the purposes of Mr Dundas' instructions," he needed access to other records: specifically, "the Company's abstracts of their Correspondence to and from Bengal & Madras" and "to and from Bombay" from the late 1760s to the establishment of the Board of Control; the abstracts of the company's Sumatra, China, and East Indies correspondence; and any further evidence of plans for the "future government, & India, or regulation of the Trade to the East Indies" that had previously been drawn up. Such material, Bruce wrote, would enable him to "give the past of the Subject as fully as possible, that [Dundas's] own plan [for the work] may come out as a result from the fullest evidence." All "papers" that Cabell could "furnish" from the company's archive would "enable" Bruce "to meet, & to fulfill Mr Dundas's orders, or general instructions to him."[37] Bruce would continue to submit further requests to Cabell for more documents from the company archive to facilitate the completion of the history.[38]

Dundas also enabled Bruce's access to the records of the State Paper Office. In May 1790, Dundas drafted a memo arguing for rearrangement of the company's records intended to facilitate the Board of Control's "superintendence" of East India affairs.[39] He tasked Bruce with drawing up a detailed proposal for arranging control of the records to this end. In September 1791, Bruce sent Dundas a plan for unifying the respective archives of company and state. If appointed as "Keeper of the State Paper Office," Bruce promised he would "in the first instance, connect Indian Affairs with that Department, and in the next, devote my future studies & industry to bring the whole of it, into a regular system."[40] He proposed a set of "Regulations for the Indian Branch of the State Paper Office" and his appointment to an office of "historiographer" to execute them. The office, which Bruce offered to fill himself, would "methodise" the company's records and place them under the direct control of Dundas. "As Keeper of this Office, when required by the Secretary of State, or by the India Board, I shall examine the archives & make reports, and upon the same plan, shall arrange the transactions, Treaties of Great Britain with the different European powers," Bruce wrote.[41] Here, he articulated his role both as defender of the company in public by making arguments based on citation of records and as archivist provisioning the government with documents useful for administration. Bruce positioned the company archive as part of the State Paper Office, enfolding the company's records into that of the archive of the Secretary of State, and placing both under his personal control. For Bruce, "state papers" would provide government with the knowledge necessary to address its present and future "business." After Dundas became home secretary in 1791, he coordinated Bruce's appointment to the position of keeper and register of state papers for life.[42] By placing control of the company and state archives in the singular hands of Bruce, Dundas thus formulated at the level of control of official records an analogue to his own union of control over both state and company administration.

The first fruit of Bruce's research in the corporate and state archives was the *Historical View of Plans for the Government of British India and Regulation of Trade to the East Indies, and Outlines of a Plan of Foreign Government, of Commercial Oeconomy, and of Domestic Administration, for the Asiatic Interests of Great Britain.* In this work, published by the East India Company in 1793, Bruce endeavored to demonstrate that its interests were historically aligned with those of the British Empire and that renewal of its charter was therefore in the best interests of the nation. The company published the work anonymously and circulated it to Parliament and the public to argue its case for renewing the charter. As Bruce explained in the introduction to the work, his method relied on arguments from "Authorities" of documents that he had "obtained either from the records of the Company and from the archives of the State, or from the communications of those whose official and local knowledge qualify them to aid their country upon this important occasion."[43] Indeed, Bruce distributed copies of the *Historical View* to key company servants and scholarly figures to facilitate such communications, presenting the work to them and requesting that in exchange, they send him "Information on the diversified Subjects of the political & Commercial History of the Countries within the Company's limits."[44]

Bruce's completion of the *Historical View* prompted Dundas to lobby the Court of Directors to formalize Bruce's role. Dundas requested that Bruce be appointed "Historiographer to the East India Company," an office that would furnish Bruce with "the benefit of a free access to the ancient records of the Company," "essential to the Work in which, under my direction, he is now engaged."[45] The office itself had been created by the court for the Orientalist Robert Orme. A longtime company servant in India, Orme wrote a heroic chronicle of the British defeat of France and its Indian allies during the Seven Years' War entitled *History of the Military Transactions of the British in India.* The company's Court of Directors sponsored the printing of the first volume in 1763 as an act of public relations. To facilitate Orme's work, the court also granted him permission to "take Copies of some Records relative to former times as he may think necessary" by requesting them from the company's secretary.[46] In 1769, the court formalized Orme's role, creating the office of "historiographer," which granted the occupant direct access to the company's records. The court modeled the position after the "historiographer royal," a largely sinecurial Crown office established in the 1660s by Charles II that allowed its appointee to access state papers in writing histories.[47] As the first company historiographer, Orme used the records to complete several other works, including the second volume of his *History of the Military Transactions,* published in 1778.[48] Following Orme's retirement, the court formally appointed Bruce to the historiographer's office on July 10, 1793.[49]

Like Orme, Bruce used the office to promote the company's interests in the public sphere through the publication of historical writing, but his approach was subservient to the ends of his patron, Dundas. For Dundas, Bruce's appointment was at once an act of sympathy for someone who had served his family, a reward to Bruce for his labor in producing the *Historical View,* and a strategic move: by installing Bruce as historiographer, Dundas gave access to the company's records to an indebted servant whom Dundas could commission to use as he advanced his power over company governance. Although Bruce offered to "make any Researches" in the India records as needed by the court, Bruce's use of the records largely served a considerably smaller audience: Henry Dundas.[50] Moreover, while the company assisted Bruce's endeavors, including through the appointment of a committee to solicit its servants in Asia for materials that would assist the historiographer in completing a general history of India, Bruce's work in office largely consisted of answering requests from Dundas for documentary precedents in the archives that would guide the administrator on responding to some proximate political or administrative issue.[51] In the tradition of early modern documentary argument, Bruce's reports were characterized by a hyper-empirical strategy of extensive citations from, and discussions of, documents as argumentative authorities, drawn from the archives of the East India Company and the State Paper Office, and provisioned from company servants. Over the course of mid- to late 1790s, Dundas commissioned Bruce to author reports establishing precedents for policymaking on issues including the suppression of domestic radicalism, the potential invasion of Britain by the French, and the reform of the East India Company's army.[52]

By the end of the 1790s, Bruce and Dundas had moved to consolidate their control of the State Paper Office. Between late 1798 and early 1799, Bruce prepared a new set of "Regulations" for the management and organization of the State Paper Office for Dundas. In mid-1799, Evan

Nepean, Dundas's undersecretary of state, drafted a letter to Lord William Wyndham Grenville, foreign secretary, in the name of his superior, summarizing John Bruce's utility to Dundas over the previous decade. Nepean wrote that Dundas had "found it indispensably necessary" in the conduct of his office "to have frequent recourse to the State Paper office, for information, on various points." Noting Bruce's patent to occupy the office, Nepean observed that Bruce's "Reports" had "opened the means, of facilitating the Dispatch of every part of the business, in the various departments of the Secretaries of State, to which the Duties of his office are in immediate subservience." The previous June, Dundas had "directed" Bruce "to draw up Regulations, for the Paper Office" "to enable him, more effectually to render the King's archives usefull" to government, regulations that it would be "of great benefit, to the public service, to adopt." Nepean concluded by asking for Grenville's support in "establish[ing] Mr Bruce fully in his office, under these Regulations" "so as to render his arrangements and Reports, not only usefull to the present Secretaries of State but the means of preserving the best materials for the future proceedings of Government."[53]

In proposing these "Regulations," Bruce was motivated by a desire to push back against a pattern of parliamentary encroachment into the state papers over the late eighteenth century. Since 1764, a parliamentary commission, independent and separate from the office of the keeper and removed from the jurisdiction of the secretary of state, had been working to methodize and catalogue the records of the State Paper Office.[54] Bruce, however, sought to undermine Parliament's claims on the records and situate control in the hands of the secretary of state's office, specifically his own: as keeper, he was the direct appointee of the secretary. His regulations and an accompanying history of the State Paper Office offered a self-serving account of the archive's development. He reported that in examining the records of the State Paper Office itself, he had been unable to locate "any authentic Documents" evincing that "any Regulations were framed, for arranging the Royal Archives," beyond the principle that the library was known as the "King's Library of Manuscripts, regarding Matters of State and Council." According to Bruce, a situation of general disorganization, including the deposit of government records across several different offices, had persisted in the management of state archives until 1714, when the then-keeper, Hugh Howard, had made the first effort to "bring the whole together," order the papers into the form of a "Library" within Whitehall, and collect official papers intermingled into the private archives of former keepers and secretaries of state. At around the same time, Bruce wrote, a "Collector and Transmitter of Papers of Council and State" was appointed as an "intermediate office" between the secretaries of state and the State Paper Office. The transmitter's role was to receive documents from the undersecretaries and first clerks of the different government departments from "20 years back" and forward them to the Paper Office to be "methodized and digested" into chronological order. But the execution of this process had proceeded in a largely haphazard manner because the keeper lacked "proper Rooms into which to receive the Papers" and no funding to hire clerks or deputies. Absent a capacity to organize them, the office's records had been dumped in "Rooms adjoining to the Board of Trade."[55]

Bruce continued his history by alluding to the parliamentary commission's ongoing efforts "to arrange and methodize the Papers" but argued that the most effective reorganization of the state papers would come by placing them under his complete custody as keeper. "Under the orders of Mr. Secretary Dundas and the Duke of Portland," Bruce wrote that he had "made researches at the Paper Office, and Reports on the different Subjects, upon which precedents were required" for the administration. "From these Authorities," he had "drawn up his Reports" advising the ministers on the appropriate action. He proposed a set of "Regulations for the State Paper Office if Made an Office of Reference," whose adoption would "render this most valuable Deposit of the King's Archives, worthy of the Sovereign of a great Nation" by making the documents "useful" to the secretary of state. He suggested altering the arrangement of the records to facilitate this end by dividing correspondence with European powers geographically by specific country and arranging documents chronologically within each series. "Abstracts" or "registers" briefly summarizing the titles of documents in each of these geographic series were also to be created, corresponding to the number of the bound volume to facilitate making "References" to the papers. Imperial records were to be organized according to a similar logic, "formed into distinct Branches, America, West Indies, East Indies, &c.," preceded by "abstracts" describing the subjects and contents of the correspondence that specifically addressed "the period and circumstances which led to the acquisition of the Territory, and to the progressive Changes and Improvements which it may have experienced, during each Reign."[56]

The keeper of state papers was to act precisely as Bruce had done for Dundas during the preceding decade: "to receive the orders of His Majesty's Ministers, upon any immediate occurring Circumstances, which may require an investigation" and "draw up Reports . . . stating the information which the Records of Office furnish."[57] Bruce suggested a precedent for this organization in what he imagined to be the approach of Louis XIV's minister Jean-Baptiste Colbert, who had reorganized the archives of the French state from being "of no use, in the actual Dispatch of Business" into a site of provisioning documentary precedents to government "when any public transaction required a Research for authorities from the State Papers."[58] Colbert had achieved this, Bruce believed, by centering both domestic and foreign administrative documents under one roof and in the hands of a single keeper. "The French always ascribed their quick Dispatch of Business, with foreign Nations, as well as the Secrecy of their Cabinet," Bruce argued, for it "prevented the bustle attending Researches in different Offices," "rendered the Answers of the King to the Memorials of Foreign Powers correct," and "prevented on all occasions, state secrets from being known to the Emissaries or Spies of Foreign Courts."[59]

Bruce's depiction of the organization of French royal archives was both inaccurate and strategic. By suggesting that the union of imperial and domestic records under the control of a single figure facilitated "correct" sovereign reason, official secrecy, and the "quick" conduct of office, Bruce proposed a vision of how state and East India Company archival administration might be united—conveniently, in his own hands—to facilitate governance. Having read, annotated, and transcribed the internal records of the state and company archives themselves, Bruce was well aware of the ways his proposal built on the deep traditions of archival political practice in Britain and its empire that this book has excavated.[60] Bruce's invocation of the mythology of Colbert as total archivist, rather than the early modern British tradition of "state papers" in which he was actually participating, therefore appears odd. Indeed, it should be interpreted as tactical. By invoking Colbert's arrangement of state archives as the reason for France's administrative "quickness," Bruce argued that mimicking the French strategy (independent of how early modern French archival practice actually worked) would enable Britain to defeat its rival, a point that might resonate with the concerns of Dundas and other officials. Like so many other early modern figures, Bruce used the practices of documentary collection, circulation, and citation to conjoin his personal advancement with policy advocacy through the institutional position of office.

Dundas endorsed Bruce's proposed "Regulations" for the State Paper Office, and the ministry prepared a new warrant officially adopting them in January 1800.[61] In the process, the authority of the parliamentary commission was revoked and the commissioners were now required to apply to the secretary of state for permission to access the records. Bruce was to manage the archive "with a View of rendering the State Paper Office more directly and immediately useful as an Office of Reference."[62] The official "Regulations for the State Paper Office" followed Bruce's plan: the keeper was "to receive the Orders of His Majesty's Secretaries of State, upon any immediate, occurring circumstance, which may require an Investigation of the King's Archives." The archive was a resource of administrative decision-making controlled exclusively by the secretary of state. According to the regulations, "No original Paper, after transmission, to be delivered out of the Paper Office, except the same shall be required by an Order, under the Hand of one of His Majesty's Principal Secretaries of State."[63] These regulations, though newly established, were in fact not new at all. Bruce had simply reasserted the older ideology of archival governance broadly embraced by early modern administrators: that the State Paper Office represented the central repository of administrative documents under Crown control, to be employed as a principal tool of government, and that archives themselves formed an empirical center to undergird policymaking.

Bruce now commenced administering the State Paper Office according to this plan. On July 31, 1800, he wrote to Dundas regarding the complications of negotiating between his own personal loyalty to the secretary of state and the function of the State Paper Office as one of more "public record." Yet another new parliamentary commission was formed to publish documents of "historical" interest for public consumption, but unlike the methodizing committee, the terms of its access to the State Paper Office were unclear.[64] The commissioners had sent Bruce two resolutions instructing him to move all the records pertaining to the House of Lords up to the year 1770 to the State Paper Office "to be arranged and indexed" and to "consider and report to this Board" a "Selection" of records intended to form a supplement to the Restoration historiographer Thomas Rymer's publication of diplomatic treaties, the *Foedera*.[65]

For Bruce, the commissioners' request challenged the remit of his office. If a parliamentary body could access the state papers directly, then the archive would no longer be under the proprietary control of the office of the secretary of state and, most importantly, the keeper himself. Bruce thus wrote to Dundas arguing that allowing the commissioners such access would turn the State Paper Office into a "Public Record Office." As with his reports, Bruce cited documents he had found in the office that demonstrated that "the History of these Papers" showed they were the exclusive custody of the secretary of state and thus properly under direct control of the secretary's designated archivist, the keeper.[66] In the moment, Bruce's position triumphed. In late August 1800, the secretary of state decided that "any directions" for supplying documents or records or abstracts and reports on records "should come from His Majesty's Principal Secretaries of State."[67] In accordance with Bruce's vision, the major demand for the office's records came from the secretaries of state through their direct orders to Bruce for documents concerning specific administrative issues, with access to others coming only via executive permission.[68] From his room in the State Paper Office, fitted with a writing table, desk, separate table for library books, inkstand, and several chairs, Bruce fielded these requests.[69] The archive continued to receive deposits of records from other parts of government, consolidating more official documents within Bruce's purview.[70]

Bruce's attitude toward government records was precisely in keeping with conceptions of other early modern officials—the archive as a source of documentary precedent for government, and the archivist as the manager of records who considered their custodianship in personalized, proprietary terms. Yet, although Bruce was now officially the manager of the records of both the State Paper Office and the East India Company, the positions did not lead Bruce to much administrative influence. Why? The immediate explanation lies in the career of his patron: once Dundas left the secretary of state's office during the fall of Pitt's government in 1801, the services of the keeper of state papers were no longer at the disposal of Bruce's protector. Dundas's return to government in Pitt's second ministry as lord of the Admiralty in 1804 precluded access to the archive that remained under the control of the secretary of state, by Bruce's own design.

The abrupt fall of Dundas from political power deprived Bruce of a key audience for his archive-based administrative plans.

But the power of archives was also undermined by a deeper change in the nature of office itself. Dundas's successors in the upper administrative echelons of the British imperial state were less committed to treating archival records as an integral tool for reasoning about policy. This hardly stopped Bruce from making use of his access to records to pursue projects: for example, with the support of the Court of Directors, he compiled and published a three-volume history of the East India Company in 1810 based on his research in both the corporation's archive and the State Paper Office.[71] Yet, seven years later, and despite Bruce's objections, the court decided to abolish the office of company historiographer. In doing so, it described the office not as part of its policymaking process but instead as engaged in activities of "a literary nature" and thus properly placed under the province of the company's librarian, who the court now entrusted to care for the records as primarily historical objects not immediately useful for policymaking.[72]

Indeed, if the proliferation and abundance of records was once viewed as integral to the work of effective governance, some company officials began to adopt a different view: records were less facilitators of rule than inhibitors of its execution. "If we consider the form of the British government in India, we shall find it ill calculated for the speedy introduction of improvement," argued the company official John Shore in 1789, for completing "official forms necessarily occupy a large portion of time, and the constant pressure of business leaves little leisure for study and reflection, without which no knowledge of the principles and detail of the revenues of this country can be obtained; true information is also procured with difficulty, because it is too often derived from mere practice instead of being deduced from fixed principles." "The multiplication of records, which ought to be a great advantage, is in fact an inconvenience of extensive magnitude," Shore continued, "for in them only the experience of others, can be traced; and reference, requires much time and labour."[73] For Shore, the proliferation of records was a burden, not an advantage, an inhibitor of effective governance rather than its facilitator. The "experience" contained within such records was, moreover, an "inconvenience," not an aid to administration. For an early modern administrator, the solution to such information overload would be to develop paper tools and

practices of archival organization—the kind of indexes, protocols of nota-
tion, and practices of filing that shaped the rhythms of early modern office
work. Shore's objective, however, was to overcome the archive entirely: to
replace the information "derived from mere practice" with that "deduced
from fixed principles."

Equally important, following Bruce's death in 1826, successive officials in the State Paper Office took different attitudes about the relationship
between government and archive. In 1844, for example, the office's senior
clerk Robert Lemon Jr. wrote to Sir Robert Peel to advise on the "extent
the public shall be admitted to have access to the priceless treasures of this
Collection" and "down to what period the papers in this Office . . . shall be
thrown open to the public." Lemon advocated for liberalization by pointing
to a notable circumstance: the state itself was increasingly disinterested in
using the records of the office. "From the year 1800 to the close of the last
year inclusive, a period of 44 years, there have been in all, 860 orders from
the Secretaries of State. Of those, exactly 450 were for official and public
purposes, and 410 for the admission of private individuals for historical
and other purposes," meaning that "only 40, not one in a year" requests
from government were for papers for actual use in decision-making. "From
these undoubted facts, powerful and incontrovertible as they are," Lemon
concluded, "no other inference can be drawn, but that the papers in this
magnificent Collection prior to the Reign of Anne, are of very trifling official importance, while they are at the same time of the very highest historical . . . value." He recommended that "a much more extended access"
by the public to these "State Papers" be facilitated.[74] The state itself was
placing decreasing value on the policy knowledge contained in the archive,
and with the papers' diminishing "official importance" to the work of government, they ought to be opened to the public.

Lemon's perspective ultimately came to be adopted by government
itself, seen especially in the issuance of an order in council in 1852, which
enabled anyone who sought to "consult the Records for literary, historical,
antiquarian, genealogical, topographical, and similar purposes" to obtain
a "card of admission" to the records office "without payment of Fees."[75]
Indeed, in the case of both the "public records" and those of the East
India Company, even more drastic moves away from at least some of the
protocols of early modern archival government were in store. In 1860, the
Public Record Office, created by Parliament in 1838, for the deposit of

"all Rolls, Records, Writs, Books, Proceedings, Decrees, Bills, Warrants, Accounts, Papers, and Documents whatsoever of a public Nature belonging to Her Majesty," formed a committee to manage the destruction of official records, which in turn made "selection[s] of useless papers . . . for conversion into pulp." The East India Company and then the India Office sought to carefully cull its records during the 1850s and 1860s. As Antonia Moon has observed, if the early modern "Company's servants had used the fact of a complete archive to boost their position as territorial administrator," "the civil servants of the India Office preserved a much weeded archive, to emphasise their claims to the same position."[76] The East India Company thus embraced a distinctively different logic of archival justification than what had preceded in the early modern period: rather than preserve everything, the idea was to preserve selectively—and to do so in a manner that made its store of collections increasingly visible, seen most vividly in the establishment and opening of a museum of "Oriental" materials collected by company servants at India House in 1801, to which admission could be obtained by applying to the Court of Directors.[77]

These concepts of the archive—as something that could be accessed by the public and indeed *should be* accessible to the public in order to help facilitate general interest in the history of government— constituted a shift away from that which had prevailed in previous centuries. Combined with the idea that state papers had diminished relevance to policymaking, they signaled a move toward a concept of government in which continued practices of institutional secrecy coexisted with gestures toward growing public expectations about the accessibility of political information and insights into the working of government. The archive increasingly came to be remade for a world that was no longer simply official but now also bureaucratic.

During the nineteenth century, the archive and the early modern protocols that had governed its use came to be confronted with a changing set of expectations about the accessibility and policymaking role of official documents. At the crux of this confrontation lay an interconnected set of shifts in how both government and society thought about the nature of political information: from a granular understanding of policy as rooted in correspondence to paper records to more abstract modes of producing political knowledge; from an account of official records as the remit of the state to an idea that they belonged to the public; and from a growing belief about the temporality of information—the idea that while official records were legitimately the privileged possession of their government creators at the time of their creation, that privilege was both temporary and connected to the office, not the officer.

This is not to imply that archives stopped being relevant to how the British Empire was governed once the likes of Chalmers and Bruce had passed from the scene. Instead, it is to suggest that the problem of the archive as it inflected practices of imperial rule in an age of bureaucracy needs to be investigated on its own terms—ones that exceed the capacities of the present study. What is clear is that many of the same structural problems and dilemmas that preoccupied early modern administrators and to which they saw archives as a solution continued to shape the concerns and practices of modern imperial government. Indeed, the question of whether non-British people should be governed in relation to British legal and political norms or in terms of some imperial-administrative conception of "indigenous" constitutions only grew in importance as a subject of political debate as the modern British Empire asserted sovereignty in the nineteenth and twentieth centuries over growing numbers of peoples in South Asia, Africa, and the Pacific. Granular concepts of precedent and history as located in specific material objects such as texts, documents, and archeological fragments continued to coexist with abstract ideologies of quantification and principle as intellectual resources that administrators and commentators drew on to devise and justify projects of rule and resource extraction over extended polities comprising peoples of diverse linguistic and cultural backgrounds.[78]

However, there were differences that rendered the archive seemingly less potent than these less-granular ways of producing political knowledge. Old problems—of the grounds on which empire could be justified and how it should be ruled—now came to be debated in relation to a set of conceptual expectations about the workings of administrative institutions, especially an expectation about their responsiveness to the demands of representative democracy, with limited applicability to the world of early modern imperial administration. The control of archives continued to be a concern of administrators but less because they saw them as resources immediately relevant to the justification and execution of policy decisions and more because they feared the consequences of the exposure of "official secrets" to public scrutiny.[79] These questions were also worked out in media environments that grew increasingly removed from the particular paper-parchment ecology of early modernity. Contra the contemporary fantasy of the paperless office, this was not because government ever abandoned the use of parchment and paper but rather because it also adopted technologies (including telegraph, internal combustion engines, photography, radio, television, and computers) whose singular as well as combined affordances for bearing authority; gathering, circulating, and storing information; and facilitating its retrieval proved far greater than the capacities of these older material forms.[80]

In the world of the early modern British Empire, then, the archive was the solution to a challenge that endures: how to govern an extended polity composed of culturally and linguistically heterogenous populations, and how to legitimate practices of rule. Taken up by administrative bodies across the empire's geographical expanse, the archive and its associated techniques of collecting, storing, and correlating written information framed the terms through which solutions to the dilemmas of asserting political order in relation to distance and difference came to be conceptualized, debated, and implemented.

Epilogue

IF EMPIRES ARE "POLITIES that maintain distinction and hierarchy as they incorporate new people," as the historians Jane Burbank and Frederick Cooper contend, then "the concept of empires presumes that different peoples within the polity will be governed differently."[1] Yet, even as empires make distinctions between the strategies deployed to govern different peoples, they determine these strategies in relation to a finite set of techniques and norms. This limited range of techniques, in turn, circumscribed the possible methods through which historical actors exercised sovereignty. Between the seventeenth and early nineteenth centuries, the archive provided the common vocabulary and shared set of practices through which the British Empire sought to solve the intertwined problems of governing different people differently and of preserving hierarchy across geographical space. No matter where or in relation to whom imperial power was deployed by the state and corporate bodies, that power and its deployment were shaped, facilitated, and constrained by the legitimating regime of records.

In the profoundly heterogeneous and polyglot world of the early modern British Empire, different people were indeed governed differently. Settler colonists were subject to common law. Outside of war, diplomatic agreements and trade structured the interactions among Native Americans, other European empires, and the British imperial state. Those who had come under the compass of imperial authorities by virtue of conquest, such as French Canadians and South Asians, were thought to be governable based on their purported "ancient" constitutions. Underlying the execution of these different governing projects, however, was a widely shared epistemology of administration that tied the authority of claims about how government should be conducted to their grounding in written precedents, contained in archives under the control of official institutions. Difference was understood by administrators according to a political epistemology that came to be applied to the very different peoples and places in which imperial power asserted sovereignty. This was the epistemology of the archive.

Not only did the archival epistemology shape the techniques of rule used by state and corporate bodies; it also structured the methods and languages that critics of empire employed to attack policies and advance alternative visions of how governance should proceed. These critics were enabled by the disjuncture between institutional aspirations to control political knowledge and the constant failure of these aspirations in practice. Governing bodies claimed to exercise the power of determining who had access to official records. They developed protocols to restrict the circulation of knowledge. They prescribed rules as to how documents were to be produced and stored. Yet, these attempts at imposing order on political information were constantly undermined, indeed often by the very same people who were tasked with upholding them. Institutional control of knowledge in the early modern British state and empire was asymptotic: relentlessly pursued by administrative bodies through the prescription and instantiation of routine yet never actually realized in practice.

By the end of the eighteenth century, forms of policy reasoning that were not contingent on reference to written records were beginning to be seen by political observers and eventually administrative institutions themselves as better tools of governance than archival methods. What were the conditions under which this shift occurred? A complete answer to that question exceeds the capacities of this book. It would require its own investigation into the information order of the modern British Empire that emerged in the nineteenth and twentieth centuries, an investigation focused, like this book, on the interface between forms of sovereignty and the political practices through which they are executed. It would also require reckoning with the implications of the expansion of representative democracy, the growing power of Parliament, and the transformation of political media by technological innovations during the nineteenth century for the relationship between administration and information. For now, I have highlighted two developments that are perhaps less obvious than these, and which seem to have contributed to a dwindling practical role for archives in governance and, consequently, enabled the emergence of new technologies of legitimation and administration.

First, there was a shift at the end of the eighteenth century in the meaning of "office," from its early modern conception as a privilege conferred upon the recipient by a sovereign to the idea that office was a service to the public. The consequence of this transformation was an increasing preference to justify policies based on publicly available information, rather than archival records whose control by statesmen and limited circulation were components of their authority. If Crown and corporate sovereigns demanded that officials produce information about what they did, we have seen that this was not just because sovereigns needed information to develop policies but also because they needed information about the conduct of their servants to monitor compliance. But once office was conceived of as a "public trust," the public availability of administrative information became crucial to ensuring that the power conferring it—the public—could monitor whether the trust was being upheld. That imperative for government to proceed on the basis of publicly available information pushed against the logics of the early modern archive: privilege, exclusivity, and secrecy. To be sure, modern imperial government continued to keep secrets and to aspire to hide from view information about its conduct. But in doing so, the modern state acted against public expectations about *bureaucratic* accountability that did not pertain in the early modern conception of *official* accountability.

The second explanation for the archive's diminishing purchase in administration lies in its displacement by other, nonarchival forms of reasoning that came to be considered better suited to the exercise of sovereignty. In a mirror image of the methodological beliefs held by those who advocated making policy on the basis of records, the proponents of these nonarchival epistemologies believed that their methods would produce certain, reliable knowledge that was either of better quality than that which came from archives or better suited to what they considered the particularities of their time. This book has pointed to the distinctive importance of one of these forms of reasoning: the idea that there were underlying principles of politics and economics that did not necessarily need reference to an archive to be known but which decisively controlled how people behaved. These principles, once known, would obviate the need to invoke the past as contained in administrative records as the authority on which policy decisions were made or justified.

What remained even with the shift away from the archival epistemology of administration was the underlying problem imperial sovereigns had used it to solve: how to govern in relation to cultural difference. Modern states continue to grapple with how to bind different people together through projecting norms whose widespread adoption, it is hoped, will help fulfill some vision of what civic harmony looks like. Modern companies also aspire to forge common preferences and desires out of which they can generate profits. Information remains fundamental to both. Increasingly, this information does not take the form of parchment or paper. But the practices of collecting, using, and storing information remain crucial to these aspirations because they allow states and companies to measure how close they are to fulfilling their goals. According to what rules should this information be gathered? How should it be used? Who should have access to it? These questions continue to preoccupy our world, much as they did the strange and remote world of the early modern British Empire. The past is at once more distant and more proximate than we may think.

Notes

Abbreviations

BL   British Library
IOR   India Office Records, Asia, Pacific, and Africa Collections, British Library
NLS   National Library of Scotland
NRS   National Records of Scotland
TNA   National Archives (UK)

Introduction

1. Harold A. Innis, *Empire and Communications,* ed. William J. Buxton (1950; reprint Toronto: University of Toronto Press, 2022).
2. Nicholas Popper, "An Information State for Elizabethan England," *Journal of Modern History* 90, no. 3 (September 2018): 503–535.
3. Noah Millstone, *Manuscript Circulation and the Invention of Politics in Early Stuart England* (Cambridge, UK: Cambridge University Press, 2016).
4. On subaltern experience and the archive, see Ranajit Guha, *Elementary Aspects of Peasant Insurgency in Colonial India* (1983; reprint Durham, N.C.: Duke University Press, 1999), 333; Michel-Rolph Trouillot, *Silencing the Past: Power and the Production of History* (Boston: Beacon Press, 1995); Saidiya Hartman, "Venus in Two Acts," *Small Axe* 26 (2008): 1–14; and Ann Laura Stoler, *Along the Archival Grain: Epistemic Anxieties and Colonial Common Sense* (Princeton, N.J.: Princeton University Press, 2009).
5. Ann Laura Stoler, "Colonial Archives and the Arts of Governance," *Archival Science* 2 (2002): 100.
6. David Armitage, *The Ideological Origins of the British Empire* (Cambridge, UK: Cambridge University Press, 2000).
7. On "styles of reasoning," see Ian Hacking, "'Style' for Historians and Philosophers," in *Historical Ontology* (Cambridge, Mass.: Harvard University Press, 2002), 178–199.
8. For this definition of "bureaucracy," see John Brewer, *The Sinews of Power: War, Money, and the English State, 1688–1783* (Cambridge, Mass.: Harvard University Press, 1989), 77. For explicit arguments that "bureaucracy" should be treated as a heuristic category transcending time and space, see G. E. Aylmer, "Bureaucracy," in *The New Cambridge Modern History: Companion Volume,* ed. Peter Burke (Cambridge, UK: Cambridge University Press, 1979), 13:164–200; and Peter Crooks, "Bureaucracy," in *Information: A Historical Companion,* ed. Ann Blair et al. (Princeton, N.J.: Princeton University Press, 2021), 343–348.
9. On the concept of the "state" in early modern Europe, see Quentin Skinner, "A Genealogy of the Modern State," *Proceedings of the British Academy* 162 (2009): 325–370.

10. Martin Albrow, *Bureaucracy* (London: Macmillan, 1970), 16–18.

11. "Courts of Justice in France," *Times of London,* November 11, 1815.

12. In this respect, J. C. D. Clark was prescient to warn scholars against using "the political vocabulary of democratic society" to interpret an early modern world in which that vocabulary's assumptions were inoperable; see *English Society, 1660–1832: Religion, Ideology and Politics During the Ancien Régime* (1985; reprint Cambridge, UK: Cambridge University Press, 2000), 5. On the origins of the phrase *ancien régime* in the late 1760s in physiocratic critiques of the French monarchy's financial policies, see Joël Félix, "Finances," in *The Oxford Handbook of the Ancien Régime,* ed. William Doyle (Oxford: Oxford University Press, 2012), 75–76.

13. On the vocabulary of "office" in early modern Europe, see Michael J. Braddick, *State Formation in Early Modern England, c. 1550–1700* (Cambridge, UK: Cambridge University Press, 2000), 20–27; Conal Condren, *Argument and Authority in Early Modern England: The Presupposition of Oaths and Offices* (Cambridge, UK: Cambridge University Press, 2006); Alexander B. Haskell, "Deference, Defiance, and the Language of Office in Seventeenth-Century Virginia," in *Early Modern Virginia: Reconsidering the Old Dominion,* ed. Douglas Bradburn and John C. Coombs (Charlottesville: University of Virginia Press, 2011), 158–184; and David Kearns and Ryan Walter, "Office, Political Theory, and the Political Theorist," *Historical Journal* 63 (2020): 317–337. On the transition to a primarily spatial understanding of "office," see Sheila Liming, *Office* (New York: Bloomsbury Academic, 2020), 13–14.

14. Robert L'Estrange, "To the Reader," in *Tully's Offices. In Three Books. Turned Out of Latin into English* (London, 1680). On Cicero and English political thought, see Markku Peltonen, *Classical Humanism and Republicanism in English Political Thought, 1570–1640* (Cambridge, UK: Cambridge University Press, 1995), 1–17.

15. Cicero, *His Offices; or, His Treatise Concerning the Moral Duties of Mankind . . . With Notes Historical and Explanatory. Translated into English by William Guthrie, Esq* (London, 1755), i.

16. Thomas Cockman, *Tully's Three Books of Offices, in English. With Notes Explaining the Method and Meaning of the Author,* 2nd ed. (1699; London, 1706), iii. On early modern rules and rule-making, see Lorraine Daston, *Rules: A Short History of What We Live By* (Princeton, N.J.: Princeton University Press, 2022), chap. 3.

17. D. C. Coleman, *The British Paper Industry, 1495–1860: A Study in Industrial Growth* (Oxford: Clarendon Press, 1958), 9–10; David Finkelstein and Alistair McCleery, *An Introduction to Book History,* 2nd ed. (2005; New York: Routledge, 2013), 35–37; Kathryn James, *English Paleography and Manuscript Culture, 1500–1800* (New Haven, Conn.: Yale University Press, 2020), 29–32.

18. On paper in Europe, see Caroline Fowler, *The Art of Paper: From the Holy Land to the Americas* (New Haven, Conn.: Yale University Press, 2019), 9–14, who observes that while "animal skin could be scraped down and erased," "paper resists erasure, and tears before the writing disappears" (9). On South Asian textual culture, see Graham Shaw, "South Asia," in *A Companion to the History of the Book,* ed. Simon Eliot and Jonathan Rose (Malden, Mass.: Blackwell, 2007), 126–137. Illustrative of the panorama of practices in the American context are the essays

in Matt Cohen and Jeffrey Glover, eds., *Colonial Mediascapes: Sensory Worlds of the Early Americas* (Lincoln: University of Nebraska Press, 2014). See also Céline Carayon, *Eloquence Embodied: Non-Verbal Communication Among French and Indigenous Peoples in the Americas* (Chapel Hill: University of North Carolina Press, 2019).

19. On "negotiation" as an interpretive framework, see Jack P. Greene, "Negotiated Authorities: The Problem of Governance in the Extended Polities of the Early Modern Atlantic World," in *Negotiated Authorities: Essays in Colonial Political and Constitutional History* (Charlottesville: University Press of Virginia, 1994), 1–24. On the limits of central state authority in the early modern world, see Mark Greengrass, ed., *Conquest and Coalescence: The Shaping of the State in Early Modern Europe* (London: E. Arnold, 1991); Charles Tilly, "Reflections on the History of European State-Making," in *The Formation of National States in Western Europe,* ed. Charles Tilly (Princeton, N.J.: Princeton University Press, 1975), 21–46; and J. H. Elliott, "A Europe of Composite Monarchies," *Past and Present* 137 (1992): 48–71.

20. See Brian Owensby, *Empire of Law and Indian Justice in Colonial Mexico* (Stanford, Calif.: Stanford University Press, 2008); Lisa Ford, *Settler Sovereignty: Jurisdiction and Indigenous People in America and Australia, 1788–1836* (Cambridge, Mass.: Harvard University Press, 2010); Tamar Herzog, *Frontiers of Possession: Spain and Portugal in Europe and the Americas* (Cambridge, Mass.: Harvard University Press, 2015); and Hannah Weiss Muller, *Subjects and Sovereign: Bonds of Belonging in the Eighteenth-Century British Empire* (New York: Oxford University Press, 2017).

21. The study of the problem of cultural difference in European political thought is now a robust endeavor; see, in particular, Anthony Pagden, *Lords of All the World: Ideologies of Empire in Spain, Britain, and France, 1500–1850* (New Haven, Conn.: Yale University Press, 1995); Uday Singh Mehta, *Liberalism and Empire: A Study in Nineteenth-Century British Liberal Thought* (Chicago: University of Chicago Press, 1999); Roxann Wheeler, *The Complexions of Race: Categories of Difference in Eighteenth-Century British Culture* (Philadelphia: University of Pennsylvania Press, 2000); Sankar Muthu, *Enlightenment Against Empire* (Princeton, N.J.: Princeton University Press, 2003); and Jennifer Pitts, *A Turn to Empire: The Rise of Liberal Imperialism in Britain and France* (Princeton, N.J.: Princeton University Press, 2005).

22. For this account of "paperwork," see Ben Kafka, *The Demon of Writing: Powers and Failures of Paperwork* (Cambridge, Mass.: MIT Press, 2012). It is also notable that many of the documents that early modern Europeans considered most important for government, such as charters, were quite literally not "paperwork" since they were written on parchment, not paper.

23. On "efficiency," see Jennifer Karns Alexander, *The Mantra of Efficiency: From Waterwheel to Social Control* (Baltimore: Johns Hopkins University Press, 2008); on "agency," see Jessica Riskin, *The Restless Clock: A History of the Centuries-Long Argument over What Makes Living Things Tick* (Chicago: University of Chicago Press, 2016); and on "freedom," see Annelien de Dijn, *Freedom: An Unruly History* (Cambridge, Mass.: Harvard University Press, 2020).

24. See "record, n.1 and adj.," *Oxford English Dictionary Online*, March 2023, https:// www.oed.com/view/Entry/159867.

25. See "archive, n.," *Oxford English Dictionary Online*, March 2023, https://www .oed.com/view/Entry/10416.

26. On the emergence of archival government in Europe, see Arndt Brendecke, "'Arca, Archivillo, Archivo': The Keeping, Use and Status of Historical Documents About the Spanish Conquista," *Archival Science* 10, no. 3 (September 2010): 267–283, esp. 268; M. T. Clanchy, *From Memory to Written Record: England, 1066–1307*, 3rd ed. (1979; Malden, Mass.: Blackwell, 2013); and Randolph C. Head, *Making Archives in Early Modern Europe: Proof, Information, and Political Record-Keeping, 1400–1700* (Cambridge, UK: Cambridge University Press, 2019). On the expansion of information-gathering and systems of collection, storage, and classification in the early modern period, see the syntheses by Peter Burke, *A Social History of Knowledge: From Gutenberg to Diderot* (Cambridge, UK: Polity Press, 2000); Daniel R. Headrick, *When Information Came of Age: Technologies of Knowledge in the Age of Reason and Revolution, 1700–1850* (Oxford: Oxford University Press, 2000); and Paul M. Dover, *The Information Revolution in Early Modern Europe* (Cambridge, UK: Cambridge University Press, 2021).

27. See W. H. Greenleaf, *Order, Empiricism, and Politics: Two Traditions of English Political Thought, 1500–1700* (Oxford: Oxford University Press, 1964), chap. 9; Noah Millstone, "Seeing Like a Statesman in Early Stuart England," *Past and Present* 223 (May 2014): 77–127; and Popper, "An Information State for Elizabethan England." On the connected development of modes of disciplining scientific observation in early modern Europe, see Justin Stagl, *A History of Curiosity: The Theory of Travel, 1550–1800* (1995; reprint London: Routledge, 2004); Joan-Pau Rubiés, "Instructions for Travellers: Teaching the Eye to See," *History and Anthropology* 9, nos. 2–3 (1996): 139–190; Daniel Carey, "Compiling Nature's History: Travellers and Travel Narratives in the Early Royal Society," *Annals of Science* 54, no. 3 (1997): 269–292; Matthew Carl Underwood, "Ordering Knowledge, Re-Ordering Empire: Science and State Formation in the English Atlantic World, 1650–1688" (Ph.D. diss., Harvard University, 2010), chap. 4; Jacob Soll, "From Note-Taking to Data Banks: Personal and Institutional Information Management in Early Modern Europe," *Intellectual History Review* 20 (2010): 363–365; Elizabeth Yale, "Making Lists: Social and Material Technologies for Seventeenth-Century British Natural History," in *Ways of Making and Knowing: The Material Culture of Empirical Knowledge, 1400–1850,* ed. Pamela H. Smith, Amy Meyers, and Harold Cook (Ann Arbor: University of Michigan, Press, 2014), 280–301; and Vera Keller, *Knowledge and the Public Interest, 1575–1725* (Cambridge, UK: Cambridge University Press, 2015), 230–240.

28. William J. Bulman, "The Practice of Politics: The English Civil War and the 'Resolution' of Henrietta Maria and Charles I," *Past and Present* 206 (2010): 44–79; Millstone, "Seeing Like a Statesman"; Millstone, *Manuscript Circulation and the Invention of Politics in Early Stuart England,* 10–12.

29. The methods applied in this book to making sense of how meanings and practices of "politics" make political history are inspired by the project of historians of science to define themselves as historians of "knowledge" to account for the

multiplicity of ways in which people have sought to know, "however remote they may be from anything resembling latter-day science." See Lorraine Daston, "The History of Science and the History of Knowledge," *KNOW: A Journal on the Formation of Knowledge* 1 (2017): 143.

30. For a concise discussion, see H. R. Woudhuysen, *Sir Philip Sidney and the Circulation of Manuscripts, 1558–1640* (Oxford: Oxford University Press, 1996), 66–71. On the formation of the Privy Council, the classic account is G. R. Elton, *The Tudor Revolution in Government: Administrative Changes in the Reign of Henry VIII* (Cambridge, UK: Cambridge University Press, 1959), chap. 5.

31. J. C. Sainty, *Office-Holders in Modern Britain*, vol. 3, *Officials of the Boards of Trade, 1660–1870* (London: Athlone Press, 1974), 3–6, 28–37. See also Oliver Morton Dickerson, *American Colonial Government, 1696–1765: A Study of the British Board of Trade in Its Relation to the American Colonies, Political, Industrial, Administrative* (Cleveland: Arthur H. Clark, 1912), 68–79.

32. J. C. Sainty, *Office-Holders in Modern Britain*, vol. 2, *Officials of the Secretaries of State, 1660–1782* (London: Athlone Press, 1973), 59–62; J. C. Sainty, *Office-Holders in Modern Britain*, vol. 1, *Treasury Officials, 1660–1870* (London: Athlone Press, 1972). For detailed discussions of the organizations of other offices with jurisdiction over overseas affairs, see J. C. Sainty, *Office-Holders in Modern Britain*, vol. 4, *Admiralty Officials, 1660–1870* (London: Athlone Press, 1975), and J. C. Sainty, *Office-Holders in Modern Britain*, vol. 7, *Navy Board Officials, 1660–1832* (London: Athlone Press, 1978).

33. On the organization of government in English America, see Leonard Woods Labaree, *Royal Government in America: A Study of the British Colonial System Before 1783* (New Haven, Conn.: Yale University Press, 1930); Jack P. Greene, *The Quest for Power: The Lower Houses of Assembly in the Southern Royal Colonies, 1689–1776* (Chapel Hill: University of North Carolina Press, 1963); Jack P. Greene, *Peripheries and Center: Constitutional Development in the Extended Polities of the British Empire and the United States, 1607–1788* (Athens: University of Georgia Press, 1986); John Murrin, "Political Development," in *Colonial British America: Essays in the New History of the Early Modern Era,* ed. Jack P. Greene and J. R. Pole (Baltimore: Johns Hopkins University Press, 1984), 442–445; Bruce C. Daniels, ed., *Town and Country: Essays on the Structure of Local Government in the American Colonies* (Middletown, Conn.: Wesleyan University Press, 1978); David Grayson Allen, *In English Ways: The Movement of Societies and the Transferal of English Local Law and Custom to Massachusetts Bay in the Seventeenth Century* (Chapel Hill: University of North Carolina Press, 1981); Bruce C. Daniels, ed., *Power and Status: Officeholding in Colonial America* (Middletown, Conn.: Wesleyan University Press, 1986); and Brian P. Janiskee, *Local Government in Early America: The Colonial Experience and Lessons from the Frontiers* (New York: Rowman and Littlefield, 2010).

34. On the patent and the structure of the company, see Rupali Mishra, *A Business of State: Commerce, Politics, and the Birth of the East India Company* (Cambridge, Mass.: Harvard University Press, 2018), 25–34.

35. See Mishra, *A Business of State,* 37–46.

36. On the company's factories and the development of its Asian trade, see, within a vast literature, Om Prakash, "The European Trading Companies and the Merchants of

Bengal 1650–1725," *Indian Economic and Social History Review* 1 (1964): 37–63; Susil Chaudhuri, *Trade and Commercial Organization in Bengal, 1650–1720* (Calcutta: K. L. Mukhopadhyay, 1975); and K. N. Chaudhuri, *The Trading World of Asia and the English East India Company, 1660–1760* (Cambridge, UK: Cambridge University Press, 1978), chap. 3.

37. Matthew S. Hull, *Government of Paper: The Materiality of Bureaucracy in Urban Pakistan* (Berkeley: University of California Press, 2012), 8.

38. Bhavani Raman, *Document Raj: Writing and Scribes in Early Colonial South India* (Chicago: University of Chicago Press, 2012), 8–9.

39. Compare Ian K. Steele, *The English Atlantic, 1675–1740: An Exploration of Communication and Community* (New York: Oxford University Press, 1986), chap. 9, with Jean Sutton, *Lords of the East: The East India Company and Its Ships* (1981; reprint London: Conway Maritime Press, 2000). For an excellent visualization of the temporal and geographic dimensions of these communication networks, see "Map 1.3 Imperial Communications," in *The Oxford History of the British Empire,* vol. 2, *The Eighteenth Century,* ed. P. J. Marshall (Oxford: Oxford University Press, 1998), 13.

40. H. V. Bowen, *The Business of Empire: The East India Company and Imperial Britain, 1758–1833* (Cambridge, UK: Cambridge University Press, 2006), 154–157.

41. Jordan E. Taylor, "Now Is the Winter of Our Dull Content: Seasonality and the Atlantic Communications Frontier in Eighteenth-Century New England," *New England Quarterly* 95 (2022): 8–38.

42. For discussions, see Clanchy, *From Memory to Written Record,* 122–127; Guglielmo Cavallo, "Book Manuscript, Production," trans. Patrick Baker, in *The Classical Tradition,* ed. Anthony Grafton, Glenn W. Most, and Salvatore Settis (Cambridge, Mass.: Harvard University Press, 2010), 139–142; and Frederick Bearman, "Parchment Booklets, the Royal Wardrobe and the Italian Connection: How the Parchment Booklet Was Adopted as an Administrative Tool in England During the Reign of King Edward I and Edward II (1272–1327)," in *Care and Conservation of Manuscripts 15: Proceedings of the Fifteenth International Seminar Held at the University of Copenhagen 2nd–4th April 2014,* ed. M. J. Driscoll (Copenhagen: Museum Tusculanum Press, 2016), 329–346.

43. Orietta Da Rold, *Paper in Medieval England: From Pulp to Fictions* (Cambridge, UK: Cambridge University Press, 2020), chap. 2. For further discussion of paper sizes, see Paul Needham, "The Study of Paper from an Archival Point of View," *International Paper History Yearbook* 7 (1988): 126; and Robin Kinross, *A4 and Before: Towards a Long History of Paper Sizes* (Wassenaar: Netherlands Institute for Advanced Study in the Humanities and Social Sciences, 2009).

44. Coleman, *British Paper Industry,* 40–49; John Bidwell, "French Paper in English Books," in *The Cambridge History of the Book in Britain,* vol. 4, *1557–1695,* ed. John Barnard and D. F. McKenzie (Cambridge, UK: Cambridge University Press, 2002), 583–601; Martyn Ould, "The Workplace: Places, Procedures, and Personnel, 1668–1780," in *The History of Oxford University Press,* vol. 1, *Beginnings to 1780,* ed. Ian Gadd (Oxford: Oxford University Press, 2013), 206–212. My account of papermaking is drawn from John Gagné, "Paper World: The Materiality of Loss in the Pre-Modern Age," in *Approaches to the History of Written Culture:*

A World Inscribed, ed. Martin Lyons and Rita Marquilhas (New York: Palgrave Macmillan, 2017), 57-58; and Dover, *The Information Revolution in Early Modern Europe,* chap. 2.

45. Answers to "Queries Respecting the Patents for Serving the Excise Office with Stationary [*sic*] Wares," July 18, 1770, T 1/475, TNA. See also Woudhuysen, *Sir Philip Sidney and the Circulation of Manuscripts,* 45-52.

46. On the founding of the Stationery Office, see J. J. Cherns, *Official Publishing: An Overview* (Oxford: Pergamon Press, 1979), 245-248; and Hugh Barty-King, *Her Majesty's Stationery Office: The Story of the First 200 Years, 1786-1986* (London: Stationery Office, 1986).

47. John Bidwell, "Printers' Supplies and Capitalization," in *A History of the Book in America,* vol. 1, *The Colonial Book in the Atlantic World,* ed. Hugh Amory and David D. Hall (Chapel Hill: University of North Carolina Press, 2007), 163-183.

48. Roderick Cave, "Early Printing and the Book Trade in the West Indies," *Library Quarterly* 48 (1978): 163-192.

49. Anant Kakba Priolkar, *The Printing Press in India: Its Beginnings and Early Development* (Mumbai: Marahty Samshodana Mandala, 1958); Indrajit Ray, *The Development of Modern Industries in Bengal: ReIndustrialisation, 1858-1914* (London: Taylor and Francis, 2018), chap. 6; Graham Shaw, "South Asia," in *The Oxford Illustrated History of the Book,* ed. James Raven (Oxford: Oxford University Press, 2020), 274.

50. Eric H. Ash, *Power, Knowledge, and Expertise in Elizabethan England* (Baltimore: Johns Hopkins University Press, 2004); Eric H. Ash et al., "Expertise: Practical Knowledge and the Early Modern State," *Osiris* 25 (2010): 1-262; Nicholas Popper, *Walter Ralegh's* History of the World *and the Historical Culture of the Late Renaissance* (Chicago: University of Chicago Press, 2012); Thomas Leng, "Epistemology: Expertise and Knowledge in the World of Commerce," in *Mercantilism Reimagined: Political Economy in Early Modern Britain and Its Empire,* ed. Philip J. Stern and Carl Wennerlind (New York: Oxford University Press, 2014), 97-116; Keller, *Knowledge and the Public Interest;* Paul Slack, *The Invention of Improvement: Information and Material Progress in Seventeenth-Century England* (Oxford: Oxford University Press, 2015); Elaine Leong, *Recipes and Everyday Knowledge: Medicine, Science, and the Household in Early Modern England* (Chicago: University of Chicago Press, 2018); Tim Riding, "Managing Expertise: The Problem of Engineers in the English East India Company, 1668-1764," *Itinerario* 45 (2021): 228-251.

51. See especially Simon Schaffer et al., eds., *The Brokered World: Go-Betweens and Global Intelligence, 1770-1820* (Sagamore Beach, Mass.: Science History, 2009); Anna Winterbottom, *Hybrid Knowledge in the Early East India Company World* (London: Palgrave Macmillan, 2016); Pablo F. Gómez, *The Experiential Caribbean: Creating Knowledge and Healing in the Early Modern Atlantic* (Chapel Hill: University of North Carolina Press, 2017); Marcy Norton, "Subaltern Technologies and Early Modernity in the Atlantic World," *Colonial Latin American Review* 26 (2017): 18-38; Alison Margaret Bigelow, *Mining Language: Racial Thinking, Indigenous Knowledge, and Colonial Metallurgy in the Early Modern Iberian World* (Chapel Hill: University of North Carolina Press, 2020); and Kalle

Kananoja, *Healing Knowledge in Atlantic Africa: Medical Encounters, 1500–1850* (Cambridge, UK: Cambridge University Press, 2021).

52. On this approach, see Vincent T. Harlow, *The Founding of the Second British Empire, 1763–1793,* 2 vols. (London: Longmans, 1952, 1964); and for an effort to revive the geographically integrative aspects of Harlow's framework while revising his distinction between a first and second empire, see P. J. Marshall, *The Making and Unmaking of Empires: Britain, India, and America, c. 1750–1783* (Oxford: Oxford University Press, 2007). On the distinction between trade and conquest in the historiography of the early modern British Empire, see Philip J. Stern, *The Company-State: Corporate Sovereignty and the Early Modern Foundations of the British Empire in India* (Oxford: Oxford University Press, 2011), 4–7.

53. See, for example, A. L. Rowse, *The Expansion of Elizabethan England* (1955; reprint Madison: University of Wisconsin Press, 2003); Theodore K. Rabb, *Enterprise and Empire: Merchant and Gentry Investment in the Expansion of England, 1575–1620* (Cambridge, Mass.: Harvard University Press, 1967); Kenneth R. Andrews, *Trade, Plunder, and Settlement: Maritime Enterprise and the Genesis of the British Empire, 1480–1630* (Cambridge, UK: Cambridge University Press, 1984); Robert Brenner, *Merchants and Revolution: Commercial Change, Political Conflict, and London's Overseas Traders, 1550–1653* (1993; reprint New York: Verso, 2003); Alison Games, *The Web of Empire: English Cosmopolitans in an Age of Expansion, 1560–1600* (New York: Oxford University Press, 2008); and Edward E. Andrews, "Tranquebar: Charting the Protestant International in the British Atlantic and Beyond," *William and Mary Quarterly,* 3rd series, 74 (2017): 3–34.

54. Rabb, *Enterprise and Empire,* esp. 108; Alison Games, *Migration and the Origins of the English Atlantic World* (Cambridge, Mass.: Harvard University Press, 1999), 35–37.

55. Narratives of empire published after Harlow's that stress a metropolitan perspective while attending to dynamics across oceanic geographies include Marshall, *Making and Unmaking of Empires;* P. J. Marshall, *Remaking the British Atlantic: The United States and the British Empire After American Independence* (Oxford: Oxford University Press, 2012); and James M. Vaughn, *The Politics of Empire at the Accession of George III: The East India Company and the Transformation of Britain's Imperial State* (New Haven, Conn.: Yale University Press, 2019).

56. Steven Pincus, Tiraana Bains, and A. Zuercher Reichardt, "Thinking the Empire Whole," *History Australia* 16 (2019): 610. This call is not new: see, for example, Philip J. Stern, "British Asia and British Atlantic: Comparisons and Connections," *William and Mary Quarterly,* 3rd series, 63 (2006): 693–712.

57. In this regard, studies such as Carl H. Nightingale, "Before Race Mattered: Geographies of the Color Line in Early Colonial Madras and New York," *American Historical Review* 113 (2008): 48–71; and Kathleen Wilson, "Rethinking the Colonial State: Family, Gender, and Governmentality in Eighteenth-Century British Frontiers," *American Historical Review* 116 (2011): 1294–1322, are exemplary.

58. This is not to deny the importance of ideas of India and Indian goods in the making of the British Atlantic world; see Jonathan Eacott, *Selling Empire: India in the Making of Britain and America, 1600–1830* (Chapel Hill: University of North Carolina Press, 2016).

59. See, for example, Linda Colley, *Captives: Britain, Empire, and the World, 1600–1850* (New York: Pantheon, 2002); Randy L. Sparks, *The Two Princes of Calabar: An Eighteenth-Century Atlantic Odyssey* (Cambridge, Mass.: Harvard University Press, 2004); Games, *Web of Empire;* Miles Ogborn, *Global Lives: Britain and the World, 1550–1800* (Cambridge, UK: Cambridge University Press, 2008); Maya Jasanoff, *Liberty's Exiles: American Loyalists in the Revolutionary World* (New York: Knopf, 2011); Emma Rothschild, *The Inner Life of Empires: An Eighteenth-Century History* (Princeton, N.J.: Princeton University Press, 2011); and João José Reis, Flavio dos Santos Gomes, and Marcus J. M. de Carvalho, *The Story of Rufino: Slavery, Freedom, and Islam in the Black Atlantic,* trans. H. Sabrina Gledhill (2010; reprint New York: Oxford University Press, 2020).

60. No matter how divergent and heterogenous their conclusions, the concept of political economy as a vector of analytical linkage among the different geographic regions of empire undergirds classic accounts of British imperial state formation such as Harlow, *Founding of the Second British Empire;* Andre Gunder Frank, *World Accumulation, 1492–1789* (New York: Monthly Review Press, 1978); and Immanuel Wallerstein, *The Modern World-System,* vol. 2, *Mercantilism and the Consolidation of the European World Economy, 1600–1750* (New York: Academic Press, 1980), as well as more recent accounts, such as Eacott, *Selling Empire;* James Vernon, *Modern Britain, 1750 to the Present* (Cambridge, UK: Cambridge University Press, 2017); and Pincus, Bains, and Reichardt, "Thinking the Empire Whole," esp. 612. Political economy is also the central analytical category of the leading frameworks for understanding "modern" British imperial expansion; see John Gallagher and Ronald Robinson, "The Imperialism of Free Trade," *Economic History Review,* 2nd series, 4 (1953): 1–15; and P. J. Cain and A. G. Hopkins, "The Political Economy of British Expansion Overseas, 1750–1914," *Economic History Review,* 2nd series, 33 (1980): 463–490.

61. Benjamin L. Carp, *Defiance of the Patriots: The Boston Tea Party and the Making of America* (New Haven, Conn.: Yale University Press, 2010); Eacott, *Selling Empire;* Elizabeth Cross, "The Last French East India Company in the Revolutionary Atlantic," *William and Mary Quarterly,* 3rd series, 77 (2020): 613–640.

62. Asheesh Kapur Siddique, "The Archival Epistemology of Political Economy in the Early Modern British Atlantic World," *William and Mary Quarterly,* 3rd series, 77 (2020): 641–674.

63. On the "economy," see Jacob Soll, "For a New Economic History of Early Modern Empire: Anglo-French Imperial Codevelopment Beyond Mercantilism and Laissez-Faire," *William and Mary Quarterly,* 3rd series, 77 (2020): 525–550.

Chapter 1. Animating Imperial Bodies

1. Edmund Burke, "Speech on Conciliation with America," March 22, 1775, in *The Writings and Speeches of Edmund Burke,* vol. 3, *Party, Parliament and the American War, 1774–1780,* ed. W. M. Elofson and John A. Woods (Oxford: Oxford University Press, 1996), 124–125, 136, 165.

2. Minutes of the Court of Directors, March 21, 1787, 1095, IOR/B/104; *Articles of Charge of High Crime and Misdemeanors, Against Warren Hastings, Esq. Late*

Governor General of Bengal; Presented to the House of Commons, on the 4th Day of April, 1786, by the Right Hon. Edmund Burke (London, 1786), front page, 32. On Hastings's trial, the classic account is P. J. Marshall, *The Impeachment of Warren Hastings* (Oxford: Oxford University Press, 1965).

3. For Burke's career as a colonial agent, see Richard Bourke, *Empire and Revolution: The Political Life of Edmund Burke* (Princeton, N.J.: Princeton University Press, 2015), chap. 6.

4. On the overlap between private interest and the executive of administrative function, see Michael G. Kammen, *A Rope of Sand: The Colonial Agents, British Politics, and the American Revolution* (Ithaca, N.Y.: Cornell University Press, 1968); Alison Gilbert Olson, *Making the Empire Work: London and American Interest Groups, 1690–1790* (Cambridge, Mass.: Harvard University Press, 1992); and Mark Goldie, "The Unacknowledged Republic: Officeholding in Early Modern England," in *The Politics of the Excluded, c. 1500–1850*, ed. Tim Harris (Basingstoke, UK: Palgrave Macmillan, 2001), 153–194.

5. See G. R. Elton, *The Tudor Revolution in Government: A Study of Administrative Changes in the Reign of Henry VIII* (Cambridge, UK: Cambridge University Press, 1959).

6. Maurizio Viroli, *From Politics to Reason of State: The Acquisition and Transformation of the Language of Politics, 1250–1600* (Cambridge, UK: Cambridge University Press, 1992); Nicolai Rubinstein, "The History of the Word *Politicus* in Early-Modern Europe," in *The Languages of Political Theory in Early-Modern Europe*, ed. Anthony Pagden (Cambridge, UK: Cambridge University Press, 1987), esp. 54–56.

7. On the English context, see W. H. Greenleaf, *Order, Empiricism, and Politics: Two Traditions of English Political Thought, 1500–1700* (Oxford: Oxford University Press, 1964), chap. 9; Noah Millstone, "Seeing Like a Statesman in Early Stuart England," *Past and Present* 223 (May 2014): 77–127; Nicholas Popper, "An Information State for Elizabethan England," *Journal of Modern History* 90, no. 3 (September 2018): 503–535; and Popper, *The Specter of the Archive: Political Practice and the Information State in Early Modern Britain* (Chicago: University of Chicago Press, 2024). Scholarship on comparable developments in early modern continental Europe and its empires is summarized in Jacob Soll, "Introduction: The Uses of Historical Evidence in Early Modern Europe," *Journal of the History of Ideas* 64, no. 2 (April 2003): 149–157; and Maria Pia Donato, "Introduction: Archives, Record Keeping and Imperial Governance, 1500–1800," *Journal of Early Modern History* 22, no. 5 (October 2018): 311–326. Accounts of the overlap between administrative and personal archives in early modern Europe include Peter N. Miller, *Peiresc's Europe: Learning and Virtue in the Seventeenth Century* (New Haven, Conn.: Yale University Press, 2000), esp. chap. 3; Kevin Sharpe, "Re-Writing Sir Robert Cotton: Politics and History in Early Stuart England" (1997), in *Remapping Early Modern England: The Culture of Seventeenth-Century Politics* (Cambridge, UK: Cambridge University Press, 2000), 294–341, esp. 314–315; and Jacob Soll, *The Information Master: Jean-Baptiste Colbert's Secret State Intelligence System* (Ann Arbor: University of Michigan Press, 2009).

8. On corporations as architects of colonial projects in the British world, see Philip J. Stern, *Empire, Incorporated: The Corporations That Build British Colonialism*

(Cambridge, Mass.: Harvard University Press, 2023). On the complexities of corporate jurisdiction in the early English Empire, see Philip J. Stern, *The Company-State: Corporate Sovereignty and the Early Modern Foundations of the British Empire in India* (Oxford: Oxford University Press, 2011), chap. 2; Rupali Mishra, *A Business of State: Commerce, Politics, and the Birth of the East India Company* (Cambridge, Mass.: Harvard University Press, 2018); and David Veevers, *The Origins of the British Empire in Asia, 1600–1750* (Cambridge, UK: Cambridge University Press, 2020).

9. On corporate recordkeeping and secrecy, see generally Joseph P. Ward, *Metropolitan Communities: Trade Guilds, Identity, and Change in Early Modern London* (Stanford, Calif.: Stanford University Press, 1997), 86–91. On the strategic use of archives by corporations to achieve specific policy or political objectives, see, for example, Jennifer Bishop, "The Clerk's Tale: Civic Writing in Sixteenth-Century London," in *The Social History of the Archive: Record-Keeping in Early Modern Europe,* ed. Liesbeth Corens, Kate Peters, and Alexandra Walsham (Oxford: Oxford University Press, 2018), 112–130.

10. For the importance of ideas of royal control to the growth of the early modern English Empire, see Ken MacMillan, *Sovereignty and Possession in the English New World: The Legal Foundations of Empire, 1576–1640* (Cambridge, UK: Cambridge University Press, 2006), chap. 3; Paul D. Halliday, *Habeas Corpus: From England to Empire* (Cambridge, Mass.: Harvard University Press, 2010), chap. 3; and Zach Bates, "The Idea of Royal Empire and the Imperial Crown of England, 1542–1698," *Journal of the History of Ideas* 80, no. 1 (January 2019): 25–46.

11. "Order for Bringing in Books &c.," May 22, 1623, CO 5/1354, fols. 206–207, TNA; Henry Montagu, Lord Mandeville, to Secretary Edward Conway, enclosing "Orders Sett down at a Meeting of the Commissioners for Virginia," July 16, 1624, CO 1/3, fol. 68, TNA. On the constitutional implications of the failure of the Virginia Company, see A. Berriedale Keith, *Constitutional History of the First British Empire* (Oxford: Clarendon Press, 1930), 18–26.

12. Charles McLean Andrews, *Guide to the Materials for American History, to 1783, in the Public Record Office of Great Britain,* vol. 1, *The State Papers* (Washington, D.C.: Carnegie Institution, 1912), 103–104; Charles Higham, *The Colonial Entry-Books: A Brief Guide to the Colonial Records in the Public Record Office Before 1696* (New York: Macmillan, 1921), 11–12.

13. On these committees, see Kathryn Anne Walker, "An English Empire of Law: Plantation Councils and the Atlantic Origins of the Imperial Constitution" (Ph.D. diss., New York University, 2016).

14. "Commission for Dissolving the Councill for Trade and Plantations," 1675, 1, CO 391/1, TNA.

15. For the order, see Minutes of the Committee of Trade and Plantations, March 13, 1675, 7, CO 391/1, TNA; and Minutes of the Committee of Trade and Plantations, March 12, 1675, CO 1/34, TNA.

16. Minutes of the Committee of Trade and Plantations, March 18, 1675, 10, CO 391/1, TNA.

17. See Minutes of the Privy Council, December 10, 1679, 311, PC 2/68, TNA, ordering "that the Severall Bundles of Papers concerning Trade & forreigne Plantations

lying in the Councill office be Lodged in the Office of the Committee of the Councill of Trade and forreigne Plantations, and that a List of them be Left in the hands of the Clerke of the Councill in wayting; That they may be ready for the Service of the Councill and that Committee upon all Occasions."

18. Minutes of the Committee of Trade and Plantations, July 11, 1676, 163, CO 391/1, TNA.

19. Minutes of the Committee of Trade and Plantations, May 24, 1675, 24, CO 391/1, TNA.

20. Minutes of the Committee of Trade and Plantations, September 24, 1675, 39, CO 391/1, TNA.

21. Hubert Hall, *Studies in English Official Historical Documents* (Cambridge, UK: Cambridge University Press, 1908), 132-133; Alan Marshall, "Sir Joseph Williamson and the Conduct of Administration in Restoration England," *Historical Research* 69, no. 168 (1996): 18-41. On the rise of the State Paper Office as the central archive of the English monarchy, see Nicholas Popper, "From Abbey to Archive: Managing Texts and Records in Early Modern England," *Archival Science* 10, no. 3 (2010): 249-266. On Blathwayt's organization of the Board of Trade's papers and his connection to Williamson, see Gertrude Ann Jacobsen, *William Blathwayt: A Late Seventeenth Century English Administrator* (New Haven, Conn.: Yale University Press, 1932), 67-95. Popper, *Specter of the Archive,* 229-235.

22. See "List of Papers Relating to Trade and Foreign Plantations, Taken of the Bundles Lying in ye Council Chambers, and Lodged in ye Plantation Office Pursuant to an Order of Council Dated the 10th of December 1679," May 6, 1680, PC 1/3128, TNA; Andrews, *Guide to the Materials for American History,* 1:esp. 104; Higham, *Colonial Entry-Books,* 16-18.

23. See, for example, "Charters and Entries Relating to Bermuda," including a copy of the Bermuda charter of June 29, 1615, 1-16, and "An Index Containing the Titles of Such Papers, Concerning ye Bermuda or Somers-Islands Company & as Are Enterd in This Book," CO 38/1, TNA; Barbados Entry Book, 1627-1669, including "Index to What Is Contained in This Book," CO 29/1, TNA; and Leeward Islands Entry Book, 1670-1671, including "A Table of Entries into This Booke," CO 153/1, TNA. See also the collection of indexes cut out of original volumes of colonial papers in OBS 1/866, TNA.

24. See, for example, "Entries for Bermuda Papers, Vol: 2.d," including "Index of ye Entrys in This Book," CO 38/2, TNA; "Entry of Papers Relating to Barbados," including "An Index Containing the Heads of All the Papers Entred in This Booke of Barbados," CO 29/2, TNA; and "Entries of Papers Relating to the Leeward Islands," including "Index Containing Heads of All the Papers Entred in This Booke," CO 153/2, TNA.

25. "Instructions for the Councill of Trade," [1660], fol. 268, Egerton MS 2395, BL. See also "Instruccons for the Councill of Trade," n.d. (ca. 1660), fol. 269, Egerton MS 2395, BL.

26. For a detailed discussion of these developments, see Asheesh Kapur Siddique, "Governance Through Documents: The Board of Trade, Its Archive, and the Imperial Constitution of the Eighteenth-Century British Atlantic World," *Journal of British Studies* 59, no. 2 (April 2020): 264-290.

27. For the implications of these challenges to the Crown's supremacy in the imperial constitution, see J. M. Sosin, *English America and the Revolution of 1688: Royal Administration and the Structure of Provincial Government* (Lincoln: University of Nebraska Press, 1982), esp. chap. 6. On the constitutional implications of the Navigation Acts, see Jack P. Greene, *The Constitutional Origins of the American Revolution* (Cambridge, UK: Cambridge University Press, 2011), 36-39.

28. Commission to Board of Trade, May 15, 1696, 3-4, CO 391/9, TNA. For the establishment of the board and its administrative powers, see Oliver Morton Dickerson, *American Colonial Government, 1696-1765: A Study of the British Board of Trade in Its Relation to the American Colonies, Political, Industrial, Administrative* (Cleveland: Arthur H. Clark, 1912), 130; Arthur Herbert Basye, *The Lords Commissioners of Trade and Plantations Commonly Known as the Board of Trade* (New Haven, Conn.: Yale University Press, 1925), 61; R. M. Lees, "Parliament and the Proposal for a Council of Trade, 1695-6," *English Historical Review* 54, no. 213 (1939): 38-66; I. K. Steele, *Politics of Colonial Policy: The Board of Trade in Colonial Administration, 1696-1720* (New York: Oxford University Press, 1968), 10-18; Peter Laslett, "John Locke, the Great Recoinage, and the Origins of the Board of Trade: 1695-1698," *William and Mary Quarterly*, 3rd series, 14, no. 3 (1957): 370-402; and Perry Gauci, *The Politics of Trade: The Overseas Merchant in State and Society, 1660-1720* (Oxford: Oxford University Press, 2003), 180-193.

29. Journal of the Board of Trade, June 25, 1696, 7, CO 391/9, TNA. On Popple's appointment to the board, see Caroline Robbins, "Absolute Liberty: The Life and Thought of William Popple, 1638-1708," *William and Mary Quarterly*, 3rd series, 24, no. 2 (1967): 210-212.

30. Journal of the Board of Trade, July 1, 1696, 8, CO 391/9, TNA.

31. Journal of the Board of Trade, July 3, 1696, 9, CO 391/9, TNA.

32. Popple's books listing the board's papers, c. 1696, CO 326/1, TNA.

33. Journal of the Board of Trade, December 22, 1699, 302, CO 391/12, TNA.

34. Andrews, *Guide to the Materials for American History*, 1:104-106.

35. General Index to Trade Papers, CO 326/2, TNA. For indexes for particular bound volumes, see, for example, CO 1/66, TNA.

36. See, for example, Subject Index to Trade Papers, CO 326/3, TNA, covering papers from 1696 to 1714 and subsequent volumes in this series, including "Plantation Office General Index Continued from the Accession of King George 1st in 1714," CO 326/4, TNA. The dates of creation are unclear but must be from about 1714. A "General Index" to Plantation Office records from 1696 to 1714 was also created around this time; see "Plantation Office General Index from Its First Establishment, in 1696, to the Accession of King George the 1st in 1714," CO 326/5, TNA.

37. "Orders & Instructions to Francis Nicholson Esqr. His Majesties Lieutenant and Governor Generall of His Majesty's Colony and Dominion of Virginia in America, and in His Absence to the Lieutenant Governour or Commander in Chief of the Said Colony for the Time Being in Pursuance of Severall Lawes Relateing to the Trade and Navigation of This His Majesties Kingdome of England and His Majesties Colonys and Plantations in America," 1698, 421, PC 5/1, TNA. On instructions in early modern European administrative and intellectual cultures,

see Garrett Mattingly, *Renaissance Diplomacy* (Boston: Houghton Mifflin, 1955), 40–43; Joan-Pau Rubiés, "Instructions for Travellers: Teaching the Eye to See," *History and Anthropology* 9, nos. 2–3 (1996): 139–190; Daniel Carey, "Compiling Nature's History: Travellers and Travel Narratives in the Early Royal Society," *Annals of Science* 54, no. 3 (1997): 269–292; Matthew Carl Underwood, "Ordering Knowledge, Re-Ordering Empire: Science and State Formation in the English Atlantic World, 1650–1688" (Ph.D. diss., Harvard University, 2010), chap. 4; and Popper, "An Information State for Elizabethan England," 509–513.

38. These other offices organized and deployed documents in similar ways; for a discussion of Admiralty and Treasury archiving in the eighteenth-century British Empire, see Asheesh Kapur Siddique, "Paperwork, Governance, and Archive in the British Empire During the Age of Revolutions" (Ph.D. diss., Columbia University, 2016), chaps. 3, 5.

39. Classic accounts of the "resumption" debate are Louise Phelps Kellogg, *The American Colonial Charter: A Study of English Administration in Relation Thereto, Chiefly After 1688* (Washington, D.C.: Government Printing Office, 1904), chap. 2; and I. K. Steele, "The Board of Trade, the Quakers, and Resumption of Colonial Charters, 1699–1702," *William and Mary Quarterly,* 3rd series, 23, no. 4 (October 1966): 596–619.

40. "Representation upon the Proposals of the Proprietors of East & West New Jersey, for a Surrender of Their Pretended Title to the Government of Those Provinces," October 2, 1701, 244–258, CO 5/1289, TNA ("severall," 244; "we do not find," 248; "Approbation," 249; "preservation," 257; "pretences," 258).

41. "Representation upon the State of His Majesty's Plantations on the Continent of America," September 8, 1721, 296–435, CO 324/10, TNA ("Copy'd," 419; "altho' the Governmt," 317; "Mischiefs," 361; "Misfeazancies," 329; "Daily Experience," 362; "might undoubtedly," 422).

42. "Copy of a Circular Letter from Earl of Nottingham to All ye Governors in America for Proclaiming War with France and Spain," May 7, 1702, fol. 353, CO 323/3, TNA. On Nottingham's exertion of control over colonial policy, see Steele, *Politics of Colonial Policy,* 85–92. For efforts to continue this practice, see Earl of Sunderland to Council of Trade and Plantations, January 3, 1707, fol. 65, CO 323/6, TNA; and Council of Trade and Plantations to Sunderland, January 13, 1707, 134, CO 324/9, TNA.

43. "Representation upon the State of His Majesty's Plantations," September 8, 1721, 422, 431, CO 324/10, TNA.

44. "Charter Granted by Queen Elizabeth to the Governor and Company of Merchants of London, Trading into the East-Indies," December 31, 1600, in John Shaw, *Charters Relating to the East India Company from 1600 to 1761* (Madras, India, 1887), 7–8.

45. On the corporate constitutionalism of the company, see Miles Ogborn, *Indian Ink: Script and Print in the Making of the English East India Company* (Chicago: University of Chicago Press, 2007), 41–46; Stern, *Company-State,* 10–13; and William A. Pettigrew, "Corporate Constitutionalism and the Dialogue Between the Global and Local in Seventeenth Century English History," *Itinerario* 39 (2016): 487–501. See also chapter 2 of this book.

46. On the company's purchase of the *zamindar,* see Farhat Hasan, "Indigenous Co-operation and the Birth of a Colonial City: Calcutta, c. 1698–1750," *Modern Asian Studies* 26 (1992): 66–70.

47. See Eric Hinderaker, "Diplomacy Between Britons and Native Americans, c. 1600–1830," in *Britain's Oceanic Empire: Atlantic and Indian Ocean Worlds, c. 1550–1850,* ed. H. V. Bowen, Elizabeth Mancke, and John G. Reid (Cambridge, UK: Cambridge University Press, 2012), 218–248.

48. *Orders and Constitutions, Partly Collected Out of His Maiesties Letters Patents; and Partly by Authority, and in Vertue of the Said Letters Patents: Ordained vpon Mature Deliberation, by the Gouernour and Company of the City of London, for the Plantation of the Summer-Islands: For the Better Gouerning of the Actions and Affaires of the Said Company and Plantation* (London, 1622), 23–24; *The Orders, Rules and Ordinances, Ordained, Devised and Made by the Master and Keepers or Wardens and Community of the Mystery or Art of Stationers of the City of London for the Well Governing of That Society* (London, 1678), 26; *By the Company of the Royal Fishery of England* (London, 1681), 5.

49. For the information order of the early company, see Ogborn, *Indian Ink,* chap. 3; and Gabor Szommer, "Parallel Expansions: The Role of Information During the Formative Years of the English East India Company (1600–1623)," *Information and Culture* 53 (2018): 303–336.

50. *The Lawes or Standing Orders of the East India Company* (London?, 1621), 2, 9, 12–13, 35. On company recordkeeping and secrecy, see Mishra, *A Business of State,* 44–52.

51. *Lawes or Standing Orders of the East India Company,* 51–54.

52. See, for example, "Rules & Directions for Ordering & Keeping the East India Accounts in England," August 12, 1664, IOR/H/15; Minutes of the Court of Directors, November 27, 1678, 58, IOR/B/35.

53. "A Comission Sett Downe by Us the Gournor, Deputie, & Comities of the Merchants," 1606, in Henry Stevens, ed., *The Dawn of British Trade to the East Indies, as Recorded in the Court Minutes of the East India Company, 1599–1603* (1886; London: Frank Cass, 1967), 116–117.

54. "Orders & Instructions Given by Us ye Governors & Company of Merchants of London Trading into the East Indies unto Mr. Charles James Whom Wee Have Chose to Be Purser of Our Ship Wellcome, in This Now Intended Voyage for Surratt, Which the Almightie Prosper," March 3, 1658, fol. 33, IOR/E/3/85.

55. "Commission & Instructions Given by Us [to] the Governour & Company of Merchants of London Having into the East Indies unto Our Loving Ffriend Capt. William Hargrave Commander of the Ship Wellcome in This Intended Voyage for Mosambique the Coast of Mallabarr & Surratt unto Which the All-mightie Bestows His Blessing," February 27, 1658, fol. 30, IOR/E/3/85. For a subsequent example of the demand for captains to return journals, accounts, and other documents on arrival from India to "any Port or place within Her Majesties Dominions," see "Orders and Instructions Given by ye Court of Managers for the United Trade to the East Indies. To Captain Samuel Hide Comander of the Northumberland Bound for Chusan in China, and to ye Comander for the Time Being," January 10, 1703, fol. 8, IOR/E/3/95.

56. "Our Agent and Factors in Bantam," May 7, 1658, fol. 58, IOR/E/3/85.

57. "Our Generall & Council of Bombay or Suratt," May 4, 1702, fol. 285, IOR/E/3/93.

58. "Our President & Counsell in Fort St. George," January 31, 1654, fol. 151, IOR/E/3/84.

59. "Our Deputy Governour and Council of Bencoolen," July 30, 1702, fol. 351v, IOR/E/3/93: "We have read over the Warehousekeepers Account and considered your clause."

60. "Our Governor & Council of St. Helena," January 3, 1703, fol. 328v, IOR/E/3/93.

61. "Orders & Instructions Given by the Court of Directors of the United Company of Merchants of England Trading to the East Indies to Capt. George Cook Commander of the Ship Howland and to the Commander for the Time Being," December 3, 1710, fol. 18v, IOR/E/3/97.

62. "Orders and Instructions Given by the Court of Managers for the United Trade to the East Indies to Mr. George Petty, Mr. Jonathan Hall, and Mr. Thomas Gott Supra Cargos of the Ship Loyal Cooke," December 1, 1703, fol. 93v, IOR/E/3/95.

63. "Instructions to Thomas Pitt Esq. President of Fort St George, Nathaniel Higginson Esq, John Syleman Esq, Mr Wm. Fraser[,] Mr. Francis Ellis[,] Mr Roger Braddyll[,] Mr Charles Barwell[,] Mr Thomas Wright[,] Mr Edward Tredcroft, and Mr Matthew Empson Councill There," January 26, 1698, fol. 6v, IOR/E/3/93.

64. "Our Deputy Governour & Council of York Fort," July 8, 1701, fol. 238v, IOR/E/3/93.

65. "Orders and Instructions Given by ye Court of Managers to Captain John Lane Comander of the Ships Herne and to the Comander for the Time Being," April 7, 1708, fol. 148, IOR/E/3/96.

66. "Our Agent and Council in Persia," April 26, 1701, fol. 225v, IOR/E/3/93.

67. "To the Deputy Governour & Council or Chief & Council for All the English Affairs on the West Coast of Sumatra for the Time Being," September 14, 1720, fol. 174, IOR/E/3/100.

68. Court of Directors to St Helena, March 21, 1717, fol. 241, IOR/E/3/99.

69. "Our Generall and Council of Bombay," April 17, 1711, fol. 116v, IOR/E/3/97.

70. "Generall Letter & Instructions for Bencoolen," January 10, 1710, fol. 85, IOR/E/3/97.

71. "Instructions to the Supra Cargo's of the Nathaniel," October 5, 1711, fol. 158, IOR/E/3/97.

72. "Our President & Council of Fort St. George," December 28, 1711, fol. 205v, IOR/E/3/97.

73. "Our President & Council of Bengall," January 18, 1716, fol. 46, IOR/E/3/99.

74. Minutes of the Court of Directors, March 18, 1708, 22, IOR/B/50A.

75. Minutes of the Court of Directors, March 29, 1706, 151, IOR/B/48.

76. Minutes of the Court of Directors, January 4, 1716, 237-238, IOR/B/54.

77. Minutes of the Court of Directors, January 11, 1716, 247, IOR/B/54.

78. Minutes of the Court of Directors, March 25, 1720, 542, IOR/B/55. For the alternating responsibilities over the management of records, see Minutes of the Court of Directors, September 9, 1724, 122, IOR/B/58; April 2, 1735, 301-302, IOR/B/63; November 8, 9, 1748, 144-145, IOR/B/70; and June 27, 1750, 94-95, IOR/B/71.

79. *Lawes or Standing Orders*, 66-70.

80. *Lawes or Standing Orders,* 75.

81. See, for example, Minutes of the Court of Directors, July 30, 1703, 155, IOR/B/44 (compensation); March 20, 1712, 346, IOR/B/52 (debts). On accounting in the company, see Vahé Baladouni, "Accounting in the Early Years of the East India Company," *Accounting Historians Journal* 10 (1983): 63–80.

82. Minutes of the Court of Directors, July 4, 1705, 15, IOR/B/46; miscellaneous account, n.d. but late seventeenth or early eighteenth century, 155, IOR/G/40/24.

83. Minutes of the Court of Directors, December 3, 1708, 309, IOR/B/49.

84. Minutes of the Court of Directors, January 4, 1711, 700, IOR/B/51.

85. Minutes of the Court of Directors, March 23, 1759, 301, IOR/B/75.

86. John Lambton to Court of Directors, June 24, 1730, fol. 142, IOR/E/1/21.

87. Minutes of the Court of Directors, November 10, 1725, 433, IOR/B/58. For an example of the court's directive that an applicant bear the expense of copying records, see Minutes of the Court of Directors, June 2, 1736, 39, IOR/B/64.

88. Catherine Pickett, *Bibliography of the East India Company: Books, Pamphlets, and Other Materials Printed Between 1600 and 1785* (London: British Library, 2011), viii.

89. *A True Relation of the Cruell and Barbarous Tortures and Execution, Done upon the English at Amboyna in the East Indies, by the Hollanders There Residing* (London, 1624), 45. On Amboyna and its legacy in imperial culture, see Alison Games, *Inventing the English Massacre: Amboyna in History and Memory* (New York: Oxford University Press, 2020).

90. *The Emblem of Ingratitude. A True Relation of the Unjust, Cruel, and Barbarous Proceedings Against the English at Amboyna in the East-Indies; by the Netherlandish Governour & Council There. Also, a Farther Account of the Deceit, Cruelty, and Tyranny of the Dutch Against the English, and Several Others; from Their First to Their Present Estate: With Remarks upon the Whole Matter. Faithfully Collected from Antient and Modern Records* (London, 1672).

91. See, for example, *A Defence of the United Company of Merchants of England, Trading to the East-Indies, and Their Servants, (Particularly Those at Bengal) Against the Complaints of the Dutch East-India Company: Being a Memorial from the English Company to His Majesty on That Subject* (London, 1762), "The Appendix."

92. Minutes of the Committee of Correspondence, November 1, 1769, 33–34, IOR/D/26. On the Examiner's Office and its drafting procedures for correspondence, see Martin Moir, "The Examiner's Office and the Drafting of East India Company Despatches," in *East India Company Studies: Papers Presented to Professor Sir Cyril Philips,* ed. Kenneth Ballhatchet and John Harrison (Hong Kong: Asian Research Service, 1986), 123–152.

93. Minutes of the Committee of Correspondence, May 20, 1770, 189–190; March 26, 1771, 342–344, IOR/D/26.

94. Minutes of the Court of Directors, April 11, 1786, 981–982, IOR/B/102. See also H. V. Bowen, *The Business of Empire: The East India Company and Imperial Britain, 1756–1833* (Cambridge, UK: Cambridge University Press, 2006), 173–174.

95. On the politics of 1773, the classic account is Lucy S. Sutherland, *The East India Company in Eighteenth-Century Politics* (Oxford: Clarendon Press, 1952),

213–328. More recently, see H. V. Bowen, *Revenue and Reform: The Indian Problem in British Politics, 1757–1773* (Cambridge, UK: Cambridge University Press, 1991), esp. chap. 11. On how these changes impacted documentary organization, see Martin Moir, "*Kaghazi Raj:* Notes on the Documentary Basis of Company Rule, 1773–1858," *Indo-British Review* 21 (1993): 186.

96. "An Act for Establishing Certain Regulations for the Better Management of the Affairs of the East-India Company, as Well in India as in Europe," 13 George 3, c. 63, in Danby Pickering, *The Statutes at Large, from Magna Charta to the End of the Thirteenth Parliament of Great Britain, Anno 1773,* 46 vols. (Cambridge, UK, 1762–1807), 30:124–143.

Chapter 2. Subjects of the Archive

1. Caroline Elkins, *Legacy of Violence: A History of the British Empire* (New York: Knopf, 2022), 10.
2. On the intellectual resources mobilized by early modern English people to justify enslavement, see Michael Guasco, *Slavery and Englishmen: Human Bondage in the Early Modern Atlantic World* (Philadelphia: University of Pennsylvania Press, 2014), chap. 1.
3. On the dynamics of the company's territorial expansion in this period, see P. J. Marshall, "British Expansion in India in the Eighteenth Century: A Historical Revision," *History* 60 (1975): 28–43.
4. Thomas Pownall, *The Right, Interest, and Duty, of the State, as Concerned in the Affairs of the East Indies* (London, 1773), 5, 7–8.
5. Pownall, *Right, Interest, and Duty of the State,* 8, 15, 40, 44, 46.
6. Pownall, *Right, Interest, and Duty of the State,* 28, 36.
7. The classic treatment of this subject is Bernard S. Cohn, "The Command of Language and the Language of Command," in *Subaltern Studies IV: Writings on South Asian History and Society,* ed. Ranajit Guha (Delhi: Oxford University Press, 1985), 276–329.
8. Linda Colley, "Britishness and Otherness: An Argument," *Journal of British Studies* 31 (1992): 309–329.
9. "Queen's Circular Letter of Recommendation of the Captains and Factors, to the Princes and States in the Countries Within the Company's Limits," 1601, in John Bruce, *Annals of the Honorable East-India Company, from Their Establishment by the Charter of Queen Elizabeth, 1600, to the Union of the London and English East-India Companies, 1707–1708,* 3 vols. (London, 1810), 1:149–150. For similar instructions for factors to cultivate local knowledge, see "A Comission Set Downe by Us," February 1607, in Henry Stevens, ed., *The Dawn of British Trade to the East Indies, as Recorded in the Court Minutes of the East India Company, 1599–1603* (1886; London: Frank Cass, 1967), 245, instructing factors "to make diligent inquirie of all things needfull."
10. "A Genrall Court the xth of February 1600," February 10, 1600, in Stevens, *The Dawn of British Trade,* 134. See also [Josiah Child], *A Treatise Wherein Is Demonstrated, I. That the East-India Trade Is the Most National of All Foreign Trades* (London, 1681), 22–23.

11. "To Mr Hawkins and the Rest of Our Factors at Suratt &c," March 15, 1609, in Stevens, *The Dawn of British Trade,* 317.

12. "Commission and Instructions Given by the Court of Managers for the United Trade to the East Indies to Mr Nathaniel Halsey, Mr. Robert Hedges, Mr. Jonathan White, Mr. Jonathan Windor, Mr. Ralph Sheldon, Mr. Robert Nightingale, Mr. John Russell, and Mr. Benjamin Boucher," March 2, 1702, fol. 30, IOR/E/3/95.

13. On the rise of Orientalist scholarship, see Alexander Bevilacqua, *The Republic of Arabic Letters: Islam and the European Enlightenment* (Cambridge, Mass.: Harvard University Press, 2018). For the role of institutions in facilitating its development, see William J. Bulman, *Anglican Enlightenment: Orientalism, Religion and Politics in England and Its Empire* (Cambridge, UK: Cambridge University Press, 2015); Simon Mills, "Scholarship," in *The Corporation as a Protagonist in Global History, c. 1550–1750,* ed. William A. Pettigrew and David Veevers (Leiden: Brill, 2018), 255–275; and Simon Mills, *A Commerce of Knowledge: Trade, Religion, and Scholarship Between England and the Ottoman Empire, c. 1600–1760* (Oxford: Oxford University Press, 2020). On early modern corporations as institutional developers of knowledge networks, see Steven J. Harris, "Long-Distance Corporations, Big Sciences, and the Geography of Knowledge," *Constellations* 6 (1998): 269–303.

14. In this regard, see especially Nicholas Dew, *Orientalism in Louis XIV's France* (Oxford: Oxford University Press, 2009); Gerald MacLean and Nabil Matar, *Britain and the Islamic World, 1588–1713* (Oxford: Oxford University Press, 2011), chap. 3; and Mills, *A Commerce of Knowledge.* Scholarship on the company's interest in Indian languages in the late eighteenth and nineteenth centuries includes Thomas R. Trautmann, *Languages and Nations: The Dravidian Proof in Colonial Madras* (Berkeley: University of California Press, 2006); and Bhavani Raman, *Document Raj: Writing and Scribes in Early Colonial South India* (Chicago: University of Chicago Press, 2012).

15. For the early interest of company servants in non-European languages, see Anna Winterbottom, *Hybrid Knowledge in the Early East India Company World* (London: Palgrave Macmillan, 2016), chap. 2. For the accommodation of European trading companies to Indian styles of diplomacy, see, among a large literature, Michael H. Fisher, "Diplomacy in India, 1526–1858," in *Britain's Oceanic Empire: Atlantic and Indian Ocean Worlds, c. 1550–1850,* ed. H. V. Bowen, Elizabeth Mancke, and John G. Reid (Cambridge, UK: Cambridge University Press, 2012), 249–281; Sanjay Subrahmanyam, *Courtly Encounters: Translating Courtliness and Violence in Early Modern Eurasia* (Cambridge, Mass.: Harvard University Press, 2012); and Guido van Meersbergen, "The Diplomatic Repertories of the East India Companies in Mughal South Asia, 1608–1717," *Historical Journal* 62 (2019): 875–898.

16. "To Mr Edward Owen Our Agent of Persia—Mr. Alexander Prescott Our Chief of Isfahan and the Rest of the Council at Both or Either of Those Places," January 9, 1704, fols. 215–215v, IOR/E/3/95. See Peter Good, *The East India Company in Persia: Trade and Cultural Exchange in the Eighteenth Century* (London: Bloomsbury, 2022).

17. Fort St. George to Court of Directors, September 16, 1713, 423, IOR/E/4/1.

18. Court of Directors to Fort St. George, January 12, 1714, fol. 252v, IOR/E/3/98.

19. "To Allen Catchpoole Esq.r President, and the Rest of the Councill in China for the Affaires of the English Company Trading to the East Indies," November 25, 1701, fols. 183v–184, IOR/E/3/94.

20. See, for example, Court of Directors to Bombay, February 9, 1766, 744, IOR/E/4/997. On Persian as the "court" language of Mughal administration, see Muzaffar Alam, "The Culture and Politics of Persian in Precolonial Hindustan," in *Literary Cultures in History: Reconstructions from South Asia*, ed. Sheldon Pollock (Berkeley: University of California Press, 2003), esp. 59–171. Recent scholarship has complicated this picture by demonstrating the centrality of Sanskrit to Mughal courtly culture; see Audrey Truschke, *Culture of Encounters: Sanskrit at the Mughal Court* (New York: Columbia University Press, 2016).

21. "Fort William Generall," January 8, 1709, 246, IOR/E/4/1.

22. "Our President and Council of Bengall," January 5, 1710, fol. 70, IOR/E/3/97.

23. "Fort William General," December 11, 1714, 537, IOR/E/4/1.

24. Court of Directors to Bengal, January 18, 1716, fol. 43v, IOR/E/3/99. See similarly "Our Agent & Council in Persia," January 5, 1710, fol. 79, IOR/E/3/97.

25. "Our Generall and Council in Bombay," April 17, 1711, fol. 105, IOR/E/3/97.

26. On Protestantism as part of the foundations of company sovereignty, see Philip J. Stern, *The Company-State: Corporate Sovereignty and the Early Modern Foundations of the British Empire in India* (Oxford: Oxford University Press, 2011), chap. 5.

27. On Boyle, translation, and the East India Company, see Miles Ogborn, *Indian Ink: Script and Print in the Making of the English East India Company* (Chicago: University of Chicago Press, 2007), preface; and Winterbottom, *Hybrid Knowledge in the Early East India Company World*, chap. 2.

28. For the relationship between the company and missionaries in the seventeenth and early eighteenth centuries, see Penelope Carson, *The East India Company and Religion, 1698–1858* (London: Boydell, 2012).

29. See, for example, Court of Directors to Bombay, March 31, 1756, 388–389, IOR/E/4/996; Court of Directors to Bombay, April 25, 1759, 751, IOR/E/4/996; Court of Directors to Bombay, February 9, 1766, 744, IOR/E/4/997.

30. On company military power and changes induced in the composition of the army after the company's military defeat of the Nawab of Bengal at the Battle of Plassey in 1757, see the recent discussion by Kaushik Roy, "The Hybrid Military Establishment of the East India Company in South Asia, 1750–1849," *Journal of Global History* 6 (2011): 195–218. For an extremely suggestive discussion of the problems that conquest introduced into the meaning of representation and sovereignty in the British Empire from the 1760s, see P. J. Marshall, "Empire and Authority in the Later Eighteenth Century," *Journal of Imperial and Commonwealth History* 15 (1987): 105–122.

31. Minutes of Fort William Committee, November 12, 1757, IOR/P/A/1.

32. Fort William (Bengal) Select Committee Consultation Minutes, September 27, 1760, IOR/P/A/3.

33. Fort William (Bengal) Select Committee Consultation Minutes, May 17, 1761, IOR/P/A/3.

34. Fort William (Bengal) Secret Department Consultation Minutes, June 21, 1764, 280, IOR/P/A/5.

35. [Alexander Dow], *Tales, Translated from the Persian of Inatulla of Delhi. In Two Volumes* (London, 1768), 1:iv.

36. Alexander Dow to Court of Directors, November 18, 1768, 212, IOR/E/1/51; Minutes of the Court of Directors, February 22, 1769, 486–487, IOR/B/84.

37. Minutes of the Court of Directors, March 17, 1769, 514, IOR/B/84; Court of Directors to Bombay, March 31, 1769, 373, 425, IOR/E/4/998.

38. Court of Directors to Bombay, April 25, 1771, 1047–1048, 1079–1080, IOR/E/4/998.

39. See Ogborn, *Indian Ink,* chap. 4. I also discuss the phenomenon in detail in the next chapter.

40. William Crichton to George Colebrooke, June 21, 1770, 302–304, IOR/E/1/53.

41. Minutes of the Court of Directors, June 22, 1770, 66, IOR/B/86. For the proposal, see "Proposals for Printing a Persian Dictionary," n.d., fols. 1–2, IOR/Mss Eur G37/17/66. For the identification of these proposals as Hamilton's and Nicol's, see Abu Taher Mojumder, "Three New Letters by Sir William Jones," *India Office Library and Records Report for the Year 1981* (1982): 32–33.

42. Minutes of the Committee of Correspondence, August 2, 1770, 222–224, IOR/D/26.

43. Minutes of the Court of Directors, August 8, 1770, 119–120, IOR/B/86. Ferguson's project was delayed because of his poor health, but the court still compensated him for the work he had completed; see Minutes of the Court of Directors, October 1, 1772, 189, IOR/B/88.

44. The proposals from Jones are transcribed in Mojumder, "Three New Letters by Sir William Jones," 29–35.

45. Minutes of the Court of Directors, January 17, 1776, 413, IOR/B/91.

46. On Jones's and Richardson's interactions, see Garland Cannon, *The Life and Mind of Oriental Jones: Sir William Jones, the Father of Modern Linguistics* (Cambridge, UK: Cambridge University Press, 1990), 40–44.

47. Richardson, unlike Jones, did not hold official employment in the company. He did, however, eventually attempt to barter his expertise into an administrative position with the Secretary of State, requesting in 1783 that Lord North grant him an office on the new Board of Control on the grounds that his "knowledge of Persian might be of use"; see Richardson to Lord North, November 27, 1783, fol. 30, HO 44/40, TNA.

48. William Richardson and John Richardson to Robert Clive, March 6, 1771, fol. 6, IOR/Mss Eur G37/61/2.

49. Minutes of the Court of Directors, January 17, 1776, 413, IOR/B/91. See John Richardson, *A Dictionary, Persian, Arabic, and English. To Which Is Prefixed a Dissertation on the Languages, Literature, and Manner of the Eastern Nations* (Oxford, 1777); and *A Dictionary English, Persian and Arabic,* 2 vols. (Oxford, 1780), 2:xiii (see also the unpaginated "List of Subscribers" in the 1780 volume). The first volume is not enumerated, and the second volume has a shorter title.

50. On the company's turn to Indian history, see J. S. Grewal, *Muslim Rule in India: The Assessments of British Historians* (New Delhi: Oxford University Press, 1970); P. J. Marshall, ed., *The British Discovery of Hinduism in the Eighteenth Century*

(Cambridge, UK: Cambridge University Press, 1970); Robert Travers, *Ideology and Empire in Eighteenth-Century India: The British in Bengal* (Cambridge, UK: Cambridge University Press, 2007); and Kumkum Chatterjee, *The Cultures of History in Early Modern India: Persianization and Mughal Culture in Bengal* (New Delhi: Oxford University Press, 2009), chaps. 5–6.

51. On Jones's legal background, see Asheesh Kapur Siddique, "William Jones, Esq.," *Global Intellectual History,* forthcoming.

52. "A Defence of the Dual System of Government in Bengal in Clive's Hand, Offering Historical Precedents," n.d., IOR/Mss Eur G37/6/20.

53. Fort William (Bengal) Revenue Department Consultation, August 8, 1777, 51, IOR/P/50/2.

54. "Mr. Jones to Mr. Thomas Yeates," June 7, 1782, in *The Letters of Sir William Jones,* ed. Garland Cannon, 2 vols. (Oxford: Clarendon Press, 1970), 1:551–554. Jones was invoking William Blackstone's description of the record-bound nature of the "unwritten" common law; see William Blackstone, *Commentaries on the Laws of England: A Facsimile of the First Edition of 1765–1769,* 4 vols. (Chicago: University of Chicago Press, 1979), 1:63–64.

55. "To the Second Earl of Spencer," February 20, 1791, in Cannon, *Letters of Sir William Jones,* 2:883–884. Jones made the same argument in a subsequent letter to Lady Georgiana Spencer; see "To Lady Spencer," October 24, 1791, in Cannon, *Letters of Sir William Jones,* 2:903.

56. William Jones, "The Preface," in *The History of the Life of Nader Shah, King of Persia* (London, 1773), c.

57. "To Edward Gibbon," June 30, 1781, in Cannon, *Letters of Sir William Jones,* 2:481.

58. The plan is printed in Garland Cannon, "Sir William Jones and Edmund Burke," *Modern Philology* 54 (1957): 185–186.

59. William Jones to William Pitt, February 5, 1785, fol. 16, PRO 30/8/362, TNA. On Jones's imperial jurisprudence, see David Ibbetson, "Sir William Jones as Comparative Lawyer," in *Sir William Jones, 1746–1794: A Commemoration,* ed. Alexander Murray (Oxford: Oxford University Press, 1998), esp. 23–30.

60. "To Elizabeth Shipley," September 7, 1786, in Cannon, *Letters of Sir William Jones,* 2:70.

61. "To John Eardley-Wilmot," September 20, 1789, in Cannon, *Letters of Sir William Jones,* 2:848.

62. On the differing ideas of an "ancient Mughal constitution" among company officials, see Travers, *Ideology and Empire.*

63. "A Charter Graunted to the Company of Royall Adventurers of England Trading into Africa," 1663, 8v, Sloane MS 205, BL.

64. "Charter Granted to the Company of Royal Adventurers of England Relating to Trade in Africa," 1663, Sloane MS 205, BL. See W. R. Scott, "The Constitution and Finance of the Royal African Company of England from Its Foundation till 1730," *American Historical Review* 8 (1903): 244.

65. "Generall Court Held at the African House the 5th February 1677/8," "Secretary's Oath," 82–83, T 70/100, TNA.

66. "Generall Court Held at the African House the 5th February 1677/8," "The Book keeper's Oath," 83–84, T 70/100, TNA.

67. "Instructions to Captain Samuel Kempthorne," May 4, 1686, in *Documents Illustrative of the History of the Slave Trade in America,* ed. Elizabeth Donnan, 4 vols. (Washington, D.C.: Carnegie Institution, 1930), 1:354.

68. Sir Humphry Morice to Captain William Snelgrave, in "Book Containing Orders & Instructions to William Snelgrave Commander of the Henry, for the Coast of Africa with an Invoice of His Cargo and Journal of Trade &c: on the Said Coast," July 15, 1721, in *Slavery, Abolition, and Social Justice,* Adam Mathew Digital, http://www.slavery.amdigital.co.uk/Contents/DocumentDetails.aspx ?documentid=2401.

69. "Circular Letter from the Council of Trade and Plantations to Governors of Plantations," April 15, 1708, 165-170, CO 324/9, TNA.

70. David Eltis and David Richardson, *Atlas of the Transatlantic Slave Trade* (New Haven, Conn.: Yale University Press, 2010), 23.

71. William Popple, "List of Papers Belonging to the African Company," c. 1696, 144-145, CO 326/1, TNA.

72. "Royal African Company to Get Due Payments," in *Royal Instructions to British Colonial Governors, 1670-1776,* ed. Leonard Woods Labaree (1935; reprint New York: Octagon Books, 1967), 2:666.

73. "Report on Number of Negroes Imported," in Labaree, ed., *Royal Instructions,* 2:667.

74. Richard Hakluyt the Younger, "Discourse of Western Planting," 1584, in *The Original Writings and Correspondence of the Two Richard Hakluyts with an Introduction and Notes,* ed. E. G. R. Taylor (London: Hakluyt Society, 1935), 2:215. On Hakluyt's emphasis on the importance of custom and locality in imperial establishment, see Peter C. Mancall, *Hakluyt's Promise: An Elizabethan's Obsession for an English America* (New Haven, Conn.: Yale University Press, 2007), chap. 9.

75. "Company of Providence Island to the Governor and Council, London," April 10, 1633, fol. 46, CO 124/1, TNA.

76. "Instructions to Our Right Trusty & Rt. Wellbeloved Cousin Richard Earle of Bellomont Our Captain Generall & Governour in Cheif of Our Province of New York and the Territories Depending Thereon in America," 1697, 346, PC 5/1, TNA. Similarly, see "New Yorke. Instructions for My Lord Cornbury the Governor," 1701, 159, PC 5/2, TNA; and more generally Labaree, ed., *Royal Instructions,* 2:463-466. On presents in New World diplomacy between Natives and Europeans, see Wilbur R. Jacobs, *Anglo-Indian Gifts: Anglo-French Rivalry Along the Ohio and Northwest Frontiers, 1748-1763* (Stanford, Calif.: Stanford University Press, 1950); Ramón A. Guttiérez, *When Jesus Came, the Corn Mothers Went Away: Marriage, Sexuality, and Power in New Mexico, 1500-1846* (Stanford, Calif.: Stanford University Press, 1991); Richard White, *The Middle Ground: Indians, Empires, and Republics in the Great Lakes Region, 1650-1815* (1991; reprint New York: Cambridge University Press, 2011); and Seth Mallios, *The Deadly Politics of Giving: Exchange and Violence at Ajacan, Roanoke, and Jamestown* (Tuscaloosa: University of Alabama Press, 2006).

77. See Robert A. Williams Jr., *The American Indian in Western Legal Thought: The Discourses of Conquest* (Oxford: Oxford University Press, 1990), 206-221; and

Daniel K. Richter, "To 'Clear the King's and Indians' Title': Seventeenth-Century Origins of North American Land Cession Treaties," in *Empire by Treaty: Negotiating European Expansion, 1600-1900,* ed. Saliha Belmessous (Oxford: Oxford University Press, 2015), 45-77. On Virginia, see Jeffrey Glover, *Paper Sovereigns: Anglo-Native Treaties and the Law of Nations, 1604-1664* (Philadelphia: University of Pennsylvania Press, 2014), chap. 1. On Massachusetts, see Jenny Hale Pulsipher, *Subjects unto the Same King: Indians, English, and the Contest for Authority in Colonial New England* (Philadelphia: University of Pennsylvania Press, 2005).

78. Lisa Ford, *Settler Sovereignty: Jurisdiction and Indigenous People in America and Australia, 1788-1836* (Cambridge, Mass.: Harvard University Press, 2010), 19-20. For the ideological roots of the exclusion of Native peoples from conceptions of English settler sovereignty, see Ken MacMillan, *Sovereignty and Possession in the English New World: The Legal Foundations of Empire, 1576-1640* (Cambridge, UK: Cambridge University Press, 2006), 34; and Craig Yirush, *Settlers, Liberty, and Empire: The Roots of Early American Political Theory, 1675-1775* (Cambridge, UK: Cambridge University Press, 2011), chaps. 4-5.

79. On the meanings of "subjecthood" in this period, see Hannah Weiss Muller, *Subjects and Sovereign: Bonds of Belonging in the Eighteenth-Century British Empire* (New York: Oxford University Press, 2017), chap. 1. On the importance of travel and migration to the creation of the early modern British Empire, see Alison Games, *The Web of Empire: English Cosmopolitans in an Age of Expansion, 1560-1660* (New York: Oxford University Press, 2008).

80. On the concepts of "protection" and "allegiance" in imperial contexts, see Muller, *Subjects and Sovereign,* 28-30.

81. Committee for Foreign Plantations, July 1670, "Instructions for Our Rt. Trusty Edward[,] Earle of Sandwich President, & Our Rt. Trusty Richard Lord George, William Lord Allignton, Thomas Grey and Henry Brounder Esq.rs Sr. Humphrey Wineh Knt . . . Whome Wee Have Appointed Our Councill for Forraine Plantations," July 1670, fol. 49, CO 389/4, TNA.

82. "An Act Incouraging the Setling of This Island [Jamaica]," April 17, 1684, 137-138, PC 5/1, TNA.

83. Colonists and Native Americans also employed hybridized vocabularies that mixed terms from different languages, which linguists call "pidgins," and physical gestures. On pidgins in the Atlantic world context, see Ives Goddard, "The Use of Pidgins and Jargons on the East Coast of North America," in The *Language Encounter in the Americas, 1492-1800,* ed. Edward G. Gray and Norman Fiering (New York: Berghan Books, 2000), 61-78. On gestures, see Céline Carayon, "'The Gesture Speech of Mankind': Old and New Entanglements in the Histories of American Indian and European Sign Languages," *American Historical Review* 121 (2016): 477-486.

84. "Instructions to . . . Mr Andrew Percivall" from the Lords Proprietors of Carolina, February 21, 1681, fol. 80v, CO 5/286, TNA.

85. "Order of the Assembly Concerning Jacob Young & the Indians," August 28, 1689, fol. 14, CO 5/718/1, TNA.

86. "Instructions for Col. Nicolson Govr. of Virginia," August 2, 1698, 410, PC 5/1, TNA.

87. "Instructions to Capt. Bennet, Lt. Gov.r of Bermudas," August 1700, 566, PC 5/1, TNA.

88. "Instructions for My Lord Cornbury the Governor [New York]," 1701, 158, PC 5/2, TNA.

89. "Mr. Dudley's Instructions as Gov.r of Massachusetts Bay," 1701, 261, PC 5/2, TNA.

90. "Col. Nicholson's Instructions [Virginia]," October 22, 1702, 73, PC 5/3, TNA ("you are to appoint fitt Officers and Commanders in the severall parts of the Country bordering upon the Indians, who upon any Invasion may raise Men and Arms to oppose them until they shall receive Your Directions therein").

91. "Col. Nicholson's Instructions [Virginia]," October 22, 1702, 79, PC 5/3, TNA ("it hath been thought fitt to permittt a Free Trade between Our Subjects of Virginia, and ye said Indians").

92. "Instructions to Lord Lovelace Gov.r New Jersey," 1708, 717, PC 5/3, TNA ("You are to encourage the Indians upon all Occasions so as to induce them to trade with Our Subjects, rather than any others of Europe").

93. See Daniel K. Richter, *The Ordeal of the Longhouse: The Peoples of the Iroquois League in the Era of European Colonization* (Chapel Hill: University of North Carolina Press, 1992), chap. 9.

94. "Instrucctons for Edward Hyde, Commonly Called Lord Cornbury . . . Our Captain Generall and Governor in Cheif of Our Province of New Yorke and the Territories Depending Thereon in America," 1702, 173, PC 5/3, TNA.

95. "Instructions for Our Trusty and Welbeloved Robert Lowther Esq.r Our Captain Generall and Governor in Chief in and over Our Islands of Barbadoes, St. Lucia, Dominico, St. Vincents and the Rest of Our Charibbee Islands, Lying to Windward of Guadolupe in America," August 28, 1710, 195-196, PC 5/4, TNA.

Chapter 3. Contentious Politics

1. For the origins of these discourses in England, see Barbara J. Shapiro, *A Culture of Fact: England, 1550-1720* (Ithaca, N.Y.: Cornell University Press, 2000), chap. 2. For developments beyond England, see Randolph Head, "Documents, Archives, and Proof Around 1700," *Historical Journal* 56 (2013): 909-930.

2. This phenomenon has been widely explored in the scholarship on early modern European knowledge practices; see, for example, J. G. A. Pocock, *The Ancient Constitution and the Feudal Law: A Study of English Historical Thought in the Seventeenth Century* (1957; reprint Cambridge, UK: Cambridge University Press, 1987); Peter N. Miller, *Peiresc's Europe: Learning and Virtue in the Seventeenth Century* (New Haven, Conn.: Yale University Press, 2000), esp. chap. 3; Kevin Sharpe, "Re-Writing Sir Robert Cotton: Politics and History in Early Stuart England" (1997), in *Remapping Early Modern England: The Culture of Seventeenth-Century Politics* (Cambridge, UK: Cambridge University Press, 2000), 294-341, esp. 314-315; Jacob Soll, *The Information Master: Jean-Baptiste Colbert's Secret State Intelligence System* (Ann Arbor: University of Michigan Press, 2009); and Alan Stewart, "Familiar Letters and State Papers: The Afterlives of Early Modern Correspondence," in *Cultures of Correspondence in Early Modern Britain,*

ed. James Daybell and Andrew Gordon (Philadelphia: University of Pennsylvania Press, 2016), 237–252.

3. Noah Millstone, "Seeing Like a Statesman in Early Stuart England," *Past and Present* 223 (May 2014): 85; Nicholas Popper, "An Information State for Elizabethan England," *Journal of Modern History* 90, no. 3 (September 2018): 505.

4. On the growing nonpolemical motivations for publishing records, see Michael Riordan, "Materials for History? Publishing Records as Historical Practice in Eighteenth- and Nineteenth-Century England," *History of Humanities* 2, no. 1 (2017): 51–77. The origins of the political practices examined here with respect to overseas affairs in the seventeenth and eighteenth centuries are explored in Noah Millstone, *Manuscript Circulation and the Invention of Politics in Early Stuart England* (Cambridge: Cambridge University Press, 2016); and Nicholas Popper, *The Specter of the Archive: Political Practice and the Information State in Early Modern Britain* (Chicago: University of Chicago Press, 2024).

5. A notable exception was the printing of the Royal Proclamation of August 1772 related to the *Gaspee* affair, wherein the *Gaspee,* a British customs ship, was run aground and then burned by colonists in protest of the Navigation Acts. The proclamation was printed in Newport by Solomon Southwick, the printer to the Rhode Island Assembly. The print is contained in Early American Imprints, 1st series, no. 42345, and a copy is held at the Rhode Island Historical Society Library, Providence. On the bibliographic history of this print, see Clarence S. Brigham, ed., *British Royal Proclamations Relating to America, 1603–1783* (Worcester, Mass.: American Antiquarian Society, 1911), 225–226. Brigham's volume also contains transcriptions of the printed royal proclamations made for the Atlantic world colonies during the colonial period.

6. See, for example, *Representation from the Commissioners for Trade and Plantations, to the Honourable Lords Spiritual and Temporal in Parliament Assembled . . . Relating to the State of the British Islands in America* (London, 1734); and *Copy of a Representation of the Board of Trade to the House of Lords* (London, 1749).

7. I deliberately omit discussion of the two works long regarded as the crowning achievements of seventeenth-century Anglo-Atlantic historiography, John Winthrop's *History of New England* and William Bradford's *Of Plymouth Plantation.* Neither text was published until well after the period under discussion (Winthrop's in 1825; Bradford's in 1901), and the extent of their circulation in manuscript form among contemporaries is unclear. On the bibliography of Bradford's account, see Douglas Anderson, *William Bradford's Books: Of Plimmoth Plantation and the Printed Word* (Baltimore: Johns Hopkins University Press, 2003); and on Winthrop, see Lindsay DiCuirci, *Colonial Revivals: The Nineteenth-Century Lives of Early American Books* (Philadelphia: University of Pennsylvania Press, 2019), chap. 2. On problems of "authorship," "canonicity," "print," and "publishing" in the seventeenth-century Anglo-American context, see generally David D. Hall, *Ways of Writing: The Practice and Politics of Text-Making in Seventeenth-Century New England* (Philadelphia: University of Pennsylvania Press, 2008).

8. Increase Mather, *A Brief History of the War with the Indians in New-England* (London, 1676), 8, 15–16, 45, "Postscript." On the construction of "King Philip's War" as a subject of political and historical discourse, see Jill Lepore, *The Name of War: King Philip's War and the Origins of American Identity* (New York: Knopf, 2009);

and Christine M. DeLucia, *Memory Lands: King Philip's War and the Place of Violence in the Northeast* (New Haven, Conn.: Yale University Press, 2018).

9. Cotton Mather, *Thaumaturgus: Vel . . . The Sixth Book of the New-English History; Wherein Very Many Illustrious Discoveries and Demonstrations of the Divine Providence in Remarkable Mercies and Judgments on Many Particular Persons Among the People of New-England Are Observ'd, Collected and Related* (London, 1702), 83.

10. Cadwallader Colden, *The History of the Five Indian Nations Depending on the Province of New-York in America* (New York, 1727), x, vii. On Colden as a historian, see William Howard Carter, "Anglicizing the League: The Writing of Cadwallader Colden's *History of the Five Indian Nations,*" in *Anglicizing America: Empire, Revolution, Republic,* ed. Ignacio Gallup-Diaz, Andrew Shankman, and David J. Silverman (Philadelphia: University of Pennsylvania Press, 2015), 83–108; and John M. Dixon, *The Enlightenment of Cadwallader Colden: Empire, Science, and Intellectual Culture in British New York* (Ithaca, N.Y.: Cornell University Press, 2016), 77–83.

11. William Smith, *The History of the Province of New-York* (London, 1757), x. On Smith as a historian, see Roger Andrew Wines, "William Smith, the Historian of New York," *New York History* 40, no. 1 (January 1959): 3–17.

12. William Gordon, *The History of the Rise, Progress, and Establishment, of the Independence of the United States of America: Including an Account of the Late War; and of the Thirteen Colonies, from Their Origin to That Period,* vol. 1 (London, 1788), unpaginated preface. For similar examples of early histories of colonies based on compilation, see Joseph E. Illick III, "Robert Proud and *The History of Pennsylvania,*" in *The Colonial Legacy,* vol. 1, *Loyalist Historians,* ed. Lawrence H. Leder (New York: Harper and Row, 1971), 164–181, esp. 172.

13. See, for example, [Richard Jackson], *An Historical Review of the Constitution and Government of Pensylvania, from Its Origin; so Far as Regards the Several Points of Controversy, Which Have, from Time to Time, Arisen Between the Several Governors of That Province, and Their Several Assemblies. Founded on Authentic Documents* (London, 1759); *An Impartial History of the War in America, Between Great Britain and Her Colonies . . . With an Appendix, Containing a Collection of Interesting and Authentic Papers Tending to Elucidate the History* (London, 1780); Samuel Smith, *The History of the Colony of Nova-Caesaria, or New-Jersey: Containing, an Account of Its First Settlement, Progressive Improvements, the Original and Present Constitution, and Other Events, to the Year 1721; with Some Particulars Since; and a Short View of Its Present State* (Burlington, N.J., 1765), vii–x; Thomas Hutchinson, *The History of the Colony of Massachusets-Bay, from the First Settlement Thereof in 1628; Until Its Incorporation with the Colony of Plimouth, Province of Main, &c. by the Charter of King William and Queen Mary, in 1691* (Boston, 1764).

14. [Charles Davenant], *An Essay upon the Probable Methods of Making a People Gainers in the Ballance of Trade* (London, 1699), 11, 9, 8.

15. [Charles Davenant], *A Discourse upon Grants and Resumptions; Showing How Our Ancestors Have Proceeded with Such Ministers as Have Procured to Themselves Grants of the Crown-Revenue; and That the Forfeited Estates Ought to Be Applied Towards the Payment of the Publick Debts* (London, 1700), 1, 306, 70, 243.

16. Lewes Roberts, *The Merchants Map of Commerce: Wherein the Universal Manner and Matter Relating to Trade and Merchandize, Are Fully Treated of . . . The Fourth Edition, Carefully Corrected, and Enlarg'd* (London, 1700), 39.

17. [John Oldmixon], *The British Empire in America, Containing the History of the Discovery, Settlement, Progress and Present State of All the British Colonies, on the Continent and Islands of America*, 2 vols. (London, 1708), 1:vii, viii–ix, xv, x, xiv. On Oldmixon's vision of commercial empire, see David Armitage, *The Ideological Origins of the British Empire* (Cambridge, UK: Cambridge University Press, 2000), 174–175. On Oldmixon as a historian, see Pat Rogers, "An Early Colonial Historian: John Oldmixon and *The British Empire in America*," *Journal of American Studies* 7, no. 2 (August 1973): 113–123.

18. The most comprehensive discussion of these documents is Heather Schwartz, "Re-Writing the Empire: Plans for Institutional Reform in British America, 1675–1791" (Ph.D. diss., Binghamton University, 2011).

19. *An Essay upon the Government of the English Plantations on the Continent of America: Together with Some Remarks upon the Discourse on the Plantation Trade, Written by the Author of the Essay on Ways and Means, and Published in the Second Part of His Discourses, on the Publick Revenues and on the Trade of England. By an American* (London, 1701), preface, 34–35, 48, 79, 80, 85.

20. William Stith, *The History of the First Discovery and Settlement of Virginia: Being an Essay Towards a General History of This Colony* (Williamsburg, Va., 1747), v.

21. *Mercator*, no. 1 (May 26, 1713), recto, quoted in William Deringer, *Calculated Values: Finance, Politics, and the Quantitative Age* (Cambridge, Mass.: Harvard University Press, 2018), 134. On the debate over the balance of trade and the rhetoric of "facts," see Deringer, *Calculated Values*, 133–136.

22. [Daniel Defoe], *A Plan of the English Commerce; Being a Compleat Prospect of the Trade of This Nation, as Well the Home Trade as the Foreign* (London, 1728), 52, iv, iii, 233–234.

23. *An Account of the Constitution and Present State of Great Britain, Together with a View of Its Trade, Policy, and Interest, Respecting Other Nations, and of the Principal Curiosities of Great Britain and Ireland* (London, [1759]), 225.

24. [Adam Anderson], *An Historical and Chronological Deduction of the Origin of Commerce, from the Earliest Accounts to the Present Time; Containing, an History of the Great Commercial Interests of the British Empire*, 4 vols. (London, 1764), 1:v–viii, title page.

25. Thomas Mortimer, *The Elements of Commerce, Politics and Finances, in Three Treatises on Those Important Subjects; Designed as a Supplement to the Education of British Youth, After They Quit the Public Universities or Private Academies* (London, 1772), vii, viii.

26. Jonathan Boucher, *A View of the Causes and Consequences of the American Revolution; in Thirteen Discourses, Preached in North America Between the Years 1763 and 1775: With an Historical Preface* (London, 1797), xviii.

27. The account that follows is indebted to Miles Ogborn, *Indian Ink: Script and Print in the Making of the English East India Company* (Chicago: University of Chicago Press, 2007), esp. chap. 4. But my argument emphasizes the com-

pany's deployment of the archival record, not (as Ogborn does) the corporation's broader relationship to print.

28. [Samuel Purchas], *Purchas His Pilgrimes. In Five Books* (London, 1625), book 3, 139–147 (charter); [Samuel Purchas], *Purchas His Pilgrimage; or, Relations of the World* (London, 1626), 484. On Purchas, see Peter C. Mancall, *Hakluyt's Promise: An Elizabethan's Obsession for an English America* (New Haven, Conn.: Yale University Press, 2007), chap. 11. On Kayll and the company, see Ogborn, *Indian Ink*, 107–120; and Richmond Barbour, *The Loss of the "Trades Increase": An Early Modern Maritime Catastrophe* (Philadelphia: University of Pennsylvania Press, 2021), chap. 8.

29. [Josiah Child], *A Treatise Wherein Is Demonstrated I. That the East-India Trade Is the Most National of All Foreign Trades* (London, 1681), 15.

30. *A Justification of the Directors of the Netherlands East-India Company. As It Was Delivered Over unto the High and Mighty Lords the States General of the United Provinces, the 22d. of July, 1686* (London, 1687). On the Anglo-Dutch corporate rivalry, see K. N. Chaudhuri and Jonathan I. Israel, "The English and Dutch East India Companies and the Glorious Revolution of 1688–9," in *The Anglo-Dutch Moment: Essays on the Glorious Revolution and Its World Impact,* ed. Jonathan I. Israel (Cambridge, UK: Cambridge University Press, 1991), 407–438.

31. *An Impartial Vindication of the English East-India Company, from the Unjust and Slanderous Imputations Cast upon Them in a Treatise Intituled, A Justification of the Directors of the Netherlands East-India Company; as It Was Delivered Over unto the High and Mighty Lords the States General of the United Provinces* (London, 1688), unpaginated, 21.

32. On the post-1688 challenges to the company's sovereignty, see Philip J. Stern, *The Company-State: Corporate Sovereignty and the Early Modern Foundations of the British Empire in India* (Oxford: Oxford University Press, 2011), chap. 7; and on the Whites and Siam, see Stern, *Company-State,* 145–146, as well as John Anderson, *English Intercourse with Siam in the Seventeenth Century* (London: Kegan Paul, 1890), 315.

33. Samuel White, *A True Account of the Passages at MERGEN in the KINGDOM of Syam, After Captain Anthony Weltden Arrived at That Port in the Curtana Frigat, for Account of the EAST-INDIA Company* ([London], [1688]), 6.

34. *An Historical Abstract of Mr. Samuel White, His Management of Affairs, in His Shabandership of Tenassery and Mergen, During Francis Davenports Stay with Him, in Quality of Secretary: Collected Out of the Said Davenports Own Private Memoirs; for the Clearer Discovery of Whatsoever May Have Relation to the Right Honourable English East-India Company Themselves, or Others Our Country Men in India, Through His Proceedings, in Pretence of His Ministration of That Publick Office Under the King of Syam* (London, n. d.), 14, 30.

35. Robert Travers, *Ideology and Empire in Eighteenth-Century India: The British in Bengal* (Cambridge, UK: Cambridge University Press, 2007), 55.

36. *An Address to the Proprietors of East-India Stock* (London, 1764), 2, 9, 13–14.

37. On company newspaper culture in Bengal, see Ogborn, *Indian Ink,* 205–206; and Ben Gilding, "The Rise and Fall of *Hicky's Bengal Gazette* (1780–2): A Study in

Transoceanic Political Culture," *Journal of Imperial and Commonwealth History* 47 (2019): 1–27.

38. See, for example, "Anecdote," *Hicky's Bengal Gazette; or, The Original Calcutta General Advertiser,* "Saturday, March 26th to Saturday June the 2d. 1781," xix, https://digi.ub.uni-heidelberg.de/diglit/hbg1781_19/0004; "Inteligence Extraordinary from Leaden Hall Street, on India Affairs," *Hicky's Bengal Gazette,* "From Saturday the June 23d to Saturday June 30th 1781," https://digi.ub.uni-heidelberg .de/diglit/hbg1781_23/0001. On the anecdote as a genre of eighteenth-century news, see Robert Darnton, "Blogging, Now and Then (250 Years Ago)," *European Romantic Review* 24 (2013): 255–270.

39. See also Ogborn's discussion of William Bolts in *Indian Ink,* 203–205.

40. On Francis's appointment, see T. H. Boyer, "Philip Francis and the Government of Bengal: Parliament and Personality in the Frustration of an Ambition," *Parliamentary History* 18 (1999): 1–21. For different accounts of Francis's radicalism, see Ranajit Guha, *A Rule of Property for Bengal: An Essay on the Idea of Permanent Settlement* (Paris: Mouton, 1963); Travers, *Ideology and Empire,* chap. 4; and Linda Colley, "Gendering the Global: The Political and Imperial Thought of Philip Francis," *Past and Present,* no. 209 (2010): 117–148. For Burke's career as a colonial agent, see Richard Bourke, *Empire and Revolution: The Political Life of Edmund Burke* (Princeton, N.J.: Princeton University Press, 2015), chap. 6.

41. Travers, *Ideology and Empire,* 142.

42. Philip Francis, *Original Minutes of the Governor-General and Council of Fort William on the Settlement and Collection of the Revenues of Bengal: With a Plan of Settlement, Recommended to the Court of Directors in January, 1776* (London, 1782), 48. On Francis's "ancient constitutionalism," see Travers, *Ideology and Empire,* chap. 4. On the disentangling of "right" from "record" in colonial American opposition ideology and the rejection of an archive-bound conception of constitutionalism in the era of the American Revolution, see Asheesh Kapur Siddique, "The Ideological Origins of 'Written' Constitutionalism," *Early American Studies,* 21 (2023): 557–599.

43. See, for example, John Zephaniah Holwell, *An Address to the Proprietors of the East India Stock; Setting Forth the Unavoidable Necessity and Real Motivations for the Revolution in Bengal, in 1760,* in *India Tracts, by Mr. Holwell and Friends,* 2nd ed. (London, 1764), which pursues its case in the familiar style of a narrative argument followed by reprinted letters and other documents from the past supposedly vindicating the foregoing.

44. Philip Francis to Gilbert Elliot, September 30, 1788, fol. 1, Minto MS 11200, NLS. For examples of Francis's editing with Elliot, in this case in support of the impeachment of the company judge Elijah Impey, see fols. 3–9.

45. Philip Francis to Court of Directors, October 12, 1780, 91, with "List of Papers" (99–101), IOR/H/215.

46. Warren Hastings to Lord North, December 4, 1774, fol. 162, Add MS 29127, BL.

47. Francis, *Original Minutes of the Governor-General and Council of Fort William,* v–vi, x, 172, 175, 186.

48. For Burke's appearances before the Board of Trade, see, for example, Journal of the Board of Trade, November 12, 1772, 167, CO 391/79, TNA; and Journal of the Board of Trade, July 1, 1773, 130–131, CO 391/80, TNA.

49. "Debate on the Clause in Mr. Burke's Establishment Bill for Abolishing the Board of Trade," March 13, 1780, in *The Parliamentary History of England*, Vol. XXI (London, 1814), 234–240, 246–247.

50. Edmund Burke to Henry Dundas, April 5, 1787, 9–10, MS 16, NLS.

51. Edmund Burke, "Speech on Conciliation with America," March 22, 1775, in *The Writings and Speeches of Edmund Burke, vol. 3, Party, Parliament and the American War, 1774–1780,* ed. W. M. Elofson and John A. Woods (Oxford: Oxford University Press, 1996), 124–125, 136, 165.

52. Edmund Burke, "Speech on Sixth Article," April 21, 1789, in *Writings and Speeches of Edmund Burke, vol. 7, India: The Hastings Trial, 1789–1794,* ed. P. J. Marshall and William B. Todd (Oxford: Oxford University Press, 2000), 35, 44, 51.

53. Edmund Burke, "Report on the Lords Journals," April 30, 1794, in Marshall and Todd, *Writings and Speeches,* 7:156, 180.

54. Edmund Burke, "Speech on Resolutions on Future of the Impeachment," May 11, 1790, in Marshall and Todd, *Writings and Speeches,* 7:78. Burke retold the story on May 28, 1794; see Burke, "Speech in Reply 28 May 1794," in Marshall and Todd, *Writings and Speeches,* 7:249–253.

55. Edmund Burke, "Speech in Reply 28 May 1794," in Marshall and Todd, *Writings and Speeches,* 7:263, 272–273, 276.

56. Edmund Burke, "Speech in Reply 30 May 1794," in Marshall and Todd, *Writings and Speeches,* 7:285–286. On Burke's attack on Hastings's interpretations of Mughal history, see Humberto Garcia, *Islam and the English Enlightenment, 1670–1840* (Baltimore: Johns Hopkins University Press, 2012), chap. 3.

57. Edmund Burke, "Speech in Reply 3 June 1794," in Marshall and Todd, *Writings and Speeches,* 7:352.

58. Edmund Burke, "Speech in Reply 11 June 1794," in Marshall and Todd, *Writings and Speeches,* 7:483.

59. Edmund Burke, "Speech in Reply 5 June 1794," in Marshall and Todd, *Writings and Speeches,* 7:394–395, 407.

60. For discussions, see notably Anna Clark, *Scandal: The Sexual Politics of the British Constitution* (Princeton, N.J.: Princeton University Press, 2004); Daniel O'Quinn, *Staging Governance: Theatrical Imperialism in London, 1770–1800* (Baltimore: Johns Hopkins University Press, 2005), chap. 4; Nicholas Dirks, *The Scandal of Empire: India and the Creation of Imperial Britain* (Cambridge, Mass.: Harvard University Press, 2006); and Chiara Rolli, *The Trial of Warren Hastings: Classical Oratory and Reception in Eighteenth-Century England* (London: Bloomsbury, 2019).

61. [Ralph Broome], *The Letters of Simpkin the Second, Poetic Recorder, of All the Proceedings, upon the Trial, of Warren Hastings, Esq. in Westminster Hall* (London, 1789), 5, 11, 32, 46, 130, 157.

Chapter 4. Records of Conquest

1. On the concept of the "extended polity," see Jack P. Greene, *Peripheries and Center: Constitutional Development in the Extended Polities of the British Empire and the United States, 1607–1788* (Athens: University of Georgia Press, 1986).

2. See Richard Tuck, "Alliances with Infidels in the European Imperial Expansion," in *Empire and Modern Political Thought,* ed. Sankar Muthu (Cambridge,

UK: Cambridge University Press, 2012), 81–83; and Edward Cavanagh, "Infidels in English Legal Thought: Conquest, Commerce, and Slavery in the Common Law from Coke to Mansfield, 1603–1793," *Modern Intellectual History* 16 (2019): 375–409.

3. "The Earl of Mansfield to Mr. Grenville," December 24, 1764, in *The Grenville Papers: Being the Correspondence of Richard Grenville Earl Temple, K. G., and the Right Hon: George Grenville, Their Friends and Contemporaries,* ed. William James Smith, 4 vols. (London, 1852), 2:476–477.

4. "The Earl of Mansfield to Mr. Grenville," December 24, 1764, in Smith, ed., *The Grenville Papers,* 2:476–478. On Quebec and the problem of law, see Philip Lawson, *The Imperial Challenge: Quebec and Britain in the Age of the American Revolution* (Montreal: McGill-Queen's University Press, 1989), chap. 3.

5. "Treaty of Paris 1763," The Avalon Project: Documents in Law, History and Diplomacy, Yale Law School, Lillian Goldman Law Library, https://avalon.law.yale.edu/18th_century/paris763.asp.

6. "Commission of Captain-General & Governor in Chief of the Province of Quebec," November 28, 1763, in *Documents Relating to the Constitutional History of Canada, 1759–1791,* ed. Adam Shortt and Arthur G. Doughty (Ottawa: S. E. Dawson, 1907), 128.

7. Hannah Weiss Muller, *Subjects and Sovereign: Bonds of Belonging in the Eighteenth-Century British Empire* (New York: Oxford University Press, 2017), 151–164.

8. For a general account of the debate over the legal foundations of the Quebec Act, see Michel Morin, "Choosing Between French and English Law: The Legal Origins of the Quebec Act," in *Entangling the Quebec Act: Transnational Contexts, Meanings, and Legacies in North America and the British Empire,* ed. Ollivier Hubert and François Furstenberg (Montreal: McGill-Queen's University Press, 2020), 101–130.

9. [Francis Maseres], "A Draught of an Intended Report of the Honourable the Governor in Chief and the Council of the Province of Quebec to the King's Most Excellent Majesty in His Privy Council; Concerning the State of the Laws and the Administration of Justice in that Province," in *A Collection of Several Commissions, and Other Public Instruments, Proceeding from His Majesty's Royal Authority, and Other Papers, Relating to the State of the Province in Quebec in North America, Since the Conquest of It by the British Arms in 1760. Collected by Francis Maseres, Esquire, His Majesty's Attorney General in the Said Province* (London, 1772), 7, 16, 20, 28, 45, 46, 43.

10. [Maseres], "Draught of an Intended Report," 41, 43, 44, 46, 47.

11. Guy Carleton and William Hey, "Report upon the Laws and Courts of Judicature in the Province of Quebec," September 15, 1769, in *Reports on the Laws of Quebec,* ed. W. P. M. Kennedy and Gustave Lanctot (Ottawa: F. A. Acland, 1931), 68, 71.

12. Alexander Wedderburn, "Copy of a Report of the Solicitor General to His Majesty on the Government of Quebec," December 6, 1772, vol. 14, R7484-326-9-E, MG30-D95, Library and Archives of Canada, Ottawa.

13. "An Act for Making More Effectual Provision for the Government of the Province of Quebec in North America," October 7, 1774, Avalon Project, https://avalon.law.yale.edu/18th_century/quebec_act_1774.asp.

14. "Instructions to Our Trusty and Welbeloved Guy Carleton Esquire," January 3, 1775, fols. 50–61, CO 5/206, TNA.

15. David Milobar, "Conservative Ideology, Metropolitan Government, and the Reform of Quebec, 1782–1791," *International History Review* 12 (1990): 62.

16. "The Constitutional Act, 1791," 31 George 3, c. 31, June 10, 1791, in *Documents Relating to the Constitutional History of Canada, 1759–1791, Second and Revised Edition by the Historical Documents Publication Board,* ed. Adam Shortt and Arthur G. Doughty (Ottawa: J. de L. Taché, 1918), 1031–1051.

17. [James Macpherson], *The Rights of Great Britain Asserted Against the Claims of America: Being an Answer to the Declaration of the General Congress,* 2nd ed. (1776; London, 1776), 47.

18. *Letter from Thomas Lord Lyttelton, to William Pitt, Earl of Chatham, on the Quebec Bill* (London, 1774), 17–18.

19. "Remarks on the Quebec-Bill: By the Author of the Farmer Refuted, &c.," *Rivington's New-York Gazette,* June 15, 1775.

20. "Remarks on the Quebec Bill: By the Author of the Farmer Refuted, &c.," *Rivington's New-York Gazette,* June 22, 1775.

21. [Alexander Hamilton], *The Farmer Refuted; or, A More Impartial and Comprehensive View of the Dispute Between Great-Britain and the Colonies, Intended as a Further Vindication of the Congress: In Answer to a Letter from A. W. Farmer* (New York, 1775), 38–39.

22. Demophilus, *The Genuine Principles of the Ancient Saxon; or, English Constitution* (Philadelphia, 1776), 7.

23. *The Constitutional Advocate: By Which, from the Evidence of History and of Records, and from the Principles of the British Government, Every Reader May Form His Own Judgment Concerning the Justice and Policy of the Present War with America* (London, 1776), 27.

24. For a further discussion of how early American constitutional discourse came to define ideas of writtenness in relation to the "British" constitution, see Asheesh Kapur Siddique, "The Ideological Origins of 'Written' Constitutionalism," *Early American Studies,* 21 (2023): 557–599.

25. *Annals of the Congress of the United States, Fourth Congress, First Session, March 7, 1796* (Washington, D.C.: Gales and Seaton, 1849), 701.

26. See especially Gregory Ablavsky, "The Savage Constitution," *Duke Law Journal* 63 (2014): 999–1089; and Claudio Saunt, *Unworthy Republic: The Dispossession of Native Americans and the Road to Indian Territory* (New York: Norton, 2020).

Chapter 5. Dueling Systems

1. John Smith, *The Generall Historie of Virginia, New-England, and the Summer Isles: With the Names of the Adventurers* (London, 1632), 68.

2. *Treaties and Grants from the Country Powers, to the East-India Company, Respecting Their Presidency of Fort St. George, on the Coast of Choromandel; Fort-William, in Bengal; and Bombay, on the Coast of Malabar. From the Year 1756 to 1772* (N.p., 1774), 64–70. On the company's treaties, see Robert Travers, "A British Empire by Treaty in Eighteenth-Century India," in *Empire by Treaty: Negotiating*

European Expansion, 1600–1900, ed. Saliha Belmessous (Oxford: Oxford University Press, 2015), 132–160.

3. Robert Clive to Court of Directors, February 23, 1757, in H. N. Sinha et al., eds., *Fort William–India House Correspondence and Other Contemporary Papers Relating Thereto (Public Series),* 13 vols. (Delhi: National Archives of India, 1949–1974), 2:208.

4. "A Defence of the Dual System of Government in Bengal in Clive's Hand, Offering Historical Precedents," n.d., IOR/G37/6/20.

5. Fort William to Court of Directors, September 30, 1765, quoted in *Report from the Committee Appointed to Enquire into the Nature, State, and Condition of the East India Company, and of the British Affairs in the East Indies* ([London], 1773), appendix no. 86.

6. On the administrative challenges facing the company after 1757, see generally P. J. Marshall, "British Officials Under the East India Company in Eighteenth-Century Bengal," 1965, in *Trade and Conquest: Studies on the Rise of British Dominance in India* (Aldershot, UK: Variorum, 1993), 95–120. On the revenue problem, see H. V. Bowen, *Revenue and Reform: The Indian Problem in British Politics, 1757–1773* (Cambridge, UK: Cambridge University Press, 1991). On the military struggle, see Seema Alavi, *The Sepoys and the Company: Tradition and Transition in Northern India, 1770–1830* (Oxford: Oxford University Press, 1995); Kaushik Roy, "The Hybrid Military Establishment of the East India Company in Asia, 1750–1849," *Journal of Global History* 6 (2011): 195–218; and Douglas M. Peers, "Gunpowder Empires and the Garrison State: Modernity, Hybridity, and the Political Economy of Colonial India, circa 1750–1860," *Comparative Studies of South Asia, Africa, and the Middle East* 27 (2007): 245–258. On law, see A. C. Patra, *The Administration of Justice Under the East-India Company in Bengal, Bihar and Orissa* (Bombay: Asia Publishing, 1962); Radhika Singha, *A Despotism of Law: Crime and Justice in Early Colonial India* (Delhi: Oxford University Press, 1998); and Robert Travers, *Ideology and Empire in Eighteenth-Century India: The British in Bengal* (Cambridge, UK: Cambridge University Press, 2007), esp. chap. 3.

7. [Warren Hastings], *A Proposal for Establishing a Professorship of the Persian Language in the University of Oxford* (London, 1766), 8–11. For Hastings's authorship of this pamphlet, see W. H. Hutton, "A Letter of Warren Hastings on the Civil Service of the East India Company," *English Historical Review* 44 (1929): 640.

8. [Hastings], *A Proposal for Establishing a Professorship of the Persian Language,* 3, 12–15.

9. David Anderson to William Collow, November 19, 1770, fol. 17, Add MS 45438, BL.

10. "Letter XXVIII, to the Hon. Warren Hastings, Esq. Governor-General of Bengal," January 9, 1781, in *The Works of Samuel Johnson, LL.D., in Fourteen Volumes,* ed. Sir John Hawkins, 14 vols. (London, 1788), 14:523.

11. See, for example, P. J. Marshall, "The Making of an Imperial Icon: The Case of Warren Hastings," *Journal of Imperial and Commonwealth History* 27 (1999): 1–16; and Kapil Raj, "From Merchants to Imperial Bureaucrats? Territorial Administration and the East-India Company, Seventeenth–Nineteenth Centuries," in *Serve the Power(s), Serve the State: America and Eurasia,* ed. Juan Carlos Garavaglia, Michael J. Braddick, and Christian Lamoroux (Newcastle, UK: Cambridge Scholars, 2016), 258 (quotation).

12. Nor was it the case that Hastings's patronage was as "new" as Johnson suggested; see chapter 2 of this book for a discussion of seventeenth-century precedents for patronage of Orientalist scholarship by governing institutions and administrators.

13. Travers, *Ideology and Empire,* 69–72, 69 (quotations). For the company's fiscal problems at the end of the 1760s, see Lucy S. Sutherland, *The East India Company in Eighteenth-Century Politics* (Oxford: Clarendon Press, 1952), 190–193; and Nandalal Chatterji, *Bengal Under the Diwani Administration* (Allahabad, India: Indian Press, 1956), 12–28.

14. Hoole's translation was published in 1783 as *Orlando Furioso: Translated from the Italian of Lodovico Ariosto; with Notes: By John Hoole. In Five Volumes* (London, 1783). The fifth and final volume concluded with a note of thanks to "the Governor-General of Bengal, and to the rest of the Gentlemen in the East India Company's service at that settlement, for their very generous patronage of my proposals" (postscript, iv).

15. See, for example, Alexander Bevilacqua, *The Republic of Arabic Letters: Islam and the European Enlightenment* (Cambridge, Mass.: Harvard University Press, 2018); and Jessica Patterson, *Religion, Enlightenment and Empire: British Interpretations of Hinduism in the Eighteenth Century* (Cambridge, UK: Cambridge University Press, 2021). On analogy as a strategy of cultural intelligibility in early modern Europe, see Lynn Hunt, Margaret Jacob, and Wijnand Mijnhardt, *The Book That Changed Europe: Picart and Bernard's Religious Ceremonies of the World* (Cambridge, Mass.: Harvard University Press, 2010).

16. Court of Directors to Fort William, June 30, 1769, in Sinha et al., eds., *Fort William–India House Correspondence,* 5:213–214.

17. Select Committee Meeting, August 11, 1769, 425–428, IOR/P/A/9.

18. Select Committee Meeting, August 16, 1769, 474–475, IOR/P/A/9.

19. Harry Verelst, *A View of the Rise, Progress, and Present State of the English Government in Bengal: Including a Reply to the Misrepresentations of Mr. Bolts, and Other Writers* (London, 1772), "To the Reader," 227–238 ("Form of Instructions to be issued by the Resident at the Durbar to the several Supervisors"). See also the discussion in Travers, *Ideology and Empire,* 77–80. For the translation of Verelst's dictates into concrete administrative activity on the ground, see the discussion of the career of George Vansittart, revenue collector, in Travers, *Ideology and Empire,* 86–99.

20. Warren Hastings to Thomas Motte, September 27, 1769, fol. 10, Add MS 29125, BL.

21. Warren Hastings to Alexander Wynch, December 9, 1769, fol. 19v, Add MS 29125, BL.

22. Warren Hastings to Major John Grant, October 18, 1770, fol. 57v, Add MS 29125, BL. On the "Shasters" in company political thought in this period, see Patterson, *Religion, Enlightenment and Empire,* chap. 3.

23. Warren Hastings to Richard Barwell, July 22, 1772, fol. 111v, Add MS 29125, BL: "You join *Vackeel* & *Embassador* as Terms synonymous—They are not altogether so."

24. *Reflections on the Present State of the East-India Trade; and Proposals to Render It of More General Benefit to the British Nation, Without Changing the Present System* (Edinburgh, 1769), "Advertisement."

25. [George Johnstone], *Thoughts on Our Acquisitions in the East Indies; Particularly Respecting Bengal* (London, 1771), iii.

26. [Alexander Dalrymple], *A General View of the East-India Company, Written in January, 1769. To Which Are Added, Some Observations on the Present State of Their Affairs* (London, 1772), 72.

27. Warren Hastings to Laurence Sulivan, October 3, 1770, fol. 47v, Add MS 29126, BL.

28. Warren Hastings to Ralph Leycester, January 23, 1771, fols. 52–52v, Add MS 29126, BL.

29. Warren Hastings to Francis Sykes, February 2, 1771, fols. 55–55v, Add MS 29126, BL.

30. Warren Hastings to Robert Holt, February 7, 1771, fol. 57v, Add MS 29126, BL.

31. Warren Hastings to Unknown, February 7, 1771, fol. 58, Add MS 29126, BL.

32. Warren Hastings to Laurence Sulivan, February 10, 1772, fols. 111v–112v, Add MS 29126, BL.

33. Warren Hastings to George Colebrooke, February 15, 1772, fols. 115v, 120, Add MS 29126, BL.

34. Warren Hastings to Lord Shelburne, July 16, 1771, fols. 73–75v, 76, Add MS 29126, BL.

35. Warren Hastings to George Barwell, July 22, 1772, fols. 113–113v, 115v, Add MS 29125, BL.

36. Warren Hastings to Laurence Sulivan, February 10, 1772, fol. 115v, Add MS 29125, BL.

37. Warren Hastings to John Graham, July 23, 1772, fol. 117, Add MS 29125, BL. See also Hastings's directives to servants to seize Mughal records: Hastings to William Rooke, May 8, 1772, fol. 154v, Add MS 29126, BL.

38. Warren Hastings to Court of Directors, November 11, 1773, 146–147, 149–150, 152–153, IOR/H/115.

39. Warren Hastings to George Colebrooke, March 26, 1772, fols. 12–13v, Add MS 29127, BL.

40. Warren Hastings to Laurence Sulivan, November 11, 1772, fols. 45v–46, Add MS 29127, BL.

41. Warren Hastings to Robert Palk, November 11, 1772, fol. 49v, Add MS 29127, BL.

42. Warren Hastings to Laurence Sulivan, March 10, 1774, fols. 119, 124v, Add MS 29127, BL.

43. "An Act for Establishing Certain Regulations for the Better Management of the Affairs of the East-India Company, as Well in India as in Europe," 13 George 3, c. 63, in Danby Pickering, *The Statutes at Large, from Magna Charta to the End of the Thirteenth Parliament of Great Britain, Anno 1773*, 46 vols. (Cambridge, UK, 1773), 30:124–143.

44. Warren Hastings to Lord Mansfield, March 21, 1774, fols. 142v–146, Add MS 29127, BL.

45. Warren Hastings to Court of Directors, March 24, 1774, 433–434, IOR/H/115.

46. Warren Hastings to Laurence Sulivan, December 4, 1774, fol. 155, Add MS 29127, BL. On the antagonism between Hastings and Francis, see Sophia Weitzman, *Warren Hastings and Philip Francis* (Manchester, UK: Manchester University

Press, 1929), esp. chap. 2. On the circumstances of Francis's appointment, see T. H. Boyer, "The Appointment of Philip Francis to the Bengal Supreme Council," *Historical Journal* 38 (1995): 145-149.

47. Warren Hastings to Lord North, January 12, 1775, fol. 169, Add MS 29127, BL.

48. Warren Hastings to Sir Gilbert Elliot, August 7, 1775, fol. 222v, Add MS 29127, BL.

49. Warren Hastings to Laurence Sulivan, February 25, 1775, fol. 177, Add MS 29127, BL.

50. Warren Hastings to Lord North, February 26, 1775, fol. 178v, Add MS 29127, BL. Hastings also sought to connect Lord North to company officials, whom he claimed held "a complete Knowledge of the Government of Bengal" and "useful Information" that would benefit "the National Interests" with respect to India; see Hastings to Lord North, August 7, 1775, January 20, 1776, fols. 214v, 234-234v, Add MS 29127, BL.

51. Warren Hastings to Lord North, November 20, 1775, fols. 228, 230v, Add MS 29127, BL.

52. Warren Hastings to Edward Wheler, August 7, 1775, fol. 216, Add MS 29127, BL.

53. Warren Hastings to Edward Wheler, August 8, 1775, fol. 220, Add MS 29127, BL.

54. Warren Hastings to Sir Gilbert Elliot, August 7, 1775, fols. 221-222, Add MS 29127, BL.

55. Warren Hastings to Laurence Sulivan, March 21, 1776, fol. 243, Add MS 29127, BL.

56. Warren Hastings to Samuel Johnson, August 7, 1775, fol. 224, Add MS 29127, BL.

57. Warren Hastings to Lord Mansfield, August 8, 1775, fol. 217, Add MS 29127, BL.

58. Warren Hastings to Lord Mansfield, January 20, 1776, fols. 231v-233, Add MS 29127, BL. See also Hastings's recommendation of officials "conversant in the Business of this Government" to Lord North, January 20, 1776, fol. 235v, Add MS 29127, BL.

59. Warren Hastings to Laurence Sulivan, January 23, 1776, fol. 238, Add MS 29127, BL.

60. "Letter from Warren Hastings, Esq., Governor-General of *Fort-William,* in *Bengal,* to the Court of Directors of the United Company of Merchants of *England, Trading to the East-Indies,*" March 27, 1775, in *A Code of Gentoo Laws; or, Ordinations of the Pundits, from a Persian Translation, Made from the Original, Written in the Shanscrit Language* (London, 1776), iii–iv. For the receipt of Halhed's code by the Court of Directors, see Minutes of the Court of Directors, January 10, 1776, 402, IOR/B/91.

61. Court of Directors to Bengal, April 5, 1776, 117, IOR/E/4/623.

62. *A Code of Gentoo Laws,* lii ("translation," "original," "Records of . . . unfathomable Antiquity"), xiii ("conjectural Doctrines"), xxi ("real Appellations," "denominated"), xxiv ("Alphabets"), xxxvii ("The Hindoos as well as the Chinese," "an Antiquity," "acquainted with Letters," "their Annals"), lxxiii ("striking Likeness," "the Laws of Moses," "many other Parts," "no Part of these Laws," "deserve the Consideration"), 6 ("Names of the Bramins"), 7 ("Glossary of such Shàscrit, Persian, and Bengal Words, as Occur in This Work"), 26-28 ("A List of the Books From whence this POOTTEE was compiled, ranked in the Order of their several Dates, as nearly as could be ascertained").

63. See, for example, Rosane Rocher, *Orientalism, Poetry, and the Millennium: The Checkered Life of Nathaniel Brassey Halhed, 1751–1830* (Delhi: Motilal Banarsidass, 1983); Thomas R. Trautmann, *Aryans and British India* (Berkeley: University of California Press, 1997); Travers, *Ideology and Empire,* 124–126; Miles Ogborn, *Indian Ink: Script and Print in the Making of the English East India Company* (Chicago: University of Chicago Press, 2007), 215 (quotation); and Patterson, *Religion, Enlightenment and Empire,* chap. 5.

64. See, among a vast scholarship, P. J. Marshall, "Warren Hastings as Scholar and Patron," in *Statesmen, Scholars and Merchants: Essays in Eighteenth-Century History Presented to Dame Lucy Sutherland,* ed. Anne Whiteman, J. S. Bromley, and P. G. M. Dickson (Oxford: Clarendon Press, 1973), 242–262; Michael S. Dodson, *Orientalism, Empire, and National Culture: India, 1770–1880* (New York: Palgrave Macmillan, 2007); Jon Wilson, *The Domination of Strangers: Modern Governance in Eastern India, 1780–1835* (New York: Palgrave Macmillan, 2008), 45–53; Jessica Ratcliff, "The East India Company, the Company's Museum, and the Political Economy of Natural History in the Early Nineteenth Century," *Isis* 107 (2016): 495–516; and Joshua Ehrlich, *The East India Company and the Politics of Knowledge* (Cambridge, UK: Cambridge University Press, 2023), chap. 1.

65. Court of Directors to Bengal, April 16, 1777, 512, IOR/E/4/624.

66. Warren Hastings to Stephen Lushington, November 15, 1799, fols. 236–236v, IOR/E/1/101.

67. Warren Hastings to Hugh Elliot, "Enclosed in Mr Elliot's Letter dated the 10th February 7, 1777," fols. 146–146v, Add MS 29128, BL.

68. Warren Hastings to Laurence Sulivan, August 23, 1778, fols. 176–177, enclosing "A Short View of the Maratta State, and a Narrative of Occurrences Relating to It, Begun and Continued at Different Periods," fols. 177–181v, Add MS 29128, BL.

69. Warren Hastings to John Graham, July 16, 1776, fols. 260v, 266–266v, Add MS 29127, BL.

70. Warren Hastings to George Johnston, September 13, 1776, fol. 272, Add MS 29127, BL.

71. Travers, *Ideology and Empire,* 156–163.

72. Warren Hastings to George Vansittart, March 3, 1777, fols. 34v–35v, Add MS 29128, BL.

73. Warren Hastings to Thomas Bates Rous, September 17, 1776, fol. 276v, Add MS 29127, BL. For Hastings's proposed reforms, see Hastings to Lord North, September 15, 1776, fols. 284–284v, Add MS 29127, BL.

74. Warren Hastings to John Purling, September 16, 1776, fol. 285v, Add MS 29127, BL; Hastings to Joseph Sparkes, September 18, 1776, fol. 288, Add MS 29127, BL.

75. Warren Hastings to Frederick Pigou, September 19, 1776, fol. 290, Add MS 29127, BL.

76. Warren Hastings to Jonathan Scott, April 20, 1781, fol. 344v, Add MS 29128, BL.

77. Warren Hastings to George Vansittart, March 12, 1777, fol. 42, Add MS 29128, BL.

78. Warren Hastings to John Graham and Lachlan Maclean, 1777, fol. 45v, Add MS 29128, BL.

79. Warren Hastings to Francis Sykes, November 21, 1777, fols. 91–91v, Add MS 29128, BL.

80. Warren Hastings to Jonathan Scott, February 5, 1781, fols. 310–312, Add MS 29128, BL.

81. *A Narrative of the Insurrection Which Happened in the Zemeedary of Banaris in the Month of August 1781, and of the Transactions of the Governor-General in That District; with an Appendix of Authentic Papers and Affidavits* (Calcutta, 1782), prefatory note, 58. On Hastings and Benares, see Bernard S. Cohn, "The Initial British Impact on India: A Case Study of the Benares Region," *Journal of Asian Studies* 19 (1960): 418–431.

82. Warren Hastings, *A Narrative of the Late Transactions at Benares* (London, 1782), 92.

83. "An Act for the Better Regulation and Management of the Affairs of the *East India* Company, and of the *British* Possessions in *India;* and for Establishing a Court of Judicature for the More Speedy and Effectual Trial of Persons Accused of Offences Committed in the East-Indies," 24 George 3, c. 25, in *A Collection of Charters and Statutes Relating to the East India Company; with an Appendix, Containing Acts and Parts of Acts, Relating to Shipping, Duties, Regulations for Export and Import, &c. &c. Which in General Do Not Solely Relate to the East India Company; Together with a Copious Index of the Whole* (London, 1817), 221–237. For the politics of the act and Dundas's appointment, see David J. Brown, "The Government of Scotland Under Henry Dundas and William Pitt," *History* 83 (1998): 265–279; and Travers, *Ideology and Empire*, 210–213.

84. "List of the Packet Sent by the Surprize," with a note that "the Packets were closed on the 12th of December and the Surprize left the Pilot on the 16th," n.d., fols. 268v–269v, Add MS 29129, BL. On the sailing of the *Surprise*, see H. V. Bowen, *The Business of Empire: The East India Company and Imperial Britain, 1758–1833* (Cambridge, UK: Cambridge University Press, 2006), 156.

85. Warren Hastings to Jonathan Scott, December 9, 1784, fol. 275, Add MS 29129, BL.

86. Warren Hastings to Jonathan Scott, December 27, 1784, fol. 270, Add MS 29129, BL.

87. For the Court of Directors' financial support for the translation's publication, see Minutes of the Court of Directors, June 9, 1785, 118–119, IOR/B/101.

88. *The Bhăgvăt-Gēētā; or, Dialogues of Krēēshnă and Ărjŏŏn; in Eighteen Lectures; with Notes. Translated from the Original, in the Sănskrēēt, or Ancient Language of the Brāhmăns, by Charles Wilkins, Senior Merchant in the Service of the Honourable the East India Company, on Their Bengal Establishment* (London, 1785), 5–10.

89. *The Bhăgvăt-Gēētā*, 11.

90. *The Bhăgvăt-Gēētā*, 13.

91. "List of the Packet Sent by the Surprize," n.d., fol. 269v, Add MS 29129, BL. For Gladwin's work on the translation, see Francis Gladwin to David Anderson, December 16, 1775, fol. 354, Add MS 45431, BL.

92. For the court's support of Gladwin's vocabulary, see Court of Directors to Bengal, April 16, 1777, 593, IOR/E/4/623. The work was published as *A Compendious Vocabulary. English and Persian Including All the Oriental Simples in the Materia Medica, Employed in Modern Practice: With Tables Subjoined of the Successions of*

the *Khaliffs, and of the Kings of Persia and Hindostan, Compiled for the Use of the East India Company by Francis Gladwin* (Malda, Bengal, 1780).

93. "Extract of a General Letter from the Governor General and Council to the Court of Directors," December 31, 1785, fols. 361–362, Add MS 29201, BL.

94. *The Hedàya, or Guide; A Commentary on the Mussulman Laws: Translated by Order of the Governor-General and Council of Bengal, by Charles Hamilton,* 4 vols. (London, 1791), 1:vii, lxxxvi.

95. Warren Hastings to Court of Directors, February 21, 1784, fol. 232, Add MS 29129, BL.

96. Minutes of the Court of Directors, May 31, 1784, 89, IOR/B/100. See also the requests listed in the minutes of other meetings contained in this same volume: Minutes of the Court of Directors, June 23, 1784, 144–145; June 25, 1784, 150–151; June 30, 1784, 159; July 7, 1784, 180; and August 4, 1784, 258–259, all in IOR/B/100. These requests from the prosecution continued throughout the trial; see, for example, Minutes of the Court of Directors, November 1, 1787, 637, IOR/B/105; April 2, 1788, 1205, IOR/B/106; May 22, 1793, 127–128, IOR/B/117.

97. William Ramsay to Warren Hastings and Nathaniel Middleton, May 30, 1786, 649, IOR/E/1/224.

98. Minutes of the Court of Directors, May 30, 1787, 138, IOR/B/105.

99. Warren Hastings to John Shore, February 19, 1787, fol. 387, Add MS 29170, BL.

100. Warren Hastings to George Nesbitt Thompson, February 8, 1789, fol. 103, Add MS 29171, BL.

101. Warren Hastings to Earl of Moira, November 12, 1812, fols. 5–5v, 16v–18, Add MS 29234, BL.

102. Warren Hastings to Earl of Moira, November 12, 1812, fol. 15v, Add MS 29234, BL.

103. Eric Stokes, *The English Utilitarians and India* (Delhi: Oxford University Press, 1959), 3–7; David Kopf, *British Orientalism and the Bengal Renaissance: The Dynamics of Indian Modernization, 1773–1785* (Berkeley: University of California Press, 1969), 238 (quotations).

104. Singha, *A Despotism of Law,* xvii (quotation); Ehrlich, *The East India Company and the Politics of Knowledge,* 11–16; Patterson, *Religion, Enlightenment and Empire,* 301–308.

105. On these commissions, see John Torrance, "Social Class and Bureaucratic Innovation: The Commissioners for Examining the Public Accounts, 1780–1787," *Past and Present* 78 (1978): 56–81; and Mark Knights, *Trust and Distrust: Corruption in Office in Britain and Its Empire, 1600–1850* (Oxford: Oxford University Press, 2021), 210–215. For the broader context of reform in which this shift in conceptions of office occurred, see Philip Harling, *The Waning of "Old Corruption": The Politics of Economical Reform in Britain, 1779–1846* (Cambridge, UK: Cambridge University Press, 1996).

106. "The Seventh Report of the Commissioners Appointed to Examine, Take, and State, the Public Accounts of the Kingdom," 1782, in William Molleson, *The Reports of the Commissioners Appointed to Examine, Take, and State the Public Accounts of the Kingdom, Presented to His Majesty, and to Both Houses of Parliament: With the Appendixes Complete. Volume the First* (London, 1783), 137–138.

107. "The Fifth Report of the Commissioners Appointed to Examine, Take, and State, the Public Accounts of the Kingdom," 1781, in Molleson, *Reports of the Commissioners*, 71.

108. "An Act That All Proceedings in Courts of Justice Within That Part of Great Britain Called England, and in the Court of Exchequer in Scotland, Shall Be in the English Language," George 2, c. 267, in Pickering, *The Statutes at Large*, 16:248–249.

109. "The Eighth Report of the Commissioners Appointed to Examine, Take, and State, the Public Accounts of the Kingdom," in John Lane, *The Reports of the Commissioners Appointed to Examine, Take, and State the Public Accounts of the Kingdom . . . Volume the Second* (London, 1785), 38.

110. "The Eleventh Report of the Commissioners Appointed to Examine, Take, and State, the Public Accounts of the Kingdom," in Lane, *Reports of the Commissioners*, 134–135.

111. On Cornwallis's embrace of the commission's recommendations, see Knights, *Trust and Distrust*, 216–218.

112. "Minute of the Governor General, Dated 11th February 1793; with Accounts Accompanying It," in *Second Report from the Select Committee on the Affairs of the East India Company* (London, 1810), 119–121.

113. "Commission for Establishing the Measures Recommended by the House of Commons Respecting the Public Records of the Kingdom," July 19, 1800, 1–2, PRO 36/1, TNA.

114. Francis Palgrave, *First Report of the Deputy Keeper of the Public Records* (London, 1840), 16.

115. Commission note, 1831, fol. 1, Add MS 52190, BL.

116. Craig Robertson, "Documents, Empire, and Capitalism in the Nineteenth Century," in *Information: A Historical Companion*, ed. Ann Blair et al. (Princeton, N.J.: Princeton University Press, 2021), 163–164.

Chapter 6. From State Papers to Public Records

1. Patrick Fraser Tytler to Lord John Russell, July 18, 1839, HO 44/34, TNA.

2. "The Present State of English Historical Literature. I. Accessibility of Our Historical Materials," *Gentleman's Magazine and Historical Review*, March 1851, 235.

3. "Answer of the Master of the Rolls to the Memorial Requesting Access to the Public Records by Literary Inquirers, Without Payment of Fees," July 31, 1851, in *Thirteenth Report of the Deputy Keeper of the Public Records, 3d June 1852* (London, 1852), 39. See also Philippa Levine, *The Amateur and the Professional: Antiquarians, Historians and Archaeologists in Victorian England, 1838–1886* (Cambridge, UK: Cambridge University Press, 1986), chap. 5.

4. Walter Boyd, *Reflections on the Financial System of Great Britain, and Particularly on the Sinking Fund; Written in France in the Summer of 1812* (London, 1815), 1–2. On the rise of the language of "data," see Daniel Rosenberg, "Data Before the Fact," in *"Raw Data" Is an Oxymoron*, ed. Lisa Gitelman (Cambridge, Mass.: MIT Press, 2013), 15–40.

5. "Political Economy," in *The Encyclopaedia Britannica; or, Dictionary of Arts, Sciences, and General Literature,* 7th ed., 21 vols. (Edinburgh, 1842), 18:260. On the relationship between "fact" and political economy, see Mary Poovey, *A History of the Modern Fact: Problems of Knowledge in the Sciences of Wealth and Society* (Chicago: University of Chicago Press, 1998).

6. On Chalmers's early life, see Grace Amelia Cockroft, *The Public Life of George Chalmers* (New York: Columbia University Press, 1939), 11–44, as well as Chalmers's memorial to the Loyalist Claims Commission: "The Memorial of George Chalmers, Formerly of Baltimore Town in Baltimore County, Maryland, Counsellor at Law, but Now of Park Street in the City of Westminster," October 14, 1783, fols. 1–8, AO 13/93, TNA. I have also discussed Chalmers in a different context in Asheesh Kapur Siddique, "The Archival Epistemology of Political Economy in the Early Modern British Atlantic World," *William and Mary Quarterly,* 3rd series, 77 (2020): 664–674.

7. "The Memorial of George Chalmers," October 14, 1783, fol. 8, AO 13/93, TNA.

8. For the significance of archives and records as sources of legal knowledge in early modern England and its empire, see Richard J. Ross, "The Memorial Culture of Early Modern English Lawyers: Memory as Keyword, Shelter, and Identity, 1560–1640," *Yale Journal of Law and the Humanities* 10, no. 2 (Summer 1998): 229–326; and Paul Halliday, "Authority in the Archives," *Critical Analysis of Law* 1, no. 1 (2014): 110–142. On the importance of law and legal reasoning to conceptions of fact in early modern English culture, see Barbara J. Shapiro, *A Culture of Fact: England, 1550–1720* (Ithaca, N.Y.: Cornell University Press, 2000), chap. 1.

9. On preserving and printing administrative records in colonial America, see H. G. Jones, *For History's Sake: The Preservation and Publication of North Carolina History, 1663–1903* (Chapel Hill, N.C.: University of North Carolina Press, 1966), chaps. 1–2; David D. Hall, "The Atlantic Economy in the Eighteenth Century," in *A History of the Book in America,* vol. 1, *The Colonial Book in the Atlantic World,* ed. Hugh Amory and David D. Hall (Chapel Hill: University of North Carolina Press, 2007), 152–162, esp. 160–162.

10. "Letter to Lord Mansfield, on the History of the American Colonies; by George Chalmers," 1780, MS Sparks 7, pp. 2–3, Houghton Library, Harvard University, Cambridge, Mass.

11. On the relationship between history and political economy in Scottish Enlightenment thought, see J. G. A. Pocock, "Cambridge Paradigms and Scotch Philosophers: A Study of the Relations Between the Civic Humanist and the Civil Jurisprudential Interpretation of Eighteenth-Century Social Thought," in *Wealth and Virtue: The Shaping of Political Economy in the Scottish Enlightenment,* ed. Istvan Hont and Michael Ignatieff (Cambridge, UK: Cambridge University Press, 1983), 235–252; John Robertson, *The Case for the Enlightenment: Scotland and Naples, 1680–1760* (Cambridge, UK: Cambridge University Press, 2005), esp. chap. 3; and Andrew Sabl, *Hume's Politics: Coordination and Crisis in the "History of England"* (Princeton, N.J.: Princeton University Press, 2012), chap. 2.

12. William Knox eventually published these documents in 1789 to vindicate his decisions in office, especially his staunch advocacy of nonconciliation with the colonies during the American crisis; see [Knox], *Extra Official State Papers; Addressed to the Right Hon. Lord Rawdon, and the Other Members of the Two Houses of Parliament, Associated for the Preservation of the Constitution and Promoting the*

Prosperity of the British Empire (London, 1789). Knox's practices of documentary collection and editing remain largely unexplored but for a brief discussion, see Leland J. Bellot, *William Knox: The Life and Thought of an Eighteenth-Century Imperialist* (Austin: University of Texas Press, 1977), 202, 213-214. For examples of Chalmers's defense of ministerial policy during the Revolutionary War, see [Chalmers], *An Answer from the Electors of Bristol, to the Letter of Edmund Burke, Esq. on the Affairs of America* (London, 1777); and [Chalmers], *Second Thoughts; or, Observations upon Lord Abingdon's Thoughts on the Letter of Edmund Burke, Esq. to the Sheriffs of Bristol* (London, 1777).

13. William Knox to Joseph Ayloffe and Thomas Astle, March 4, 1780, 301, CO 5/251, TNA.

14. Chalmers's collections were broken up in an 1841 auction; for a contemporary listing, see *Catalogue of the Very Curious, Valuable and Extensive Library of the Late George Chalmers, Esq., F.R.S., F.S.A., Author of Caledonia Antiqua, Life of Mary Queen of Scots* (London, 1841). His personal correspondence, manuscripts, and collected books are now dispersed among several archives, with especially sizable deposits at the New York Public Library; the British Library, London; the National Library of Scotland, Edinburgh; and the National Records of Scotland, Edinburgh.

15. George Chalmers to George Germain, March 1780, fol. 64, CO 5/157, TNA.

16. George Chalmers to J. Forster, September 19, 1783, fols. 26-26v, AO 13/93, TNA.

17. George Chalmers, *An Estimate of the Comparative Strength of Britain during the Present and Four Preceding Reigns; and of the Losses of Her Trade from Every War Since the Revolution* (London, 1786), iii-iv.

18. George Chalmers, *Opinions of Eminent Lawyers, on Various Points of English Jurisprudence, Chiefly Concerning the Colonies, Fisheries, and Commerce, of Great Britain: Collected, and Digested, from the Originals, in the Board of Trade, and Other Depositories*, 2 vols. (London, 1814), 1:iv-vii, title page.

19. On the dissolution of the Board of Trade and the founding of the new Privy Council committee, see Vincent T. Harlow, *The Founding of the Second British Empire, 1763-1793*, vol. 2, *New Continents and Changing Values* (London: Longmans, 1964), chap. 5.

20. Meeting "of the Committee of Council, Appointed for the Consideration of All Matters Relating to Trade and Foreign Plantations," April 6, 1784, fols. 82-84v, Add MS 38388, BL.

21. For Chalmers's appointment and role as custodian of the papers, see Council of Trade Minutes, August 25, 1786, 15-16, BT 5/4, TNA.

22. "Art. IV. *An Estimate of the Comparative Strength of Great Britain, During the Present, and Four Preceding Reigns . . . By George Chalmers*," *Monthly Review*, March 1787, 213-217.

23. Chalmers, *Opinions of Eminent Lawyers*, 1:ii-iii.

24. George Chalmers, *The Life of Mary, Queen of Scots; Drawn from the State Papers*, 2 vols. (London, 1818), 1:iii (quotations), 315.

25. George Chalmers, *The Author of Junius Ascertained: From a Concatenation of Circumstances; Amounting to Moral Demonstration* (London, 1817), 31, 3-4, 1.

26. Thomas Mortimer, *The Elements of Commerce, Politics and Finances, in Three Treatises on Those Important Subjects; Designed as a Supplement to the Education of British Youth, After They Quit the Public Universities or Private Academies* (London,

1772), viii; Thomas Mortimer, *Lectures on the Elements of Commerce, Politics, and Finances* (London, 1801), 161.

27. George Chalmers, *An Historical View of the Domestic Economy of G. Britain, and Ireland, from the Earliest to the Present Times* (Edinburgh, 1812), xv–xvi.

28. Jane Haldimand Marcet, *Conversations on Political Economy in Which the Elements of That Science Are Familiarly Explained* (1816; reprint Cambridge, UK: Cambridge University Press, 2010), 20.

29. Sir John Sinclair, *Specimens of Statistical Reports* (London, 1793), viii, x–xi. For the manifestations of these shifts within offices, see David Eastwood, "'Amplifying the Province of the Legislature': The Flow of Information and the English State in the Early Nineteenth Century," *Historical Research* 62, no. 149 (October 1989): 276–294; Ian Hacking, *The Taming of Chance* (Cambridge, UK: Cambridge University Press, 1990); and Zoë Laidlaw, *Colonial Connections, 1815–45: Patronage, the Information Revolution and Colonial Government* (Manchester, UK: Manchester University Press, 2005), chap. 7.

30. "Act of Council Appointing Messrs. Bruce and Duncan to Teach Classes in the College," October 26, 1774, fol. 187, MS 3431, NLS. I have also discussed Bruce in Asheesh Kapur Siddique, "Mobilizing the 'State Papers' of Empire: John Bruce and the Bureaucratic Archives of Britain," *Journal of Early Modern History*, 22, no. 5 (October 2018), 392–410.

31. Roger L. Emerson, *Academic Patronage and the Scottish Enlightenment: Glasgow, Edinburgh, and St Andrews Universities* (Edinburgh: Edinburgh University Press, 2008), 339.

32. On Dundas's offer to Bruce, see Charles Hope to John Bruce, May 16, 1788, GD 152/215/14/29–31, NRS; and Henry Dundas to James Finlayson, November 2, 1790, GD 152/104/13/16, NRS. For the review, see "Art. XI. The Elements of the Science of Ethics, on the Principles of Natural Philosophy. By John Bruce," *Monthly Review*, June 1787, 500. On Dundas's patronage in facilitating the entry of Scots into East India Company and government service, see P. J. Marshall, *East India Fortunes: The British in Bengal in the Eighteenth Century* (Oxford: Clarendon Press, 1976), 12–13; and George K. McGilvary, *East India Patronage and the British State: The Scottish Elite and Politics in the Eighteenth Century* (London: Bloomsbury, 2008).

33. Henry Dundas to Thomas Morton, September 10, 1784, 2, IOR/E/2/29; September 10, 1784, 350; January 12, 1785, 785–786, IOR/B/100.

34. See, for example, Francis Russell to Thomas Morton, January 11, 1785, 45–48; and William Cabell to Morton, April 22, 1785, 85, IOR/E/2/29.

35. "Mr Bruce's Plan for Forming a History of British Affairs in the East Indies," September 6, 1789, fols. 467–469, GD 51/3/30/1, NRS.

36. John Bruce to Henry Dundas, September 6, 1789, fol. 471, GD 51/3/30/2, NRS.

37. John Bruce to William Cabell, "about 1791," fols. 475–476, GD 51/3/30/4, NRS.

38. John Bruce to William Cabell, n.d., fols. 478–480, GD 51/3/30/5, NRS.

39. "Memorandum, Dated May 27, 1790, by Henry Dundas . . . Concerning the Management of the Records of the East India Company," Mss Eur D. 849, BL.

40. John Bruce to Henry Dundas, September 24, 1791, GD 152/51, NRS.

41. "Regulations for the Indian Branch of the State Paper Office," September 1791, GD 152/51, NRS.

42. "Patent to John Bruce Esqr, Keeper and Register of Papers of State," November 15, 1792, Private Register, State Paper Office, 1–6, SP 45/75, TNA.

43. [John Bruce], *Historical View of Plans, for the Government of British India and Regulation of Trade to the East Indies, and Outlines of a Plan of Foreign Government, of Commercial Oeconomy, and of Domestic Administration, for the Asiatic Interests of Great Britain* (London, 1793), vii.

44. John Bruce to Alexander Adamson, May 16, 1793, 1–2, IOR/H/456e. See also Bruce to John Shore, May 17, 1793, 5–7; Bruce to William Jones, May 17, 1793, 9–10; and Bruce to Sir Charles Oakeley, May 18, 1793, 13–14, IOR/H/456e.

45. Henry Dundas to John Bruce, [July 9], 1793, GD 152/104/13/25, NRS. For Dundas's attainment of the royal patent for Bruce's appointment, see Dundas to George III, September 26, 1792, fol. 67, Add MS 40100, BL.

46. Minutes of the Court of Directors, July 18, 1764, 138, IOR/B/80; Minutes of the Committee of Correspondence, August 14, 1764, fol. 134, IOR/D/23.

47. George Colebrooke to Robert Orme, August 2, 1769, 221, IOR/E/1/214; Minutes of the Court of Directors, August 2, 1769, 137–138, IOR/B/85. See also Orme to Colebrooke, August 3, 1769, 452, IOR/E/1/52, thanking the Court of Directors for the appointment and its granting of "permission . . . of consulting their records." On the "historiographer royal," see Denys Hay, "The Historiographers Royal in England and Scotland," *Scottish Historical Review* 30 (1951): 15–29.

48. On Orme, see Asoka Tammita-Delgoda, "'Nabob, Historian and Orientalist': The Life and Writings of Robert Orme (1728–1801)" (Ph.D. diss., University of London, 1991).

49. Minutes of the Court of Directors, July 10, 1793, 258, IOR/B/117.

50. John Bruce to William Devaynes, October 30, 1793, 31–32, IOR/H/456e.

51. For the company's solicitations for materials on Bruce's behalf, see Bengal Public Department Records, "Circular," March 29, 1797, 329–331, IOR/E/4/646; and "List of Papers Collected by the Committee Appointed at Bombay . . . for Procuring Information for the Use of the Company's Historiographer," 1798–1799, IOR/H/46.

52. See, for example, John Bruce, "Progress of the Levelling Opinions in Great Britain," 1794, GD 152/40, NRS; [John Bruce], *Report on the Arrangements Which Have Been Adopted . . . When France Threatened Invasions of Britain or Ireland* (London, 1798); John Bruce, "Observations on Lord Cornwallis' Dispatches . . . for the Right Hon. Mr Dundas," 1790, IOR/A/2/11A; "Proposed Establishments as First Drawn Up by Mr Bruce," July 4, 1795, fols. 105–139, IOR/H/453; and Bruce, "Plan of a Dep.t for the Recruits of the East India Company's Army," n.d., 1–52, GD 152/189, NRS. Bruce's sources included his brother Robert, an artilleryman in Bengal, and Henry Dundas's nephew Philip, governor of Bombay: see John Bruce to Philip Dundas, May 27, 1794, 55, IOR/H/456e; and Robert Bruce to John Bruce, June 2, 1795, fols. 1–2, GD 152/21/5/6/2, NRS. For more details on Bruce's information networks, see Asheesh Kapur Siddique, "Paperwork, Governance, and Archive in the British Empire During the Age of Revolutions" (Ph.D. diss., Columbia University, 2016), 243–249.

53. "Mr. Nepean's Draft of a Proposed Letter Between Mr. Dundas to Lord Grenville," 1799, GD 152/39, NRS.

54. Charles F. Mullett, "The 'Better Reception, Preservation, and More Convenient Use' of Public Records in Eighteenth-Century England," *American Archivist* 27 (1964): esp. 205. For an earlier effort to organize the state papers in 1732, see *A Report from the Committee Appointed to View the Cottonian Library, and Such of the Publick Records of this Kingdom* (London, 1732).

55. John Bruce, "No. 1 Sketch of the Origin and Present Situation of the State Paper Office," 1799, SP 45/75, TNA.

56. Bruce, "No. 1 Sketch of the Origin and Present Situation of the State Paper Office," 1799, SP 45/75, TNA.

57. John Bruce, "Regulations for the State Paper Office If Made an Office of Reference," 1799, SP 45/75, TNA.

58. Bruce's account of Colbert was inaccurate; for a discussion of Colbert's archival strategies, see Jacob Soll, *The Information-Master: Jean-Baptiste Colbert's Secret State Intelligence System* (Ann Arbor: University of Michigan Press, 2009).

59. "Note," "Regulations for the State Paper Office If Made an Office of Reference," 1799, SP 45/75, TNA.

60. For Bruce's reading and annotations of the original papers relating to the establishment of the office, see SP 45/20 and 9/30, TNA.

61. John Mitford to Henry Dundas, May 28, 1798, GD 152/39, NRS; "Form of Application to the King in Council Respecting the State Paper Office," July 7, 1799, SP 45/75, TNA.

62. "King's Warrant Revoking the Establishment of Commissioners for Methodizing and Arranging the Records of the State Paper Office," Private Register, State Paper Office, no. 1, 7–8, SP 45/75, TNA. The commissioners were now required to apply anew and directly to the Secretary of State for permission to access the records. See Michael Riordan, "'The King's Library of Manuscripts': The State Paper Office as Archive and Library," *Information and Culture* 48 (2013): 190–191.

63. "King's Warrant: Establishment of the State Paper Office," Private Register, State Paper Office, no. 1, 9–12, SP 45/75, TNA.

64. On the commission, see Peter Walne, "The Record Commissions, 1800–1837," *Journal of the Society of Archivists* 2 (1960): 8–16.

65. John Topham to John Bruce, July 30, 1800, SP 45/50, TNA.

66. John Bruce to Henry Dundas, July 31, 1800, SP 45/50, TNA.

67. John King to John Bruce, August 28, 1800, SP 45/50, TNA. For the Secretary of State's ordering Bruce to furnish records to the commissioners, see King to Bruce, October 1, 1800, SP 45/51, TNA.

68. For an example of such requests from the Secretary of State, see John King to John Bruce, May 15, 1800, SP 45/50, TNA. For applications for records from other government officials, see John Mitford, Attorney General, to Bruce, May 28, 1800, SP 45/51, TNA; and J. H. Addington to Bruce, May 1, 1817, SP 45/52, TNA.

69. "Order for Furniture for Mr. Bruce's Room at the State Paper Office," 1800, SP 45/50, TNA.

70. John King to John Bruce, June 30, 1803; Charles Williams-Wynn to Bruce, February 16, 1807, SP 45/50, TNA.

71. John Bruce, *Annals of the Honorable East-India Company, from Their Establishment by the Charter of Queen Elizabeth, 1600, to the Union of the London and English East-India Companies, 1707–1708*, 3 vols. (London, 1810).

72. "Extract of a Letter from W. Ramsay Esq.r to Mr. Bruce," March 31, 1817, 332–333, IOR/H/456e; Minutes of the Court of Directors, April 8, 1817, 1180–1181, IOR/B/164.

73. "Appendix, No. 1. Minute of Mr. Shore, Dated 18 June 1789; Respecting the Permanent Settlement of the Lands in the Bengal Provinces," in *The Fifth Report from the Select Committee on the Affairs of the East India Company* (London, 1812), 169.

74. Robert Lemon Jr. to Sir Robert Peel, April 3, 1844, fols. 60–61, Add MS 40542, BL.

75. *The Twenty-Sixth Annual Report of the Deputy Keeper of the Public Records,* February 16, 1865 (London, 1865), iv.

76. Antonia Moon, "Destroying Records, Keeping Records: Some Practices at the East India Company and the India Office," *Archives* 33 (2008): 114–125. For the formation of the Public Record Office, see "An Act for Keeping Safely the Public Records," August 14, 1838, 1 & 2 Victoria, c. 94, in *The Statutes of the United Kingdom of Great Britain and Ireland* (London, 1838), xiv, 883–886, 886 (quotation). For the pulping of papers, see *The Twenty-Third Annual Report of the Deputy Keeper of the Public Record, February 22, 1862* (London, 1862), 7–8.

77. Ray Desmond, *The India Museum, 1801–1879* (London: Her Majesty's Stationery Office, 1982), 20–21. See also Jessica Ratcliff, "The East India Company, the Company's Museum, and the Political Economy of Natural History in the Early Nineteenth Century," *Isis* 107 (2016): 495–517.

78. The scholarship on how that debate unfolded is vast, but key interventions include Eric Stokes, *The English Utilitarians and India* (Delhi: Oxford University Press, 1959); Ronald Robinson, John Gallagher, and Alice Denny, *Africa and the Victorians: The Official Mind of Imperialism* (London: Macmillan, 1961); Francis G. Hutchins, *The Illusion of Permanence: British Imperialism in India* (Princeton, N.J.: Princeton University Press, 1967); Thomas Metcalf, *Ideologies of the Raj* (Cambridge, UK: Cambridge University Press, 1994); Uday Singh Mehta, *Liberalism and Empire: A Study in Nineteenth-Century British Liberal Thought* (Chicago: University of Chicago Press, 1999); Jennifer Pitts, *A Turn to Empire: The Rise of Liberal Imperialism in Britain and France* (Princeton, N.J.: Princeton University Press, 2005); and Karuna Mantena, *Alibis of Empire: Henry Maine and the Ends of Liberal Imperialism* (Princeton, N.J.: Princeton University Press, 2010).

79. On secrecy and colonial violence, see Erik Linstrum, *Age of Emergency: Living with Violence at the End of the British Empire* (Oxford: Oxford University Press, 2023).

80. Even parchment was, until 2017, still used to record parliamentary legislation; see Dan Bilefsky, "Britain's Lords Turn the Page on Parchment," *New York Times,* February 11, 2016, sec. A, p. 4.

Epilogue

1. Jane Burbank and Frederick Cooper, *Empires in World History: Power and the Politics of Difference* (Princeton, N.J.: Princeton University Press, 2010), 8.

Index

accountability, 7, 48, 179

accounting, 49, 121

Act of Union (1840), 111

Address to the Proprietors of East-India Stock, An, 93

affidavits, 11, 92

Africa, 70–73, 175. *See also* Royal African Company (RAC)

Africans, enslaved, 3–4, 9, 54–55, 70, 71, 72, 73, 79

Ain-i Akbari, 145, 146, 148

Akbar (Akber), Emperor, 145, 148

Alam II, Shah (Mughal emperor), 56

Albiville, Marquis of, 92

Aleppo, 18

Alinagar, 116; Treaty of, 117. *See also* Calcutta

Allah, 'Inayat, 63

Allahabad, Treaty of, 56

Amboyna massacre, 50–51

American colonies: Burke's speech regarding, 26; Carolina, 112; charters of, 29, 31–32, 37, 38, 75, 112–13; communication in, 18; East and West New Jersey, 37; constitutions of, 16; Georgia, 89; governing structure of, 16–17; governors of, 16; Jamestown (Virginia Company), 23; Maryland, 112, 114, 156, 158; Massachusetts Bay Colony, 38, 75, 83, 85, 112; New York, 78, 84, 112–13, 116; paper mills in, 21; proprietary, 37, 38–39; Virginia Company, 16, 23, 24, 29, 41, 75, 112

American Indians. *See* Native Americans

American Revolution, 5, 98

Anderson, Adam, 89

Anderson, David, 121

Anderson, James, 145

Anglo-Dutch Wars, 50–51

Anne (Queen), 173

archives: access to, 6, 153, 156, 171, 173, 174, 178; of the Board of Trade, 72, 90, 96–97, 101, 104, 158, 160; colonial, 32, 79, 90; control of, 175–76; creation of, 4–5, 30–40, 69–70, 171; and the creation of knowledge, 21–25; defined, 11–13; dwindling role of, 178–79; ecclesiastical, 27, 29; of the English East India Company, 40–53, 92, 93, 95, 101–2, 161, 162, 164–66, 171, 172, 173; epistemology of, 177–79; exclusions from, 54–55, 72, 103; expanded definition of, 54–55; of the French state, 107, 108, 109, 111, 169; functions of, 3; of Hinduism, 135; imperial/royal, 4, 22, 24, 79, 167, 169–70; of local knowledge, 153; materials of, 19–21; non-English/Indian, 5, 99, 104–5, 118, 124–25, 129, 131–38, 143, 146, 147; official, 158; organization of, 30, 31, 34–35, 36, 45, 46–47, 173; personal, 140, 157; and politics, 28–29; private, 81–82, 168; provincial, 87–88; as records of governance, 55; records of legislative decisions, 68; scholarship on, 4, 79; as sites of "history," 6, 68, 151–52, 161; as source of political knowledge, 95; and sovereignty, 26, 113–15, 152, 175, 176, 177. *See also* documents; records

archivists, 6, 151

Aristotle, 13

Asia, 56, 91. *See also* South Asia

Astarabadi, Mahdi Khan, 65

auditors, 48

Aurangzeb, 47

authority, 22, 24–25

Azim-ush-Shan (Prince), 40

Bank of England, 71

Bantam, 18, 42, 92

Barwell, Richard, 52, 96, 131

Basra, 117

Bay of Bengal, 17, 18

Benares, 141

Dundas, Henry, 97, 142, 162, 164, 165, 166,
167, 168, 169–70, 171
Dundas, Robert, 162
Dutch East India Company (VOC), 50, 92

East India Company. *See* Dutch East India
Company (VOC); English East India
Company
East Indies, 17, 56, 57–58, 163
Eden, William, 97
Elements of Commerce, The (Mortimer), 90
Elements of the Science of Ethics (Bruce), 162
Eliot Bible, 61
Elizabeth I, 17, 28, 40, 58, 154
Elkins, Caroline, 54
Elliot, Alexander, 134, 135
Elliot, Gilbert, 95
Empire and Communications (Innis), 2
Empire of India. *See* India (Bengal)
England: Anglo-Dutch Wars, 50–51;
bureaucratic documentation in, 12; and
the Seven Years' War, 165; treaties with
European powers, 164; wars with France,
33. *See also* British Empire
English colonies (American). *See* American
colonies
English Constitution, 26, 57, 98, 113
English East India Company: accounting
practices, 49; archives of, 24, 40–53, 79,
161, 162, 166, 169, 171, 172, 173; in Bengal,
26, 115; Bengal council, 62, 100, 119, 123,
133, 136, 138, 140; Bruce's history of, 165,
166, 172; charter of, 10, 40, 47, 56, 79, 91,
129, 162, 163, 165; commercial privileges
of, 50; corporate constitution, 40–41;
correspondence of, 17–18; Court of Committees, 42, 48; critique of, 130; culling
of records, 174; defending and debating,
91–102; Fort William council, 131, 132,
133; in India, 10, 23, 42, 55, 93, 103, 116,
127–28; empire of, 17–18, 148; learning
local languages and customs, 58–62, 63,
65–66, 68–69, 116–17, 119–21, 125–26, 137,
142–43; London headquarters, 23–24;
military branch of, 62, 118, 166; paper
used by, 21; publication projects, 63–64;
recordkeeping by, 42, 43, 44, 46; records
of, 17, 26, 27, 41–44, 46, 47–48, 92, 93,

98, 99, 100, 104–5, 132, 133, 136, 147,
162, 163, 165, 166, 173; Regulating Act
(1773), 51–52, 97, 130–31; sovereignty of,
55, 56–58, 62–63, 66; Supreme Court of
Judicature, 52, 66, 131, 134; takeover of
rival company, 47; Treasurer's Office, 42.
See also Court of Directors
English law, 67–68, 77, 104, 108–11, 112, 130,
134, 158
English Reformation, 29
enslaved people, 3–4, 9, 54–55, 70–73, 79
entry-books, 30
*Essay upon the Government of the English
Plantations on the Continent of America,
An* (Davenant), 87, 88, 90
*Estimate of the Comparative Strength of
Britain during the Present and Four
Preceding Reigns; and of the Losses of Her
Trade from Every War Since the Revolu-
tion* (Chalmers), 157, 158, 159
experience, defined, 12
expertise, 22

Ferguson, John, 64
finance, 155
First Peoples, 9, 115. *See also* Native
Americans
Five Nations, 78
Foedera, 171
Foreign Office, 15
Fort St. George (Chennai), 44, 46, 60, 62,
119, 122, 125
Fort William, 51–52, 62, 63, 93, 131, 132, 133,
134
France: imperial recordkeeping by, 12, 24,
108, 109, 169; laws of, 112, 118; Native
Americans allied with, 78; state records
of, 107, 108, 109, 111, 169; wars with
Britain, 33, 62, 165
Francis, Philip, 52, 94, 95, 131, 132, 133, 140, 141
Franklin, Benjamin, 18
French Canadians, 177. *See also* Quebec
French laws, 105, 107–9, 112, 118

Gaspee affair, 206n5
Gates, Horatio, 85
Gayer, John, 47
Gayer, Mary, 47